THE WILD ROVER

ROVER

MIKE PARKER

A BLISTERING JOURNEY ALONG BRITAIN'S FOOTPATHS

Collins

To my parents:
Jane, David, Anne

First published in 2011 by Collins
HarperCollins*Publishers*
77–85 Fulham Palace Road
London W6 8JB

www.harpercollins.co.uk

1 3 5 7 9 10 8 6 4 2

Wolverhampton canal shot in Chapter 8 courtesy of Roger Kidd

Cardiff Hospital shot in the endpiece courtesy of Peter Finch

'The Path' by Ivor Cutler, reproduced by agreement of The Estate of Ivor Cutler. See www.ivorcutler.org for more on the old genius.

Excerpt from 'Slough' © John Betjeman by permission of The Estate of John Betjaman

The author asserts his moral right to be identified as the author of this work

A catalogue record for this book is available from the British Library

ISBN: 978-0-00-737266-9

Printed and bound in Great Britain by Clays Ltd, St Ives plc

Mixed Sources

Product group from well-managed forests and other controlled sources
www.fsc.org Cert no. SW-COC-1806
© 1996 Forest Stewardship Council

FSC is a non-profit international organization established to promote the responsible management of the world's forests. Products carrying the FSC label are independently certified to assure consumers that they come from forests that are managed to meet the social, economic and ecological needs of present and future generations.

Find out more about HarperCollins and the environment at
www.harpercollins.co.uk/green

CONTENTS

1.   (Not in) My Back Yard   1

2.   On the Warpath (North)   21

3.   Blazing the Trail   55

4.   The Old Ways   93

5.   On the Warpath (South)   129

6.   . . . Now Walk the Walk   169

7.   And Did Those Feet   197

8.   Where Dirt Meets Water   245

9.   The Stile Police   281

10. Lark Rise to Cameron   305

Acknowledgements   323

Bibliography   325

Index   327

THE PATH

Many feet make one path.
I like to walk on a foot path.
I walk over the grass
and turn to see if I have made a path.
Two feet once only
is not enough.
I return to the foot path
to fill one of the bunch.
I add my feet.
I look back.
What a path we made.

Ivor Cutler

The primrose path gives way to the garlic path on Gower

1. (NOT IN) MY BACK YARD

Of all the things you least want to come face-to-face with on an early morning dog walk, your own hypocrisy comes quite high on the list.

It was the wooden fingerpost that caused the first twinge. Bright and shiny, brand new and leaking fresh pine sap, the arrow and the motif of the little walking man picked out in gleaming yellow paint. A Public Footpath, it screamed. But I knew that already: I'd been walking this path, across the rushing river and through the fields, for years. Along the way a tributary stream funnels down a tiny valley, crossing the path at a ford overhung by my favourite oak. Moss-covered rocks huddle around the ford, each one a warm seat on which to rest and take the day's sunshine or rain. In eight years of walking the path and pondering life at the ford, I'd only ever been disturbed once at my special place by a fellow walker. And now everyone was going to be pointed towards it.

Over the next few days, I walked the other paths that surround the village, each one seemingly tailor-made for any subtle difference of mood, season or weather. If I need a good stretch after too many hours slumped in front of a screen, I'll take the hill track, a steep climb up an old holloway, past thorn trees twisted into animal shapes – the guardians of the village, according to some of the older residents – and up to a lofty viewpoint that never fails to give back some perspective to a foggy brain. In the autumn, I'll take the wooded path that forks off the back lane for its rusting colours and musky smells. If it's a bright morning, I'll take the short-sharp-shock path up through the forestry and on to a circular hilltop track that gets blasted by early sunshine. On a summer's afternoon, I'll ramble through the riverside fields, chucking sticks into the water for the dog, and then we'll both take a dip in one of the deep pools that sparkle green in the late day's sun. But the path over the little bridge and to the magical ford is the one I'll do on any day, at any time, in any weather, for it combines exactly the right amount of wood and water, shelter and open skies, grass and rock.

The new signs had materialised on every single track. Out of nowhere, little yellow men had appeared all over the village, pointing eagerly down driveways and farm tracks. Brand new zinc gates, their Travis Perkins price tag still glued on, had been rammed in too, replacing those held together only by twine, rust and local know-how. An ancient network of paths, some trodden for centuries and known to generations in intimate detail, had been suddenly thrown open to the world. I was bloody furious, and felt as if a load of complete strangers had stomped into my kitchen, and were sniggering at my smalls drying over the fire. It was nothing short of violation.

Even as those first feelings of outrage bubbled up in a stew of bile, I was well aware that they were laced with the even more corrosive ingredient of raging hypocrisy. For decades, I'd been sounding off about blocked footpaths and rights of way that appear on the map in crisp certainty but which, on the ground, are nowhere to be found. I'd cursed planners and councils for their lethargy in keeping paths marked and walkable. In 2001, when the foot-and-mouth crisis closed every path in the land, I'd written angry articles about the lightning speed with which the No Entry signs had gone up and compared it with the years that it took to remove them again. In every corner of the country, I'd hurled my hands up in horror at getting lost during the seemingly simple task of spotting a good path on the map and attempting to follow it. I'd ranted in print, on the radio, on TV, and to anyone who would listen, that councils really should take their respons- ibilities more seriously, not only to the walking public but as guardians of the hefty weight of history that had carved out such a cherished network of rights of way on our small island.

But that was There. Beyond, away, on someone else's patch, in places where I was a visitor and expected some modicum of consideration. And this was Here. Not for a moment did my spleen accommodate the obvious truth that my Here was nearly everyone else's There, and that they should perhaps be afforded the same hospitality that I so noisily demanded.

A few months on, the signs and the gates still look too new, too sharp, too much like prodnosed intruders. A couple of Welsh winters should batter them a little more comfortably into the landscape, but that's scant consolation, for they are already doing their damned job. Neighbours who live along the newly signposted tracks tell me that the footfall of passing cagoule- wearers has increased noticeably. So it seems: I keep finding complete strangers on my paths, ambling uncertainly along and fretting visibly about the cows in the next field. On my better days, I manage a smile and a hello, even as I wish they'd vanish into the sweet air. On my rather less charitable days, I do my best to look like the surliest farmer of popular paranoia and glower at them from across the hedgerows. It doesn't work. Even my scariest facial expressions cannot compete with the signposted certainty that they are there by right – their ancient, inalienable right of way.

Is there anything that combines simple utility and quiet beauty better than a footpath? There it goes, just the lightest of touches across a field or through a wood, the sum total of countless feet over countless years. At one and the same time, it is the humblest of all our imprints on the landscape, yet one of the sturdiest too. And not just physically so, but culturally and emotionally too. We need our paths, like we need to breathe.

Britain's network of paths is unique in the world. Nearly all countries have their waymarked trails and designated tourist routes, but we have something so much better: a filigree network of rights of way that snakes through every landscape and connects every town and village. Our paths, bridleways, byways and green lanes are threads of common land in an increasingly privatised countryside, hidden grooves of peace and beauty through the chaos, short cuts into our history and identity. They are democracy at its most fundamental, open to all, where you don't have to pay , and they will take you as far as you could possibly wish to go. All you need are a pair of feet and the urge to use them.

In England and Wales, there are around 150,000 miles of off-road rights of way, together with over 6,000 square miles of 'right to roam' Access Land (about three-quarters of one of those famous international units of measurement, a Size of Wales). In Scotland, the situation is even better, for there is a natural presumption of access to all land, including tens of thousands of miles of path and track. This astounding resource is something of a shrinking violet, however. While roads and railways, airports and interchanges howl for our attention and our wealth, the paths slip by almost unnoticed.

Like most Brits, having a bit of a walk is in my DNA. It was what you did on a Sunday afternoon, wrapped up snug against the autumn winds or giving your skin a laundering in the first warm rays of spring. We weren't, thank God, one of those rambling families, mum and dad in matching cagoules, kids moaning unheard at a distance. In our house, even the dog's favourite walk was to the pub. But the paths, and the hills and woods, rivers and fields, were always there, and always within walking distance.

Once, my dad told me that we were all going on a walk, and that I could choose where. Of course, I rushed to the map to pick somewhere that looked interesting, and fastened immediately on the Clee Hills, midway between our home in Kidderminster and the Welsh border. 'Are you sure?' Dad said. 'It's a bit grim.' His job often took him out that way, and he'd come back with stories of dribbling inbreds and ancient feuds. Which is almost certainly exactly why I wanted to go there.

Stubbornly, I refused to change my mind, and, good to his word, Dad packed us all into the car, grumbled only slightly, and set off for Clee. I can't remember much of the walk, save for some filthy quarry tracks and a burnt-out 54-seater coach halfway up a hillside, the grass scorched and still smelling of petrol.

As we stood, rather nervously, looking at it, someone pointed out the black sky heading our way. About thirty seconds later, a biblical deluge of hail, with balls of ice big enough to bruise, exploded over us. I wasn't asked to choose a walk again.

Mind you, Dad had some pretty leftfield ideas of his own as to what constituted a good walk. When the West Midland Safari Park opened, we were living on a new estate only a few hundred yards away. There was great excitement in the area at the opening of something so thrilling on our doorstep; in school, competition was fierce as to who'd yet been. Those that had would swan in, flamboyantly showing off their souvenir pencil case emblazoned with a lion. The rest of us would crowd round the lucky beggar, and pump them for titbits about the animals, the amusements, the food and whether their car aerial had been snapped off by a baboon. I couldn't wait to go, and kept begging my parents to take us there. The answer was always no, qualified with things like 'just look at the queues' or 'we'll wait until the crowds have died down', rather than the more unpalatable truth that it was because money would have to be spent.

We must have all nagged pretty thoroughly, because Dad one day announced that we were finally going to the Safari Park. I very nearly combusted with excitement. At last, I was going to be able to hold my head up high at school, and join in the exclusive conversations about whether we preferred giraffes or tigers. Off we walked down the road towards the entrance, before suddenly turning off too soon and heading instead up to the perimeter fence. We then spent hours, largely in the rain, being frogmarched around the park's outer limit, peering through the fence at occasional intervals and trying to work out if that distant blur was a cheetah or a leopard. Or perhaps an Austin Allegro.

Only gradually did the realisation dawn that some paths were allowed, and some weren't. As a child, I roamed as free as I dared, by bike and on foot, out into the woods and fields around the town, along canal and river tow-paths, country lanes and muddy bridleways, with no thought as to whether it was officially sanctioned or not. Occasionally, I'd get shouted at by someone, but that happened most days anyway, so I thought nothing of it. Thanks to my growing collection of Ordnance Survey (OS) Landranger maps, I was soon aware of what the little lines of red dots and dashes meant, that these were official rights of way, as intrinsic a part of the Queen's Highway as any trunk road or motorway. Learning that was fascinating, and tracing their route across the map and on the ground was a joy, but it necessitated a loss of innocence that would never return.

These rights of way have only been marked on OS maps for the last fifty years (and only in their entirety for the last twenty-five or so), but today, they are unquestionably the main reason that anyone still buys paper versions of the Landrangers (1:50 000) and Explorers (1:25 000). The orange-covered Explorer maps, in particular, have become the walker's best friend, as they are at the smallest possible scale where field boundaries can be shown, an essential help on the many occasions when the dotted line on the map refuses to reveal itself on the ground.

Where better to start an inventory of the state of our rights of way than on your home patch? I sat by the fire one winter's night and gazed at the local Explorer map, mentally totting up the little green dashed lines that wriggled and wormed their way across it, picturing the routes and their views that I knew as I followed the map. There were so many – but just as many again that I didn't know. Whole footpaths and bridleways that I'd never once tried, of which I had no visual image or memory. As the fire crackled and spat, I resolved to draw a circle on the map, centred on my house, and to walk every single right of way – or at least, attempt to walk every one – within it. I pictured myself sallying forth from the doorstep like an ocean-going liner down the slipway, plunging with a happy splash into the fields, forests and hills that surround me. I would conduct a thorough audit of my own back yard.

I started by drawing a five-mile circle around where I live, and swiftly realised that it presented a little too much of a challenge, one that looked as if it would take many months to complete. I pulled the circle in a little, taking a three-mile radius instead. Three miles sounds nothing. It *is* nothing: I habitually walk four-and-a-bit miles into town, and it's a doddle, taking only a shave over an hour if I go at a decent lick. But looking at the six-mile-wide circle on the map was really quite disorienting. Within it, there were whole valleys, farms and woods that I'd never been near, whose names I'd never even consciously digested. I had no idea who lived there, what their lives were like, who they were related to or were friends with and – most pressingly – whether they'd welcome a map-wielding rambler or set their dogs on me.

Every day for the first week of my audit, I set off on foot in a different direction, and found footpaths and bridleways that I'd never seen before. I still can't quite believe it, for I've been in this house for nearly a decade, and have been out walking almost every single day (the lot of the dog owner: so bloody what if it's lashing with rain). Yet, here were old holloways and green lanes, paths bumping down through woods and tell-tale darker lines of grass winding their way across fields that I'd never clapped eyes on before. It was nothing short of thrilling.

Then the snows came, and stayed. This perked up the experience even more, for I was clearly able to see from the footprints just how many other creatures, human and otherwise, were sharing the paths. All kinds of birds, rabbits galore, a few hares, dogs, foxes, cats and some that were intriguingly difficult to pin down. Ever since I've lived here, there have been occasional rumoured sightings of big cats. A few years back, the mutters swelled to a climax one spring, and whispered second- and third-hand sightings were a regular topic of almost every conversation. One day during that time, a friend and I were walking in the forest when a black shape shot across the path, paused and then vanished into the undergrowth some hundred yards ahead. We both inhaled sharply and squealed, 'What was *that*?' It hadn't much looked like a puma or panther to me, rather a wild boar, and I said so. 'Oh thank God,' my friend said. 'That's exactly what I thought, but I thought it sounded mad to say so.' Scrutinising the snowy paw- and hoof-prints, I've not been able to make any out that are distinctly porcine, but there were plenty that looked thrillingly mysterious.

This being rural Wales, the cloven footprints of sheep were to be seen everywhere. Sheep paths are always a useful way of traversing rough ground, for the animals follow each other with such dependability that a groove is soon worn into a hillside or through a wood, enough to take a careful walker. In the snow, the phenomenon was even more pronounced. Little indented paths, eight or nine inches wide, were scoured deep into the white stuff, as regular and as ordered as if they'd been carved out by tyres. In fact, at first I mistook them for tyre-tracks, the

9

remnant of some mysterious single-wheeled farm vehicle that had been paraded drunkenly through every field. I might have lived the *Escape to the Country* dream for a decade, but that's how much of a thick townie I still am. Only after a few days of walking through countless sheep fields, and noticing many such tracks and how they were made up of hundreds of cloven-hoof indentations, did the truth dawn. Presumably, one started walking in a particular direction (the Alpha Ewe, as we'll call her), and the others all fell in behind her, excitedly wondering where they were going. And still they follow.

As I pounded the paths and hills around, the mystery of the new signs and gates only deepened. They were everywhere, on seemingly every right of way, even those that are barely ever walked. And on those that *can't* be walked: gates – even bridges – to nowhere. The oddest example was a sparkling new pine footbridge, straight off the shelf, gracefully spanning a small river between a dirt-track lane on the one bank and a tight thicket of brambles and pines on the other. There is an old right of way here, which, as part of my audit, I attempted to walk from the other end. It's a soggy old holloway, but it soon vanishes altogether in the conifer plantations. On the late nineteenth-century large-scale OS maps, it was the main track along the valley, but no-one has walked or ridden it in decades, and no-one could now, however hard they tried. But they would have a lovely new bridge to not take them there.

There was a pretty clear hierarchy at work in the correlation between gates and signs as well. Evidently, the local Rights of Way officer had trotted around the local farms with a mixed bag of news. 'On the up side,' I could imagine him saying, spreading his fingers across an old oak table or stone wall, 'I'll refit every gate on every path on the farm – all free, all brand new, straight out the factory.' Farmers like free, but they would know that there's a catch. There always is. The down side was that they would also have to have new signs pointing out paths and bridleways that have been unsignposted – and largely unused – for generations. You get yourself shiny new fences and gates, but you also get an increase in the footfall of passing ramblers, eager to pound their newly recognised rights of way. Or not, as it seems. Although every path in the vicinity seemed to have new gates and fences, far from every one was now signed.

There was the inevitable rural hierarchy at work. The longer your family had been in the area, or the further up the local greasy pole you had shinned, the fewer signs were deemed necessary on your land. Any farm or estate owned by incomers or the recently arrived (and by recent, I mean at least second generation) was subject to the full range of signs. The older local families just got the free gates and fences. If you're wondering how I knew whether it was locals or incomers living in every remote property I passed, there is plenty of tell-tale evidence. You don't usually have to look further than the farm's nameplate sign at the top of the track. Incomers have some lavish wood affair, usually embellished with a few flowers or butterflies, and hand-carved by a nice boy called Oliver. Locals generally use a vehicle number plate.

That said, almost all of the paths across the old farms were eminently walkable, and, with the help of the map and asking for the odd bit of guidance, easy to follow. They just don't particularly want to advertise them, and I can understand that. No-one gave me any grief; quite the opposite. I had numerous illuminating, sometimes hilarious, conversations with gnarled old farmers and their pink-cheeked wives in some of the outlying valleys and up in the hills, and learned plenty of new angles on the history of the area and its fiercely self-sufficient inhabitants. Had all the paths been smooth and signposted, I could perhaps have steamed on through, imperious and impervious to the land and the people on it. As it was, and as it should be in remote rural areas like this one, I had to engage with them, and the walks were all the richer and more enjoyable for it.

In fact, outside of the forests, the only paths that were absolutely blocked were on the land not of the old farming families, but of a particular breed of incomer. Most of us rat-race refugees in an area like this fall into one of two camps: vaguely hippyish or vaguely Ukippyish, sometimes a bizarre hybrid of both. The hippies want organic veg, chickens in the yard and Enid Blyton adventures. The Ukippies want to escape the brown and black faces of their home town and hole themselves into their compound. There are strange similarities between them, for the impetus driving both groups is often the same misplaced search for a fantasy version of their own childhoods, a prospect condemned to remain for ever out of reach. They differ hugely in their approach to paths, however: the hippies embrace (sometimes, all too literally) anyone wandering across their land, the Ukippies retreat behind barbed wire and stern, monolingual English signs telling you to keep out. The fact that they have become the immigrants that they so despise at home is an irony that never seems to trouble them.

From my audit, the dubious accolade of biggest path-blockers of all went to the Forestry Commission, whose wholesale re-ordering of the local map has been little less than Stalinist in its scope and execution. Dozens of paths on the map failed to appear in reality and, often, there was no trace whatsoever of their former selves. Of course, the need for timber was desperate, especially when the Forestry Commission was created in the aftermath of the First World War. And areas like this one, with mile upon mile of thinly populated, marginal land of no great potential for crops or livestock, were obvious candidates for afforestation. As a major local industry, it swept in on the back of the slate quarries and mines just as they were juddering to the end of their working lives. Forestry was much-needed work, and real work at that too: sweaty, bloody, outdoor and bursting with the kind of manly camaraderie that makes my generation, most of whom click a mouse for a living, go a bit weak at the knees.

In the village where I live, the Forestry Commission took over an old prisoner-of-war camp and filled it with workers, their families, a kids' playground, a village hall and community centre, a snooker club, a sports field, a library and the inevitable tin tabernacle. Events were plentiful and enthusiastic. Whist drives, am dram, jumble sales, WI meetings, eisteddfodau, parties and concerts whirled by in a cloud of gossip and giggles. In the winter, the Christmas concert was a must for all, but the big annual event was the summer gala, where folk donned fancy dress (dragging up and blacking up were especially popular) and schoolgirls were crowned as Forest Queens and paraded around on the back of logging trucks. Newspaper reports of the day make it sound like something straight out of 'Hansel and Gretel'. The lorries were decorated with 'evergreens and flowers of the forest', while the young Queen herself was clad in a white satin gown and a 'fur-collared mantle of dark green – symbolic of the forests'.

The first Forest Queen was crowned in 1954, the year that the Forestry Commission took over the camp and created the village-within-a-village. Queen Blodwen was her name, a 15-year-old from a big local family. 'This is a happy village,' gushed the area's lady of the manor to the county newspaper, but she was largely right, and so it remains. The local vicar went even further, thanking the Forestry Commission for stemming the exodus of locals: 'It was true to say,' he went on, 'that the neighbourhood was one of the few in North Wales which was not seriously suffering from the modern rural malady of depopulation.' Other Welsh towns and villages watching their slate industries slowly die were going the same way, but until the Commission's money began to run out in the 1970s, our village blossomed.

Before its brief hiatus housing captured German officers, the camp had been built in the 1930s as an instructional centre for the unemployed of Birkenhead and Liverpool. They were bussed out of Merseyside and made to work for three months in the hills, blasting the new forestry roads through whatever got in their way: farms, walls, houses, woods and mile upon mile of ancient path. It goes on still today, albeit without the jobless Scousers.

For most local people, then, the Forestry Commission is seen as a benevolent force, for it gave work, self-respect, homes, high days and holidays. Arriving here long after the party ended, however, has given me a far sourer view of the Commission and its effects locally, for the blanket destruction and alteration of the landscape – the power to play at tin gods – created some serious arrogance in its protagonists. It always does.

On my bookshelves are numerous old guides to Wales. Some, when talking about this area, mention something that sounds quite dazzling, a cave called the Siambr Wmffre Goch (the Chamber of Red Humphrey). This had given its name to an obscure local stream, only a mile or so long, and it's by that name that it appears even today on the OS map. A Ward Lock guide from the 1970s records the *siambr* as 'a cave behind a waterfall which long served as a highwayman's hide' – Red Humphrey being that highwayman. *The Shell Guide to Wales*, from 1969, is a little more effusive, calling it 'an extraordinary place', and going into some more detail: after passing through a cluster of ash trees, you come to 'apparently a simple, caved entrance into the hillside, but on passing through the arch you find yourself under the open sky, with a pool and a fall of water and a further cave-like formation ahead of you'.

The siambr sounded magical, like something out of a fairy story, and I've searched for it on a number of occasions. The valley of the little stream named after it has since been heavily forested, and it is a difficult search, necessitating either numerous scrambles and slides down sheer banks, or an attempt to walk along the stream and hop from slippery rocks to fallen timber. And all to no avail. How on earth can you lose a cave and a waterfall in a small Welsh valley?

I was keen to feature Siambr Wmffre Goch in one of my TV programmes and, having exhausted enquiries around the village, I wrote a piece asking for help for the local freesheet, delivered to all the nearby villages. Our most celebrated local naturalist got in touch to suggest we go and search for it together, as he too has always been intrigued by the siambr's reputation. Whereas before, when I'd been searching alone, I'd wussed out at the really scary bits, with Jack it was different. The man is fearless. When I met him at the bottom of the little valley, he took one look at how ill equipped I was for a proper search, wandered over to a stout young hazel tree, lopped off a straightish branch with his knife, swiftly pruned it of all twigs and presented it to me as the ideal tool to hack our way through the thick under-growth. From tree part to bespoke walking-cum-scything stick in about 45 seconds.

Over the next few hours, we hacked, slashed and hopped our way up every last inch of that stream. Branches and brambles snapped across me, slashing my arms like a teenage goth. As Jack (a man nearly 30 years my senior) nimbly galloped between rock and tree trunk, I crashed along in his wake like a hippo chasing a gazelle. We found nothing. I was prepared for the guidebooks to have exaggerated the elfin appeal of the cave and waterfall, but to have conjured it out of thin air seemed bizarre, impossible. Jack was as mystified as I was, and we finished our day with a handshake and a solemn promise to share any infor-mation that might yet bubble to the surface.

Months later, I was walking through the next village up the valley, when an elderly man waved at me. 'You're the fella wanting to know about that highwayman's cave, aren't you?' he wheezed in an accent as thick as Welsh rain. I nodded eagerly. 'We blew it up,' he said, with an air of triumph in his voice. It transpired he had been part of a team planting the trees in that valley in the early 1970s. A supply of explosives, to blast out occasional rock faces, was part of the kit, and one day they'd egged each other on to blow poor old Wmffre Goch's hideout into the skies. 'Why did you do that?' I asked him. He looked at me as if I were a simpleton. 'Because we could,' he said, and shuffled off down the street.

My footpath audit had been a revelation. Within three miles of my front door, I walked nearly 70 miles of rights of way, from gloomy squelches through dank forestry to hawthorn-trimmed holloways high over the hills. I found lakes, woods, views and neighbours that I never knew existed. And I don't think that the experience was unique simply because I live deep in the country-side. Have a look at the map of your own back yard and, unless you live in the middle of a big city (or the more agro-industrial parts of East Anglia), there will be dozens of rights of way too within your own three-mile radius.

If my little local project had been such an eye-opener, just how much better could it get if I went further afield? The idea possessed me. I was desperate to go and see more, to open the circle across the whole of the country, and to discover the many stories of England, Scotland, Wales and Ireland, as told by their paths. I wanted to see the finest, the oddest and those most steeped in their own lore and custom. It was time to bring to life some legendary names off the map: Kinder Scout, the Pennine Way, the Elie Chainwalk, Framfield, the Lyke Wake Walk, the Thames Path, Offa's Dyke, the Ridgeway, Winnats Pass, the Tóchar Phádraig. I took the maps out, and started dreaming.

By now, I felt quite ashamed of my early churlishness. Someone said to me that the British footpath network is worthy of being listed as a UNESCO World Heritage Site, so rare and extraordinary is it. They're right. And there was I wishing it, if not away, then certainly where it could be seen and not heard. Some kind of penance was called for.

The answer was obvious. I must sweat my misanthropy out by working on the repair of a public footpath, perhaps clad in sackcloth. I should go out and dig, hammer and saw with one of the many voluntary footpath-upkeep societies in Britain. Without them, the network would have disappeared under a siege of bramble and barbed wire years ago, and we would be left with the kind of situation found in most other countries, namely a few well-used, showpiece paths, glistening with signs, benches and nut-brown pensioners, but very little else. Online, I found a group in Kenilworth, which seemed like a suitably Middle England kind of destination, an Everyplace that might slyly reveal universal truths about us and the land secreted in its red soil. Furthermore, it was still part of my extended back yard, in that my grandparents had lived either side of the town in post-war Coventry and then Leamington in retirement, and my mum still lived half of the time in the spa town. So, even if I learned nothing, I could see some old haunts and my old mum.

As I left hers, we discussed what we imagined the members of the Kenilworth Footpath Preservation Group (KFPG) to be like. I predicted an all-male group, mostly bearded and mostly older than me. Mum disagreed on all scores, and she was right. Swinging my van into a large car park that Sunday morning, the first thing that struck me about the cheery-looking group in fluor-escent yellow tabards was just how many of them were women. Segregation came swiftly, though: the ladies were sent off on their regular task of affixing yellow arrows to everything and a little light pruning, while the men and I gruffly headed into the spring sunshine to dig out a couple of stiles and replace them with gates.

The KFPG was set up in 1974 by one man, and he runs it still today. Meeting him, you'd think he was a fit 65-year-old, but in fact, he's passed 80. His passion was undimmed, although the increasing amount of red tape and regulation from the council was doing its best to quash it for him. His group now look after around a hundred miles of Warwickshire paths, and it has pro-voked a huge upsurge in their usage. He was a quiet evangelist – the best kind – for the rights of way network, channelling his drive into something so positive and constructive.

Fun, too. I had a brilliant morning with them, digging away into the cold earth and sharing jokes at each other's expense. Many of the most ribald comments between the men were about each other's politics, for it was evident that the group was a very Kenilworth hybrid of old-school Tories doing their bit for tradition, idealistic Liberals and dyed-in-the-wool socialists, inching forward the proletarian revolution by giving them access to the land. Love and concern for our rights of way seem to go right across the political spectrum. In the pub afterwards, I was shocked to learn that one of my fellow co-diggers, who'd left us by then, was a BNP activist. My shock obviously showed, for one of the younger members said to me, 'Yeah, I know. If anyone had told me I'd be spending my Sunday mornings working alongside a BNP member, I'd have refused to believe it. But you know, the greater good . . . well, it's bigger than any of us, and that's what I have to keep reminding myself.' After the shock had subsided, I felt quietly awed by their easy-going tolerance, and that in itself is the best argument against the likes of the BNP.

The physical graft made for an exhilaratingly different kind of Sunday morning to my usual one, which generally consists of bacon, eggs, tea, fags, the papers and *The Archers*. I'd managed not to smoke for the previous couple of months: that, and the up-hill, down-dale exploration of the paths in my part of Wales, had helped me feel so much fitter. It was time to get out there and explore the country along its byways and bridleways, to sharpen my body and my mind on the nation's contours, as seen from close-up and at walking pace. As I raised my pint to the effusive path-clearers of Kenilworth, I knew exactly where I had to go next.

An unlikely crucible for revolution: the Bottoms path, Flixton, Greater Manchester

2. ON THE WARPATH (NORTH)

'We're just bolshie buggers. Especially when you see your boss swanning around on the moors, moors that you can't even get on to, poncing around with his mates and a twelve-bore, shooting grouse.' It's 1931, and a determined Lancashire voice pierces through the excited chatter bouncing off the roof of Manchester's Victoria station, as flat-capped hordes swarm forward on to the train that will take them out of the city, into the hills for an afternoon's fresh air and freedom.

Actually, I lie. It's 2010 in a suburban semi in Stockport, the offices of the Peak & Northern Footpaths Society (PNFS), Britain's most venerable rights of way campaigning group, and the words are those of Clarke Rogerson, their chairman. He's answering a simple question that has ricocheted around my head for weeks: just what is it with Lancastrians and their precious footpaths?

Almost every battle and campaign of any significance about access or rights of way has taken place in north-western England, with a few contemporaneous flare-ups across the Pennines in the smoke-and-eckythump bits of Yorkshire. The names of Kinder Scout, Winter Hill, Bleaklow and Winnats Pass roll around the mouth of a northern folk singer like a religious incantation. And in a way, that's exactly what they have become: totemic names of battles hard fought and even harder won, their status growing with every re-telling. Each story has the full roster of Victorian melodrama heroes and villains: moustache-twirling landowners cackling with evil glee as they clout a couple of peasants round the ear and shoot a few more defenceless grouse, pitted against salt-of-the-earth workers who just want five minutes gasping fresh air on't moors before they drop dead from a lifetime of eating and breathing nobbut soot.

Being bolshie buggers is hardwired into north-westerners, and they take enormous pride in the fact. They also take moment-ous pride in their landscape, the tussocky moors and rain-lashed hills that loom large as the backdrop to almost all of the region's towns and cities. Put the two together, and you get a swank that threatens to burst, it's that bloated with decades of padding. How did anyone ever think that they were going to keep these people off their hills? You might as well try and stop them shouting, or shitting.

To understand the place of the path in our national make-up, a visit to the north-west is essential. It is not just a casual visit, however, some light Sunday afternoon stroll, topped off with a cup of tea you could trot a mouse across. To go to the north-west seeking answers to the many questions about our relation-ship with paths and landscape is to embark upon nothing short of a pilgrimage, a search for some kind of holy grail that can only possibly be found here. This is where paths become no less than stairways to heaven, and I was genuinely excited by the prospect of seeing the paths soaked in the blood and sweat of those who'd fought for the right to walk them.

The starting point of my north-west pilgrimage had to be the very right of way that's generally accepted as the birthplace of the modern footpath preservation movement. I'd like to report that, as would befit its historical stature, it's a glorious hilltop track clambering up to a panorama of eight counties, or, failing that, at least a stony path inching its way up through the mist alongside a peaty burn. It's neither. In fact, it's a gentle trot across a golf course, sandwiched between two other golf courses, in one of those outer parts of Greater Manchester that would far prefer to call itself Cheshire. The story, as is the case with nearly all tales of footpath derring-do in this part of the world, is indeed a tale of class war, but not the brawny, horny-handed version of *The Ragged Trousered Philanthropists* – it's much more *Keeping Up Appearances*.

For this is Flixton, in the true-blue borough of Trafford, a gin'n'Jag suburb of smart semis, Tudorbethan piles, tanning salons and the languid air of somewhere that doesn't have to fret itself overly much, except perhaps about a broken nail extension. Slap in the heart of this leafiest of suburbs are the 218 acres of Flixton Park, once common land threaded by numerous well-walked paths and tracks. Today it's a golf course and public park, its primroses and pansies mathematically spaced and much enjoyed by strolling families and smiling couples. Even the gangs of hoodies are polite and quiet. Yet between these two incarnations as public property, Flixton Park closed in on itself, shut itself away and inadvertently created the hydra-headed monster of the rights of way protest movement.

The Flixton Footpath Battle hissed and spat for three years, from 1824 to 1827. Ralph 'Vegetable' Wright provoked it, after making big money in agriculture and ploughing it into the creation of a small stately home, Flixton House, in the first few years of the nineteenth century. This flat, fertile plain south-west of Manchester, a world away from the mills and smoke-stacks, was already dotted with medieval mansions: Flixton House, and Wright himself, were the Johnny-come-lately neighbours to Shaw Hall (dating from 1305), Davyhulme Hall (c.1150), Newcroft Hall (c.1270) and Urmston Hall (c.1350). Flush with his fine new house and bulging bank balance, Wright fully expected to be welcomed into their drawing rooms, but it was not to be. Old money, as ever, peered imperiously down on new money, and Wright grew increasingly bellicose as their doors continued to remain shut to him. Every Sunday, the big house families would sweep past him stuck in his pew at the back of Flixton's twelfth-century parish church, as they made their stately progress up to their ancient family boxes at the front. 'Vegetable' Wright sat and stewed in the cheap seats, dreaming up ways of getting his revenge.

The parish church, in whose graveyard Wright lies buried within the most massive mausoleum of all, had already acted as the cauldron for Flixton's petit bourgeois tensions. In 1804, a public appeal was launched to recast the church's four bells, but such was the urge amongst the local gentry to outdo – and, more importantly, to be seen to outdo – each other, the appeal raised way more than was needed, and it was decided to have eight brand new bells cast for the church instead, at a cost of over £750 (around £60,000 at today's prices). 'Vegetable' Wright ostentatiously paid for the biggest bell of the lot, setting him back £101 12/6. No-one had thought to check that the fabric of the church could take such weighty munificence and, seven years later, the walls fell in. Less than a decade after they were rebuilt, the tower threatened to collapse. It was partially rebuilt, and then declared unsafe again in 1863. This time, it was obvious that the overly heavy bells were the culprit, and they were silenced until 1888, by which time a new and reinforced tower had been built from scratch.

After the first rebuilding of 1814, a row erupted about a stove that had been placed in the church's chancel for 'the accommodation of the congregation generally, and the scholars attending Sunday school in particular'. One prominent parishioner, a Mr Norris, objected, but nothing was done, so he persuaded a friend, Conyers Bale, to attempt to prove legal ownership of the chancel by dint of the fact that he was a parish lay rector. This was ignored, so Norris and Bale employed a gang to rip the stove out. The churchwardens sued at the Police Court for trespass and 'wilful spoil', and won. Norris and Bale appealed to the Sessions, who overturned the decision, which was then subject to an appeal by the other side and finally settled, nine expensive years later, at the Lancaster Assizes, Bale having turned the charge of trespass back on to the churchwarden for installing the stove in the first place. The great Church Stove Battle, chased through every court and getting a lot of people in a fierce palaver about – quite literally – a lot of hot air, was a prescient pointer to the footpath struggle ahead, for it was evidently the Flixton way of doing things. Looking at the place today, I suspect that little has changed.

When Flixton House was finished in 1806, 'Vegetable' Wright acquired, in various parcels, some 15 or 16 acres to go with it. Flushed with the notion that he needed to hone it into a parkland befitting his newly acquired status of gentleman, he sealed his land piece by piece, despite the fact that it was crisscrossed by a network of old paths. Some were little missed, but one in particular, known as the Bottoms, was the only dry path to church for people of all classes on the regular occasions that the nearby River Mersey flooded. The Highways Act of 1815 ruled that a path could only be extinguished by the signed order of two magistrates, but this proved no problem for Wright, who was also on the bench. The odd dinner for fellow JPs (church-stove battler and inveterate litigant Mr Norris being a regular) was held in Flixton House's gaudy dining room, before some fine port and a footpath closure order slipped in to follow. Oftentimes, he barely even bothered with that perfunctory process, shutting up the paths, even ploughing and planting them with oats, before any official decision had been made.

This was just the opportunity that Wright's many enemies needed, and when the Manchester Society for the Preservation of Ancient Footpaths was founded in 1826 in direct response to the Flixton case, virtually every local bigwig queued up to join. Although a similar organisation had been founded for comparable reasons two years earlier in York, the Manchester one continues to this day. Its considerable funds were used as the basis for the foundation of the Peak & Northern Footpaths Society in 1894, making it by far the oldest extant footpath campaigning group in the world.

The newly formed Society eagerly took on 'Vegetable' Wright. Court cases galore ensued, many of Wright's witnesses being bribed or plied with drink to get them to attend. He tried to raise the spectre that enemies of footpaths always fall back on, namely that the Bottoms path was a hotbed of immorality. To that end he persuaded the governor of Flixton workhouse, William Eccles, to give evidence, which proved perhaps less than helpful to his cause. 'I think use of the Bottoms encourages vice,' simpered Eccles in court. 'I only see disorderly ones going that way.' He paused, and continued: 'I once saw Mr Stephenson the clergyman going that way to church.'

After huge legal costs had been racked up on both sides, the ultimate result was defeat for Wright. A delighted party broke into his parkland and walked the paths that had been off-limits for two years. Archibald Prentice, proprietor of the *Manchester Gazette* and a committee member of the Society, arrived to witness the end of the celebrations. Although he wrote that he had been sad to miss the moment when the fences were smashed through and the paths walked once again, he was moved to say that 'I experienced a higher pleasure in observing the fresh marks of the saw, the little two-feet wide opening, and the newly made track through the tall grass, than such sights might be thought capable of giving.' So intoxicated was Prentice by the result that he published a 60-page victory pamphlet on the Flixton Footpath Battle, and gave it away with copies of the *Gazette*.

Wright had reaped a tailwind of trouble, but perhaps not quite all of it of his own making. The industrial towns of the north-west had ballooned in size in recent decades (Manchester's population had risen sevenfold to 150,000 in just 50 years), but the endless boom and expansion had hit its first set of buffers, and times were fearsomely tough. The Napoleonic Wars were fresh in every mind, especially those of the nervous authorities. Manchester was still simmering from the brutal attack of August 1819 that became known as the Peterloo Massacre. A massive crowd, estimated to be around 70,000 people, had gathered in St Peter's Field in the city centre to hear radical firebrand Henry Hunt speak in favour of sweeping political reform. A jittery set of city magistrates – Ralph Wright amongst them – unleashed the militia on the unarmed demonstrators, whom they scythed through mercilessly. Between ten and twenty people were slain, and hundreds injured. It was a defining moment in British history and, overlain with the lacy snobbery of Flixton society, made for a toxic cocktail.

Despite being blessed with an advanced sense of the melodramatic, even I couldn't whip up much emotion from the Flixton footpaths as they stand today, however historic their significance. In my head, I imagined a Soviet-style monument to the victory of common access, but instead there's a very modest little plaque, placed by the PNFS, half-way up a lamp-post, half-way along the Bottoms path. This is the track that caused the kerfuffle in the first place, although the building of the railway from Manchester to Warrington in the early 1870s necessitated its slight straightening. The railway, and the golf course on the other side, have hemmed the path right in. Each side is policed by a massive fence, with the footpath low between them, just wide enough for two people to pass if they angle themselves correctly (if they don't, Mr Eccles at the workhouse might just have had a point). Walking it, you feel as if you're in the perimeter no-man's-land of a high-security prison.

Monotonous as it may be, there is something strangely comforting in walking it too. The only views you get are those through the bars (on the railway side) or the mesh (on the golf course side), but it's all very familiar, ubiquitous even. There are a million paths just like it all over the land, those that duck along the bottom of people's gardens, run atop rubbish-strewn railway banks, squeeze down alleyways between 1960s houses, get caked in the footprints and fag ends of persons unknown. The Bottoms is Everypath, and that seems entirely fitting.

Leaving sleek little Flixton, I was hungry for some proper Lancastrian blood and strife, a slab of red meat, under the red flag in this, the red rose county. Clarke Rogerson at the busy HQ of the PNFS had mentioned a couple of important footpath battles that had taken place on the moors above Bolton and Darwen, old mill towns to the north of Manchester. To him, they were of far greater significance than the showpiece mass trespass at Kinder Scout, and considerably earlier to boot. The Bolton struggle, which culminated in a series of mass trespasses in September 1896, was the most noteworthy. It had centred on access to Winter Hill, a swollen moor to the north of the town, and was an archetype of the kind of struggles so lovingly eulogised in Lancastrian socialist memory.

At Winter Hill, there was the full cast of goodies and baddies. In the boo-hiss corner was Colonel Richard Ainsworth, lord of Smithills Hall and boss of a huge bleaching works. With all the nearby cotton mills, there was mucho brass in bleach, especially for the company that pioneered the use of chlorine in the process. People who breathed in a daily diet of chlorine and smog were understandably keen to get a little of the fresh stuff come the weekend, and Winter Hill had long been a popular place for Boltonians to do just that. The early- to mid-Victorian period had seen a flowering of working-class interest in outdoor life, and not just among ramblers. Societies of amateur botanists, birders, geologists and naturalists were booming in all the northern industrial towns; they gathered libraries, specimens, collections and herbaria, wrote authoritative textbooks and papers. Elizabeth Gaskell, in her 1848 novel *Mary Barton*, described the

'. . . weavers, common hand-loom weavers, who throw the shuttle with unceasing sound, though Newton's *Principia* lies open on the loom, to be snatched at in work hours, but revelled over in meal times, or at night . . . There are botanists among them, equally familiar with either the Linnaean or the Natural system, who know the name and habitat of every plant within a day's walk from their dwellings; who steal the holiday of a day or two when any particular plant should be in flower . . .'

Ainsworth had taken over the Hall and the family firm in 1865. Fiercely anti-socialist and anti-union, he adored the trappings of the gentleman's life, none more than pointing a gun at a grouse. On his favourite shooting ground of Winter Hill, part of his Smithills estate, he built a shooting hut and decided to close an old track, known as Coalpit Lane, that led across it. A gate was placed across the track further back towards town, employees were placed around the moor's perimeter to warn people off and numerous 'Trespassers Will Be Prosecuted' signs appeared.

Within days, word had spread and Bolton was seething. Together, the Bolton Socialist Party (BSP) and the town's Social Democratic Federation (SDF), a Marxist outfit, decided to organise a mass trespass across Winter Hill, and advertised it for the next Sunday, 6 September 1896. Much to their amazement, over 10,000 people came. A small band of policemen and gamekeepers was quickly overwhelmed, and with great excitement, the crowds charged through the now broken gate, tramped over the hill and down the other side to the village of Belmont, giving the landlord of the Wright's Arms a day he'd never forget.

The protest electrified Bolton, and the tiny revolutionary groupings of the BSP and SDF could scarcely believe their luck. They had located a deep nerve amongst the people, had hit it with pinpoint precision and were now ready to take it up a gear. Capitalism was trembling! Today a footpath across a Lancashire moor, tomorrow the world! It was decided to repeat the mass trespass on the following Sunday. Despite pouring rain, even more people came this time, around 12,000. A few tooled-up lads came looking for a dust-up with the law, but the law wisely decided to step aside before it came to that. More euphoria, Defence Committees, feverish chat, public meetings, the letters' pages in the local papers raging one way and the other.

Then Ainsworth bit back. On the morning of the third demonstration – the next Saturday this time, to appease Sunday worshippers – his land agent trotted around Bolton in a hansom cab, doling out writs against ten named men from the first trespass. Nervousness about getting nabbed, combined with the inevitable tailing off of interest by some and another day of terrible weather, reduced the numbers to around 5,000. Another 32 writs were served, which only made the central core of organisers dig in deeper, returning to Winter Hill the very next day to do it all again. Joseph Shufflebotham, a leading light of the SDF and one of the original ten pursued by Ainsworth, was scathing in his assessment of his fair-weather comrades: 'On Sunday I took my wife and three children . . . but about 200 were afraid of losing their names, and turned back – but of course, they were not socialists. No socialist can be afraid of paper warnings.'

Winter Hill, and the impending trial of those Ainsworth had named as the agitators, became a *cause célèbre* in northwestern socialist circles. National names came to the town to speak, and *Justice*, the journal of the tiny SDF, could barely contain its excitement: 'Bolton is now an A1 Lancashire town for socialist propaganda . . . hurrah for the revolution!' You've got to love the eternal optimism of the hardcore left in the face of all the evidence – and still it goes on. Every demo I've ever been on has been full of excitable activists from the Socialist Workers' Party and other even tinier Trotskyist off-shoots, convinced that this rally against the poll tax, the Iraq war, government cuts, tuition fees or whatever is the start of the revolution. Meanwhile, the demonstrators happily accept the free placards, and just tear off the words '*Socialist Worker*' from the top.

The trial of the original ten protagonists began in Manchester on 9 March 1897, Ainsworth's aim being to prevent them 'trespassing' on his estate, the moor in particular, at any point in the future. The 44 witnesses for the defence were largely older locals who recalled using the path unhindered across Winter Hill in their youth; the 33 witnesses for the prosecution were almost all employees of Ainsworth. Nonetheless, it went his way. The ten men had injunctions served against them, and the two who were seen as ringleaders were ordered to pay costs of over £600.

Having been such a bright flash in the pan, the Winter Hill protests – amongst the largest access demonstrations ever seen in Britain – soon faded from memory, and it wasn't until 1982 that local activist and historian Paul Salveson unearthed the story from a brief paragraph in Allen Clarke's book *Moorlands and Memories*. By this time, far smaller protests – most notably at Kinder Scout in 1932 – had reached near mythological status, and there was much feeling in Bolton that they should claim their proud place in the saga of the ongoing march towards open access to our moors and mountains. Meetings were held, talks given, a play written and performed outside the Wimpy Bar in Bolton town centre, and a commemorative march planned for the first weekend of September, the 'Winter Hill 1896 Trespass Anniversary' as the leading banner had it. True, though unusual to make such a splash for the 86th anniversary.

Paul Salveson expected a couple of hundred to come on the march, but in the event nearly 2,000 made it, confirming Bolton's historic ability to mobilise numbers when needs be. Benny Rothman, the public face of the Kinder protest, came along, as did Labour MP Andrew Bennett, a brass band and Mike Harding, comedian, folk singer, soon-to-be President of the Ramblers' Association and all-round professional Lancashire Lad (the title of his first album). Further celebrations were held in 1996, the centenary of the mass trespass, including the long-awaited dedication by the local council of Coalpit Lane as an official right of way. Having been so strangely forgotten, Winter Hill 1896 is now firmly etched in the folklore of both Bolton and the access movement.

On a chilly March Sunday morning, Paul met me at Belmont, the end of the protest route, and ferried me back to its start, at the disputed gate on Coalpit Lane. He had to rush off, but pointed me on my way up to the soggy, still-snowbound peak of Winter Hill. Not that you could miss it: a cluster of massive telecommunications masts occupies the summit now, making it even more desolate than nature alone has managed. There is something powerfully gloomy about the place: famous for a gruesome murder in 1838, regular sightings of UFOs and a litany of plane crashes. In the worst one, on a grim winter's day in 1958, a flight from the Isle of Man mistook its position and smacked into the hillside, killing 35. The impact was only 350 yards from the summit transmitter station, yet so severe was the weather that the men working there didn't even realise that there had been a crash.

If you're blessed with a clear day on Winter Hill, and mercifully my cold March morning was one such, it's the view that stuns, all the way over the whole of Greater Manchester. A few silent chimneys are the only reminder that, not so long ago, this would have been a view over Hades itself, a seething, smoking cauldron of humanity crammed into every crevice. Now, the most obvious landmark, glittering Teutonically in the cold sunlight, sits right over the other side of Manchester: the Chill Factor indoor ski slope, next to the candy domes of the Trafford Centre.

Walking down the other side to Belmont, I couldn't shake from my head the chorus of Ewan MacColl's 'The Manchester Rambler', a song written from his personal experience of the Kinder protest. Checking there was no-one within earshot, I even bellowed it out a couple of times, swelling to a climax on the immortal chorus, 'I may be a wage slave on Monday / But I am a free man on Sunday.' It felt brilliant to be high up on the Lancashire moors on a bright, blustery Sunday morning, and I was far from alone. Since first thing, I'd been aware of ramblers everywhere, alone, in couples and in joyful groups of all ages. It was particularly thrilling to see so many kids and teenagers along with their parents and grandparents, and none of them looked grumpy or bored. Perhaps, though, if I'd been near enough, I might have heard '*Graaaan*, next time can we go to t'Chill Factor? *Pleeeeeease*.'

By that strange law of universal coincidence, on the very day of the first Winter Hill trespass, Sunday, 6 September 1896, another hill just up the road was witnessing its precise antithesis. The people of Darwen, a smaller mill town less than ten miles north, were celebrating the end of a long access battle with a procession, mayor, corporation, brass bands, banners and all, up on to the moor above the town. There too, generations of locals had been used to walking, but had suddenly found that it was ruled off-limits by the landowner, in this case a vicar who rarely even made it to Darwen, as his parish was in Dorset. Two years later, another procession headed up the hill, this time to open a viewing tower that looks to be the very epitome of the Victorian age – dark, severe, yet lofty and ambitious, and built to celebrate its apogee, the Queen's Diamond Jubilee in 1897. Nominally, that is. The florid plaques on the tower's base all celebrate the Queen's longevity and list the aldermen who shuffled up the hill to applaud the dignitaries on that day in September 1898, but a more recent addition gives the game away. That is a plain crest that celebrates the 1996 centenary of the victory for the townspeople in gaining access to the moor that glowers above their streets.

It may have taken nearly a century to get the real reason for the Darwen Tower inscribed on its side, but the ambition was explicit from the start. Letters in the local press supported the idea of a Jubilee Tower, but as long as it also served as a celebration of the townsfolk's victory over their absentee landlord, the Rev. William Arthur Duckworth. With sweet irony, it was Duckworth himself, on one of his rare forays north to Darwen, who had to preside over the opening ceremony of the very symbol of his recent defeat. As I walked towards the tower earlier on that windswept Sunday morning, the mist whipping across the moor brought its shape in and out of focus. At a certain stage of semi-visibility, it looked like nothing more than a fat, raised middle finger, quite probably from the people of Darwen to the good reverend. From another angle, and in another stage of atmospheric opacity, there's something undeniably phallic about it, and that's probably aimed at him too.

This is hard country. Old snow lay curdled in piles in north-facing clefts and gullies, or packed up against the dry stone walls, sullen lines of dirty sandstone augmented by concrete blocks and broken paving slabs wherever they'd collapsed. It's a well-worn path, but you have to keep your eyes on the ground, as ankle-turning ruts and rocks litter the way. Wherever I looked, the whole scene appeared to have been painted by an artist with just three colours in his palette: olive green, battleship grey and a mucky ochre. Even calling it olive green gives it a continental raffishness that the month of March over Darwen can never possibly fulfil, but you get the picture.

Around the top of the tower there are optimistic little toposcope plaques, telling you what you might be able to see if only the mist would thin a while. It won't. Everyone who writes about Darwen Tower mentions not seeing anything. Official boasts claim that, on a clear day, you can see Snowdonia, but someone I read said that he's been up there dozens of times, and never caught sight of it. The plaque facing Wales has long since been jemmied off the tower, but the other two are still there. I looked out into the fog that was zipping past like a battalion of ghosts, willing myself to see, as promised, the Old Man of Coniston or Kinder Scout, my ultimate destination on this tour of the northwest's much fought-over footpaths. A couple walking a pair of very fat Labradors loomed out of the mist instead.

Just for a minute, it suddenly cleared. Only enough to see the town of Darwen below, but given that I'd only been able to see for about 20 yards prior to that, the effect was startling. The town is a sprawl, but a sprawl of straight lines and right angles: long terraced streets in blocks and grids, angular great buildings, a vast chimney or two. It looked sharp and harsh, as if you might cut yourself on one of its edges. Suddenly, the cheerless moor and pompous little Victorian tower looked like softness itself, the swirls of tracks and billowing clouds of heather a vital antidote to all that lay beneath. Something clicked in my head about the umbilical urgency of these wild open spaces to the people locked in that once-teeming grid on the valley floor. Down below, the smog, the chapels, the factories, the watchful eyes, the gossip, the iron rules. Up above, a transitory freedom, nature red in tooth and claw, redder still in unshackled loins. Blake's line about 'these dark Satanic Mills' was never far away as I drove through these towns, all the more so when every turn seemed to take me back on to the A666.

The people have not been slow in marking their victory in the battle for access. All over Darwen Tower, and in the benches around it, names and initials, going right back to the tail end of the nineteenth century, are carved into the sandstone, into the wood, or scribbled in marker pen. Snow-haired old gentlemen, pillars of the town, can still find the initials they carved as bullish youths. And it was good to see too that the modern identity of Darwen, and that cluster of towns nearby, is well represented in the daubings and chisellings. There's football rivalry, of course (Darwen Scum '97), and heartfelt scratchings of love and lust (Jak Is Fit As by Nicola H, Mick + Gail, Pat & Stace, Lisa ♥ Kev), but there's also Haleema, Radek and Irmina, Wrocław and Ian ♥ Antony.

And so to Kinder Scout, the name that looms largest of all, not just over the many struggles in the north-west to get into the wild places, but over the entire history of the British access movement. Even its name – half chocolate egg, half bob-a-job – seems wholesome and aspirational; it's hard to imagine that the names of nearby Bleaklow, which suffered even stricter prohibition, or Winter Hill would have galvanised public support quite so effectively, and consistently over the past 80 years and counting. It is the British rambling community's holy relic, and has inspired dramas, books, school projects, paintings, films, TV and radio programmes, poetry and music. In the proud bastion of the north-west itself, I fully expected to see eyes mist over and voices get a little croaky at the first mention of Kinder. I was very wrong.

Clarke Rogerson at the Peak & Northern Footpaths Society was the first to set me straight. 'I get a bit peed off with people going on and on about Kinder all the time,' he declared. 'It was a small event, and in some ways an ill-conceived event. Certainly, this society was opposed to it at the time, and we weren't the only ones. The Snake Pass [a path from the north across Kinder], for instance, we got that open through negotiation, not by guerrilla tactics or threats. There are those who say that the Kinder trespass put the whole cause back thirty years, that it did more harm than good. I have mixed feelings about it. Was it the Kinder trespass that changed the law? No it wasn't. It was hours and days and months and years of toil by lots and lots of people that got our moors open.' And in answer to my question as to whether the five men imprisoned after the trespass were treated unduly harshly, he has an immediate response: 'No. Not for what they did at the time.' Following the success of a 2007 exhibition commemorating the 75th anniversary of the mass trespass, there are plans to establish a permanent museum about the access struggles of the north-west, but it was proving difficult to get people excited about anything other than 'bloody Kinder'.

Neither was this a bit of modern revisionism. Tom Stephenson (1893–1987), another man carved out of Lancashire grit, was a giant of twentieth-century land-access campaigns. His dogged persistence, encyclopaedic knowledge of the law and social-ist drive saw him in the thick of the action from the First World War, when he was imprisoned in Wormwood Scrubs as a con-scientious objector, to the Thatcher years. Through the turbulent 1950s and 1960s, he led the Ramblers' Association, and drove the establishment of the Pennine Way, the country's first official long-distance footpath. In his memoir *Forbidden Land*, he pulls no punches in assessing the success, and otherwise, of the century's many access tussles. On the 1932 mass trespass of Kinder Scout, he is unambiguous, describing it as 'the most dramatic incident in the access to mountains campaign. Yet it contributed little, if any-thing, to it.' He goes further, becoming positively snicky when he nicknames Benny Rothman, the highly voluble leader of the tres-pass, as 'General' Rothman, and sneering on numerous occasions that it wasn't a proper protest, because they didn't make it to the absolute top of Kinder Scout.

Clarke Rogerson was not understating it when he said that there was little support at the time for the mass trespass amongst more middle-class ramblers. An official of the Manchester & District branch of the Ramblers' Federation wrote to the press to condemn it before it had even happened, and the organisation very publicly disassociated itself from it in its raucous aftermath. Their successors, the Ramblers' Association, tend to gloss over that one. To those seeking a more softly-softly approach of polite parliamentary lobbying, the demonstration was pure anathema, and many howled that it had set the cause back, rather than progressed it any. To the young firebrands who organised the trespass, this just proved that they were right, especially when you remember that attempts to lever greater access through

Parliament had been a major cause for half a century by then, and yet had delivered precisely nothing.

All the same, I was inexplicably excited to be tackling Kinder for the first time, and to see in the dark flesh a part of the world that I'd often gazed at on the map. Despite never having been there, I'd always been intrigued, even slightly intimidated, by the look of the High Peak on my Ordnance Surveys. The summit of Kinder is a vast, almost contour-free plateau 2,000 feet up and in the rough, elongated triangle shape of a primitive arrowhead (or, if you prefer, as seventeenth-century poet Charles Cotton had it, 'nature's pudenda'). Technically, of course, it does have an absolute summit (636m), but that's just a slight swelling of elevation over the neighbouring ground and with little difference discernible between that and the plateau's three scattered trig points, at 624, 633 and 590 metres, an obvious fact that make Tom Stephenson's sneer about them not having reached the summit look unnecessarily bitchy. The trig points delineate the outer edge of the summit plateau, almost as if they were guarding it; the miles of moor in between, an elevated void of very little indeed.

Look on the larger-scale Explorer map, however (number OL1, appropriately enough, for this has long been the biggest seller of all OS paper maps), and a whole load of new detail leaps out. Dozens of tiny peaty brooks fan out like the capillaries on a wino's nose, followed by a few contours that look like the marks made by mould as it sneaks its lacy way up a damp wall. Pretty, but kind of downbeat, and that was how I imagined the area itself to be. All around the flat arrowhead summit, contours tumbled down to the farms and settlements below. The outer limits of the plateau looked thrillingly sharp, and with suitably crisp names: Blackden Edge, Seal Edge, and across the north-ern perimeter, simply The Edge. Other names to chew on like old-fashioned blocks of toffee – Cluther Rocks, Kinder Downfall, Fairbrook Naze, Grindslow Knoll, Madwoman's Rocks – were scattered around this bizarre, extraordinary-looking mountain.

My plan was to camp the night in Edale, then take the train to New Mills the following morning and walk back over the Kinder plateau, following the route of the trespass. I'd wanted to go to the Vale of Edale, tucked down below the south-eastern edge of Kinder, for decades, again all thanks to the map. No main roads pass through, but there's still a railway, the high route between Sheffield and Manchester, and a village station. Viewpoints and campsites are dotted liberally amongst the contours, and of course, Edale is the starting point of the Pennine Way, its deeply scored route striding west out of the village and up on to Kinder. That would be my way back off the mountain in a day that would have me touch the soul of what walking means to the British.

If the glorious myth of the mass trespass has rather over-taken the reality, then so has the status of Kinder Scout itself. When I mentioned to various people locally that I was going to walk across Kinder, with thick snow still visible against the black peat of its top, the same reaction came almost every time. 'Tha's walkin' oop Kinder? A'this time uh yur? Dear God, tha wants to be curful, tha knows – thur's feet o'snow still on top. Can change in'n instant oop thur. Mek sure tha's got plenty o'provisions, wurterproofs, torch, whistle, map, coompuss – eeh, be curful, lad.' They made it sound like the Eiger, and it got me very excited indeed.

The train journey to New Mills took just 15 minutes, and getting off, the near-holy status of the Kinder mass trespass loomed large, in the shape of a mural at the station depicting a romantic tableau of the events of Saturday, 24 April 1932. It was the visual equivalent of a book that I'd happily devoured the previous evening, Fay Sampson's *A Free Man on Sunday*, her imaginative reworking of the event into a children's story. In it, she invents a sixth trespasser who was imprisoned, and gives him a back story that mainly revolves around a feisty little daughter who loves nowt more than to dubbin her dad's boots and accompany him on his moorland rambles. It's charming, heart-warming stuff, where every rambler is kindly, and every copper and gamekeeper a bloodless bully. In it, Benny Rothman is sainted before we even get to the trespass, as poor little Edie, the heroine, tumbles off her bike on the way to the gathering point at Hayfield. Sure enough, it's Rothman who swoops by to the rescue.

Looking at the way different anniversaries of 1932 have been celebrated, there's an undoubted sense that, the further it retreats into history, the more bloated the myth becomes. Now that all of the protagonists have died, the anchor of reality has been cut loose and the story is free to float where it wants. We need Kinder Scout as a totem, a crystal-clear symbol of good versus evil, and everyone – with the possible exception, it seems, of the footpath professionals of the north-west – is keen to make it their own. On a website about the protest, you can find videos of the 75th anniversary rally, held in April 2007 in New Mills. Inevitably compèred by Mike Harding, the keynote address was given by David Miliband, then the Secretary of State for the Environment. His bug-eyed enthusiasm to appropriate the mass trespass as the kind of thing the New Labour government admired and encouraged is received in near stunned silence, save for a solitary cry of 'Bollocks!' from somewhere off-camera. In a not untypical piece of statistical mangling, he also manages to inflate the number of trespassers to 4,000, ten times the actual figure. Even that, though, doesn't quite reach the level of awkwardness achieved by Harding's rousing singalong of 'The Manchester Rambler' as the zenith of the celebration. Harding himself does a fine enough job, but it's ruined by the sight of Lord (Roy) Hattersley slumped in a too-small chair behind him, silent and immobile, imperiously unwilling to join in and with his arms folded across his ample bosom, looking for all the world like Les Dawson's gossipy housewife.

Leaving New Mills station, my first path on a day of many was exhilarating. The town's Millennium Walkway is a 175-yard-long steel trajectory, pinned to a massive embankment wall some 20 feet above the churning waters of the River Goyt. This is a path that gives a perspective never available before, and it absolutely enchanted me, even more so because this audacious piece of civic bling sweeps through the middle of staggering post-industrial putrefaction. As I continued through the town, it became clear that this kind of vertiginous engineering was no new thing, for houses and factories teetered on top of cliffs, sheer rockfaces sprouted chimneys and windows like strange plants, tunnels vanished into the gloom while viaducts swooped overhead. It seemed that meaty buttresses and bolts were holding the whole place together.

The old railway line to Hayfield is now a path, so it was an easy, flattish canter to breakfast. There was, it seemed, plenty of choice: pubs, cafés and hotels all with 'RAMBLERS WELCOME' displayed prominently on their signs. It was a very different picture back on the day of the mass trespass, when legions of police filled the town and bristled up against the gathering hundreds intending to reach the peak above them. Reports from the day suggest that nearly all the residents of Hayfield shut themselves indoors, terrified of trouble.

The Peak and Northern might be a little standoffish about the whole Kinder protest, but they weren't missing a trick in terms of potential recruitment at this ramblers' holy grail, for their lovely cast-iron signs were everywhere up the Kinder Road. As I climbed, I started to recognise landmarks from the photographs taken in 1932. On rounding a corner, a stab of déjà-vu announced the Bowden Bridge quarry, where perhaps the most famous Kinder photo of all was taken, of an improbably youthful Benny Rothman addressing his troops from atop a rock before they set off up to the moor. Apart from the fact that it now acts as a car park, the quarry really hasn't changed much, and I lingered for a good fifteen minutes, soaking up the atmosphere that, in my charged state, was beginning to feel almost sacred. Thankfully, another piece of rubbish Kinder art was on hand to break the spell, in the shape of some excruciating doggerel inscribed proudly on a bench:

> As I trudge through the peat at a pace so slow
> There is time to remember the debt we owe
> To the 'Kinder Trespass' and the rights they did seek
> Allowing us freely to ramble the Dark Peak.

On that Saturday nearly 80 years ago, the protestors could not, in their wildest fantasies, have imagined that their little adventure would be so massively, passionately remembered. The idea had first germinated a few weeks earlier, when a youth camp organised by the British Workers' Sports Federation (BWSF) had taken place at Rowarth, a couple of miles north-west of Hayfield. Some of the campers had gone for a walk up to Bleaklow and had got into an argument with a gamekeeper. Back at camp, discussing the event, the idea of a well-publicised mass trespass on Kinder Scout was floated, and enthusiastically adopted. The date was set, and Benny Rothman, a 20-year-old unemployed mechanic, used his considerable flair for publicity to ensure that knowledge of the event was spread to the winds. To that end, he wrote and distributed leaflets, organised posters, inscribed chalk advertisements on pavements and went to visit the offices of the *Manchester Evening News*, who duly obliged with a sensationalist spread about the bust-up to come.

After the rally in the old quarry, the trespassers marched up past Kinder Reservoir, which was being heavily patrolled by officials of the water corporation, and thence into open country, along a rising valley called the William Clough. This was the disputed territory: once open to all, but through the nineteenth and early twentieth centuries, gradually closed off for grouse shooting. The grouse are still there today, and as you walk through, they squawk and fly off suddenly, but soon return unperturbed to their original spot. They are not, as gamekeepers and landowners have so stridently claimed over the years, much bothered by ramblers. In the William Clough, the first skirmishes took place with stick-wielding keepers, one of whom was slightly injured in a fall. The trespassers broke through and made it to the top of the Clough, on to the hallowed summit plateau of Kinder Scout. There they met a contingent from Sheffield who had walked unimpeded up the other side from Edale station, whereupon a short victory meeting was held, before the Manchester contingent returned to Hayfield. The police and keepers were waiting, and six ringleaders, Benny Rothman included, were picked off and arrested. At Derby Assizes three months later, five of them were imprisoned for a few months apiece, by a jury that comprised of two brigadier-generals, three colonels, two majors, three captains and two aldermen.

Had they not been arrested and imprisoned, the mass trespass would probably have been remembered only by Ramblers' Association archivists and local historians. But Kinder proved to be the inevitable flashpoint in a smouldering fire of resentment and agitation that had been building up since the end of the First World War. As is hinted on the famous Ellis Martin covers of OS maps of the time, this was the first great age of the rambler. Walking clubs were everywhere, from groups of well-to-do middle managers tramping the lanes and hills of the Home Counties to the great working-class mass movements of the north, furiously campaigning for access to their nearest open spaces. Inevitably, there was more mutual suspicion dividing the two than any sense of comradeship uniting them. No surprise, perhaps, for this huge chasm was not just circumstantial, but deeply ideological as well, and gave the Establishment press plenty of ammunition against the trespassers. In the Derby court case, the prosecution claimed that demonstrators had sung 'The Red Flag' (probably true) and chanted 'Down with the landowners and ruling classes!' and 'Up with the workers!' (probably not) as they clambered on to the moor. Counsel noted that a book by Lenin was found in the home of one of the defendants, to which the judge, Mr Justice Acton, responded. 'Isn't that the Russian gentleman?' In a foretaste of much that has happened since, youthful naïveté and exuberance were portrayed as something much darker and more disreputable. And the case pandered to darker instincts still, for the fact that three of the six defendants had demonstrably Jewish names did not go unnoticed.

Read any number of accounts of that distant April day, including first-hand ones, and they differ quite markedly, even in basic facts such as the number of participants. Benny Rothman claimed 600–800. The reporter from the *Manchester Guardian*, who accompanied the protest, stated it to be in the region of 400–500. The *Daily Express* went with 500 too, while the prosecution case at the trial in Derby put it at between 150 and 200.

In the north-west, I'd heard a fair few disdainful things said about the Kinder trespass, and Benny Rothman in particular. He had a terrific, unabashed flair for promotion, self-promotion included, a tendency guaranteed to upset those of more oatmeal tastes, if only because of their secret envy of his showmanship and shamelessness. As he got older, though, he was treated increasingly as a holy relic and, almost until his death in 2002, was regularly wheeled out to inject a little Kinder stardust into ramblers' meetings, rallies and photo-calls. And as I followed his footsteps up past the reservoir and into the William Clough, I looked up at the snow-smeared black pillows of the summit plateau, and any antagonism dissolved. Off to my right, the spray of water coming over Kinder Downfall was catching the wind and being blown upwards like smoke. An intoxicating jolt of freedom surged through my veins, and all I could do was thank him.

I thanked him and his comrades again when I reached the top. Despite the wide-eyed warnings of some locals, it had been a relatively simple ascent, following an easy track up the side of a peaty brook. The reward was magnificent. Views were endless, as was the sea of black peat rippled and cut into chunks and slabs by streams the colour of an old-fashioned porter beer. In the keen sunlight, the great slabs of millstone grit glittered like black diamonds, presenting themselves as terrific impromptu picnic tables, chairs and even sunbathing platforms. I stopped to munch my sandwiches by Kinder Downfall, watching the spray of the water tumble over the edge, vaporise and float free into the sharp sky.

Melting snow had swollen the river and, to cross it, I joined with a group of others in trekking upstream to find a spot where it could be forded. We nearly lost one braveheart, who strode out, shouting 'Follow me!,' on to a packed shelf of hard snow over the river. Just as he reached a point where he could almost jump to the other side, the shelf groaned and cracked, dropping with a splash into the rushing water. Looking like a surprised polar bear in a nature documentary, our man flailed downstream towards the fall, but managed to jump free back on to the rocks before cartoon calamity struck. We were all a bit hysterical by then, wheezing laughter and shouts of ribald piss-taking at each other in clouds of wintry breath. There was, I realised, a different atmosphere on these northern peaks: far more comradely, much less pompous than you'd sometimes find elsewhere. And more than anywhere I'd walked in years, Kinder looked and felt like a completely different world to the one below, a world that would never fail to lift sagging spirits or inspire new ways of seeing things. It had been a peak well worth fighting for, even if the fight had been a little overcooked by the Chinese whispers of constant retelling.

The descent back down into the Vale of Edale was equally delicious, down the boulder-strewn track that serves as the first (or, less commonly, the last) stretch of the Pennine Way. Well-worn tracks, smooth gates, numerous discreet signs and little wooden fingerposts make it impossible to lose your way. Not for the first time, I marvelled at the ruthless, yet generally cheerful, efficiency with which the Peak District National Park deals with its many visitors. It has to: situated as it is between the great metropolises of the north and Midlands, with well over a quarter of the British population within an hour's drive, it receives easily the greatest number of visitors of all 15 British national parks, something over ten million annually (the next most popular are all in northern England too: the Yorkshire Dales, the Lake District and the North York Moors, in that order). Yet despite this overwhelming influx, the annual spend of those visitors in the Peak District is the second lowest of all 15 parks: at £97 million per annum it's higher only than lowly Exmoor, which receives around an eighth of the Peak's number of visitors. The annual spend in the Lake District, by comparison, is nearly £700 million, and from two million fewer people.

On all the leaflets and notice boards locally, I'd clocked the phrase about the Peak being 'one of the family of National Parks', and as I climbed down towards Edale and a pint in the Old Nag's Head, the traditional starting point of the Pennine Way, I pictured this strange, diverse family. The well-loved grandparents of the clan, whom I imagined as a sort of Phil and Jill Archer, were undoubtedly the Lake District and Snowdonia, offering their venerable wisdom to the eager whippersnappers around them. Equally aged, if a little more bellicose, was Great Uncle Cairngorms, glowering by the fire in a big leather armchair and cradling a fine malt. Pembrokeshire and the Norfolk Broads were two flash cousins glued to their iPhones, one a surf dude, the other a braying yachtie. Pony-mad little sister, the

New Forest, was something straight out of a Thelwell cartoon. The Yorkshire Moors and Dales were two of your favourite aunties, who always baked the best cakes, but who also told the filthiest jokes after a couple of sweet sherries at Christmas. Hovering ethereally in the shadows was Northumberland, a mysterious distant cousin that everyone's heard of, but no-one's really met. And judging from the statistics, the Peak District was the staple of every family, the good time had by all, but who rarely gets so much as half a shandy bought for her afterwards.

In the Old Nag's Head, Pennine Way and Kinder Scout ephemera coated the walls of the Hikers' Bar, a name announced on the door. Another front door led into the Locals' Bar, and it was evident that the divide was pretty absolute. It probably has to be: Edale has been so thoroughly consumed by the Great Outdoors industry that the locals need to create and police their own corners, from a bar in the pub to a section of the vast village car park that was marked as 'VILLAGE PARKING ONLY'. I camped the night in my van at the top of the car park (it's not encouraged, of course) and was mildly amused to see that, even when the whole place was empty save for me and one other camper van, locals very pointedly made sure that they still used their designated spaces.

Immediately south of Edale is the 'shivering mountain' of Mam Tor, somewhere else that I'd wanted to visit for years. It's almost my ultimate destination, as a spiritual pilgrimage to one of the great mother mountains of Britain, but also as a far more prosaic, positively spoddy one too, a chance to see our most spectacular abandoned modern highway. Mam Tor's colourful nickname comes from its sheer precariousness as a vast pile of regularly shifting shale, just as it meets the firmer limestone to the south. Landslips are commonplace, which makes it a feat of towering optimism to have lain a trans-Peak road across its southern flank in 1810. This grew into the A625, a stretch of road notorious for its hairpin bends, unyielding gradient and harsh winter weather. Bits of the carriageway collapsed regularly and were patched up until the next slip, all causing terrible headaches for the Highways Agency and Derbyshire County Council. In February 1977, at the end of a wet winter that had itself followed a drought summer, the mountain shivered and the road buckled. Cracks and steps, some two foot deep, appeared in the asphalt. It was stitched back together once again, but as a single carriageway controlled by traffic lights. With more slips inevitable, the road was finally closed to all traffic in 1979. I can well remember the intriguing gap on the map in road atlases of the time: two thick red lines of main road failing to meet in the middle, and with the legend 'No Through Road at present' between them. I'm really quite ashamed that it had taken me this long to visit.

Getting there 30 years late was no anti-climax. In truth, it was way better than I'd dared hope, even after looking at so many photostreams of it from my fellow nerds on the internet. The old A625, after just three decades of abandonment, is a salutory lesson in the vanity of hoping to conquer Mother Nature, here on one of her very own named peaks. The shattered road drops away in cliffs, its layers of make-do-and-mend tarmac giving it the look of geological strata that had been painstakingly laid down over millennia. Faded white lines and Cat's-eyes point into cracks, holes and sheer nothingness. Above sat Mam herself, calmly waiting, occasionally shivering, and in total control of all she surveyed.

One unfortunate by-product of the A625's closure was that the adjacent Winnats Pass, a narrow defile through limestone turrets, has seen a considerable rise in traffic thundering through. The thin road is a 1:5 hairpin rollercoaster, and on a bright March day it was plenty busy enough; it must be a nightmare on a bank holiday Monday. Winnats Pass has an honourable place too in the story of our fight for access to our wild places, for it was here that national Access to Mountains rallies were held annually from the late 1920s through to the outbreak of the Second World War. They were generally fairly polite affairs, a few hundred or thousand picnicking happily in the natural amphitheatre of the Pass and applauding the rambling lobbyists and sympathetic politicians of the day. The events on Kinder Scout of April 1932 galvanised the event, with 10,000 turning up for the rally two months later, many of them young Kinder veterans and their friends noisily demanding support from the more timorous wings of the access movement. The rather diffident and polite world of rambling had changed for good.

Winnats Pass, and the neighbouring tourist honeypot of Castleton, were the perfect places to bring my northern footpath odyssey to an end, for I wanted to kick off the walking boots and place all these stories in their wider context of how folk up north like to relax. If Edale, with its cute train station and no main road or street lights, comes across like something off a 1930s OS map, all knobbly knees, mess tins, bad teeth and the tantalising chance of a fresh air-assisted leg-over, then Castleton is its twin in Sunday best. Castleton is where you take your aunties on a day trip, and although I'd never been there before, it felt somehow like the embodiment of my 1970s childhood, all lacquered hairdos, gift shops that have you clucking at the prices, ice-cream faces and lacy doilies. It's famous for its spectacular caves, and the unique local stone, called Blue John, that comes from them. Blue John is, you are regularly assured, one of the most prized of decorative rocks, but to my eyes its garish swirls looked tailor-made for clunky 1970s ashtrays, and not much else. Entirely fittingly, it was to Castleton that one of the earliest *Coronation Street* outings took place, a 1965 jaunt to the Blue John mine organised by upright Emily Bishop (or Nugent as she was at the time). In the shop at Speedwell Cavern, there's a lovely photo of them filming Hilda and Stan Ogden, Len Fairclough, Elsie Tanner, and Mr and Mrs Walker as they tottered off the excursion coach. I pulled on my cardy, channelled the spirit of Annie Walker and went for a cup of tea. Loose leaf, in a china cup.

There were countless other paths I could have walked, innumerable hills, forests and moors that had witnessed the north-west's struggle for access, but I felt that I'd seen and walked the most important, and that, in themselves, they represented a fine cross-section both of the issues and the landscapes involved. The trip had been superb, as much for the warm-hearted humour and easy-going chattiness of the locals as the imposing scenery. The umbilical link between the people of the north-west and their wild places had inspired me hugely, and it is as strong now as it ever has been. I had to admit that the bolshie buggers are quite within their rights to go on about it.

Follow the beige brick road on Mam Tor, Peak District

3. BLAZING THE TRAIL

Pub-quiz time: which UK number one record included quotations from Noam Chomsky, William Ewart Gladstone and Albert Camus? A clue – it wasn't by Westlife, but you probably guessed that. It did, however, storm straight in at number one and knock out the little Irish poppets, who'd been there for the previous four weeks with yet another damp ballad. It was the first new number one of the twenty-first century; over a decade on, it still pounds through you like a blast of amphetamines.

You know, I'm sure. Who else but the shamelessly precocious Manic Street Preachers, Gwent's finest in eyeliner, would attempt to weave words by such an unlikely triumvirate into a massive hit record? Gladstone gave it its title ('All the world over, I will back the masses against the classes'), Camus its coda ('A slave begins by demanding justice, and ends by wanting to wear a crown'), whined out at the dying fall by lead singer James Dean Bradfield, but it was the words of Chomsky that grab you by the throat at the very outset, and launched us into the new millennium on a surge of pure adrenaline.

'The country was founded on the principle that the primary

role of government is to protect property from the majority – and so it remains,' intones Chomsky, before the guitars and drums storm in and speed us into submission. It's a great line, and one that the linguist-philosopher-guru expands upon on his website, saying, 'American democracy was founded on the principle, stressed by James Madison in the Constitutional Convention in 1787, that the primary function of government is *to protect the minority of the opulent from the majority* [his italics]. Thus he warned that in England, the only quasi-democratic model of the day, if the general population were allowed a say in public affairs, they would implement agrarian reform or other atrocities, and that the American system must be carefully crafted to avoid such crimes against *the rights of property*, which must be defended (in fact, must prevail).'

Strong stuff, but look at the agonised history of legislation around the issue of access to our hills and paths, and it's hard to disagree with any of it. Inspired by my trip to the north-west, I wanted to read up on the turbulent background that had sparked the fights at Flixton, Bolton, Darwen and Kinder, especially how they had been conducted within the political discourse of the day. It was an illuminating, and not terribly inspiring, search.

Since huge tracts of the countryside were enclosed, particularly during the eighteenth and nineteenth centuries of massive industrial expansion and concomitant urbanisation of the population, public rights of access have only ever been grudgingly returned, and only in the most piecemeal of ways. Scores of pieces of legislation, each one chipping just a fragment off the granite block of our obsessions with property and privacy, have occupied Parliament for months at a time. Helped perhaps by listening to 'The Masses Against the Classes' at full volume, reading up on this interminable struggle was a fine way of making the sludgy blood of a lapsed lefty fizz once more through my veins.

The bottom line is that, had it been left to the Conservative Party, we'd still be peering through the gates. Every single advance in our rights of access has come about because of the dogged persistence of campaigners, their willingness to break the law and their often few friends in Parliament. Such members have invariably been drawn from the radical fringes of the Liberal and Labour parties, and often faced considerable opposition on their own benches, let alone the scarlet-faced opprobrium of those on the opposite side of the chamber. At every measure, Tories have spluttered indignantly and tried to bat away progress with a well-worn litany of disingenuous half-truths, perverse speculation, scaremongering and a persistently nasty seam of hatred towards the lower orders. As a result, it has taken well over a hundred years of constant new legislation to reach the point we are at today, with a half-decent public footpath network and a modest right to roam, mainly on uncultivated land, in England and Wales. In Scotland, there's a rather bolder presumption of access to the land (and, importantly, to waterways too), one that brings the country into line with the age-old Scandinavian ideal known in Swedish as *Allemansrätt*, or 'every man's right'.

The first parliamentary attempt to claw back some of the land came in 1884, with James Bryce's Access to Mountains (Scotland) Bill. Scotland's story is even more remarkable than that south of the border, for the most liberal access rights today have come out of a background that was the most generally repressive anywhere in these islands. With the infamous

Highland Clearances fresh in the popular memory, the late nine-teenth century saw something of their ghostly echo, as vast swathes of the Highlands were cleared and closed off for deer forests, in which a growing numbers of wealthy industrialists, from America as well as Britain, would hunt. Ghillies and stew-ards policed their perimeters, and innumerable instances were recorded of people being forcibly barred from entering land and using old paths that had been open to all since anyone could remember.

As is nearly always the way, it took a startling headline to bring the situation to a head. The 'Pet Lamb Case', as it became known in the Fleet Street papers that covered it with breath-less excitement, came about when a lamb owned by Highland crofter Murdo Macrae strayed into the 300-square-mile deer forest rented as a shooting estate by American railroad mil-lionaire William Louis Winans. Bearing in mind that Winans's estate (although called a 'forest', it was mainly mountain and moor) engulfed the small hamlet where Macrae and his family lived, the lamb needed to go not much further than the end of the garden to be on forbidden turf. Winans turned the full force of the law on to Macrae, ultimately unsuccessfully. Worse, he made himself a laughing stock – even the landowner from whom Winans rented the estate publicly denounced him. Not that it much dented his swagger: *The Times* reported that, while he was travelling through the Highland village of Tomich, some stones were thrown at his carriage. He stopped and immediately offered a reward of £500 – a quite unimaginable sum to Victorian croft-ers – for the capture or discovery of the guilty people.

It was at this time that Bryce was attempting to introduce his bill to Parliament. Public opinion could not have been more on his side. Editorials in *The Times* and other newspapers detailed the historical grievances in the Highlands and used the 'Pet Lamb Case' as the ultimate example of how skewed the situation had become. The time, it seemed, was ripe, but no-one had told members of Parliament. Bryce presented his bill, but it was dismissed without debate.

A year later, in 1885, James Bryce's constituency of Tower Hamlets was abolished and he headed to Scotland for a newly created one, becoming the Liberal MP for Aberdeenshire South until 1907, whereupon he took up the post of British Ambassador to the USA. The first MP to have his name scribed on the walkers' roll of honour was a fascinating individual, fulsomely bearded, fearsomely intellectual and a prolific author on topics as varied as botany, ancient history, sociology and modern political theory. In his earlier years, he'd walked and climbed much in the Alps, Scandinavia, Russia and beyond, even climbing Mount Ararat in an 1876 expedition. At over 13,000 feet, well above the tree-line, he found a large piece of carved timber, four or five feet long, and deduced it to be a remnant of Noah's Ark.

Bryce resubmitted his Access to Mountains (Scotland) Bill on an almost annual basis, but it was not actually debated until 4 March 1892, some eight years after its parliamentary debut. He gave his long-awaited introduction to the measure with relish, as he described how difficult getting into and around the Highlands was at that time for the hiker, artist or scientist. So assiduous are the landowners in protecting their vast estates (which, at their peak, accounted for around 6,000 square miles, a fifth of Scotland), he said, that 'one is obliged to stalk ghillies as the ghillies stalk the deer.' Tory members opposite could not take him, or the idea, seriously. After Bryce claimed he had 'climbed mountains in almost every country', some buffoon shouted 'Holland?', to loud guffaws. Incidentally, even that was an ill-informed heckle: Holland has some fairly significant hills in its south-eastern corner around Maastricht, with Mount Vaals topping a thousand feet (321m). The micro-states of Monaco and Vatican City excepted, Europe's flattest country is, by some distance, Denmark, where three 'peaks' scrap it out for national supremacy. They are all around 170 metres high, but, since 1998, have been topped by a new, man-made loftiest point in the country, the towers of the Great Belt suspension bridge between the islands of Funen and Zealand, each more than 80 metres taller. If we're being really pedantic, there's a TV mast even higher.

In his opening speech, Bryce stated that ideally, the measure he proposed would cover the whole of the United Kingdom, but that for now, he felt it necessary to concentrate on Scotland. He gave honourable members a history lesson, reminding them that the problem of access to the Highlands 'is practically a new grievance. Eighty years ago everybody could go freely wherever he desired over the mountains and moors of Scotland. Eighty years ago was the time when Scott made Highland scenery familiar to the world, the time when Wordsworth displayed the effect of his sympathetic studies of nature, and it was just at that time when Scott and Wordsworth's poems exercised such powerful spiritual and moral influences on the people that the policy of debarring people from the search after the truths of nature and intercourse with nature began to be pursued.'

'I cannot help remarking,' he continued, 'that the exclusion of the people from the enjoyment of the mountains of Scotland began just at the time when the love of nature and of the sciences of nature had been most widely and fully developed. The scenery of our country has been filched away from us just when we have begun to prize it more than ever before. It coincided with the greatest change that has ever passed over our people – the growth of huge cities and dense populations in many places outside those cities – and this change has made far greater than before the need for the opportunity of enjoying nature and places where health may be regained by bracing air and exercise, and where the jaded mind can rest in silence and in solitude. It is at this very time when these needs are so deeply felt, that the thoughtlessness or selfishness of the few has debarred the lover of scenery and science from those enjoyments and pleasures they desire.'

The Bill's seconder, Dr Robert Farquharson, the member for Bryce's neighbouring constituency of Aberdeenshire West, eloquently echoed the point. 'Light and air are two of the greatest necessaries of life. Light was taxed at one period of our history; there has been no attempt to tax air, because the process would be so difficult. If it were possible to reduce the air we breathe to a commercial commodity, we should soon have joint stock companies to deal with it, as in gas and water, and paying dividends more or less large – generally large'. In reply, the Solicitor General for Scotland, Andrew Graham Murray, the Conservative Unionist member for Buteshire, could not see what all the fuss was about. It was quite possible, he loftily stated, for anyone to walk in the deer forests 'if only they ask permission and are accompanied by a forester'. He turned his sights on the motives of some supporters of Bryce's bill, stating that 'members who know anything of Scotland will be aware that there is a certain class of questioner whose desire to put a candidate at a difficulty is greater than his thirst for information. I am afraid the honourable gentleman's Access to Mountains Resolution has become part of the stock-in-trade of the ordinary and unimaginative heckler. It is put forward by that class of person because they think that an unqualified answer in the negative would savour not at all of that platform generosity which gives away with lavish hand everything in the world save that which belongs to the speaker himself.'

Now, I've read that dozens of times, and I still don't have a clue quite what he was on about in that final rambling sentence. It's almost as if he's lost in some bitter, private memory; a public meeting somewhere in Buteshire, perhaps, where the Honourable Andrew Graham Murray was made to look like a complete idiot by some gobby constituent. It doesn't sound as if it would have been too hard to wind the old buffer up (actually, quite young buffer; he was only 42 at the time), and he probably didn't meet real members of the general public very often, so the chances of an epic culture clash would have been high indeed on such occasions. I miss Tories like that. Now that they have learned how to impersonate members of the human race, it's quite difficult to nail the bastards down. Old-school Tories were so palpably, radiantly condescending and pompous. They still are, of course, but apart from the occasional misfired tweet, they know now to keep it behind closed doors.

It had taken James Bryce eight years to get his bill even debated in the House of Commons, though in the meanwhile, another attempt, this time to open up land in Wales, had briefly flickered into life in 1888. The protagonist was another brilliant and highly individual Liberal MP, Tom Ellis, the member for his native Merionethshire in north Wales. In moving the Mountains Rivers and Pathways (Wales) Bill, he said that 'the object of it was to secure public right of access to the mountains and waste lands in Wales, and also to the rivers, lakes, and streams. It provided that any pathway that had been used for any five successive years during the last 49 years should be again used by the public.' Ellis conjured up ancient Welsh custom and law in support of his proposal, but this was denounced as 'simple fancy' by the veteran Tory MP for Caernarvon Boroughs, Edmund Swetenham. Swetenham fulminated at length against Ellis's proposal, eventually talking the bill out under the 12 o'clock rule, whereby debate is automatically adjourned as midnight strikes. It never returned.

James Bryce, and then his younger brother John Annan Bryce, the Liberal MP for Inverness Burghs, continued to present the Scottish Bill to Parliament, but to no avail. It was also presented, covering the whole of Britain, in 1908 by another renegade Liberal firebrand, Charles Trevelyan, the young member for Elland, West Yorkshire. His rhetorical introduction to the debate has become something of a poster slogan and rallying *cri de coeur* for British ramblers: 'Who has ever been forbidden to wander over an Alp? Who has ever been threatened with an interdict in the Apennines? Who has ever been warned off the rocks of the Tyrol? Who has ever been prosecuted for trespassing among Norwegian mountains?'

A little prone to earnest high-mindedness they may be, but the Trevelyan family are a fine example of the kind of dippy Liberal gentry who have forged and steered our national relationship with the land. True to his upstanding words, Charles was an enthusiastic vice-president of the Ramblers' Association and, when he inherited the family pile of Wallington Hall near Newcastle, set up Northumberland's first youth hostel in a stable block. He then donated the entire estate to the National Trust, thus disinheriting his son George, who nonetheless went on to become one of the leading New Age gurus of the twentieth century. Charles's daughter Katherine was also a notable free spirit, walking solo across Canada in 1930, aged just 20 and equipped only with a tent and a revolver. On writing of her experiences in a book, *Unharboured Heaths*, she became something of a transatlantic celebrity and a potent symbol of emancipated young womanhood.

Charles's younger brother, another George (usually known as G. M. Trevelyan), was an equally committed pedestrian who wrote one of the finest essays ever published on walking. Its opening words – 'I have two doctors, my left leg and my right' – are another motto often found pinned to a rambler's kitchen cupboard. He continued in deft explanation: 'When body and mind are out of gear (and those twin parts of me live at such close quarters that the one always catches melancholy from the other), I know that I have only to call in my doctors and I shall be well again.' His essay is especially good on the mental benefits of a good walk, when 'my thoughts start out with me like bloodstained mutineers debauching themselves on board the ship they have captured, but I bring them home at nightfall, larking and tumbling over each other like happy little boy-scouts at play, yet obedient to every order to concentrate for any purpose . . . I may wish.' His book – *Clio, a Muse and Other Essays* – was published almost a century ago, but the condition, and the cure, are timeless.

It is after this George, not his hippy nephew of the same name, that Trevelyan House, the St Albans headquarters of the Youth Hostel Association, is named, for he was their first president, in post for 18 years from the organisation's launch in 1930. He's left a rather less sober mark too, in one of the country's oldest and oddest extant outdoor events, the Trevelyan Man Hunt. A boisterous hurrah for the upper classes, the idea was dreamed up in 1898 by Trevelyan and two Cambridge friends, having been inspired by the flight from the authorities of the two young heroes in Robert Louis Stevenson's tale of derring-do, *Kidnapped*. Since then, the format has changed little: it is an exhilarating three-day scramble that still sees posh boys and their paters (the 'hounds') galloping over the fells of the Lake District in hot pursuit of a handful of young stablehands and jockeys in red sashes (the 'hares'). The Trevelyan Man Hunt, or Lake Hunt as it's sometimes known (naked swimming is an integral ingredient of the chase, for in common with many other aristocratic pursuits, it's a thin excuse for a chap to get his kit off with his chums), sounds terrific.

Defecting from the Liberals to become a Labour MP and Cabinet minister under Ramsay MacDonald, Charles Trevelyan was always astute in seeing which way the wind was blowing, and by becoming one of the first stately home owners to present his pile to the National Trust, pre-empting it as best as possible. More importantly, his gift came from a profound belief that owning huge tracts of land brought responsibility to ensure some measure of public access to it. Other politicians were neither as prescient nor as philanthropic, and the sound of the landed and wealthy resisting inevitable change continued to echo through Parliament and the press right up to the outbreak of the Second World War.

Trevelyan's 1908 access bill seemed at first to be successful; the Commons voted heavily in its favour. But for all the fine words in the chamber, as soon as it was shunted into committee, the bill was quietly sidelined and left to gather dust. In the press, only the *Manchester Guardian*, predictably enough, made enthusiastic noises; *The Times* seemed to forget its earlier support for Bryce and retreat into its Establishment lair, from where it shouted grumpily, in an editorial headed 'Mountains and Molehills', that the whole access issue was a 'bogey', and that every 'man or woman or child who wishes to explore the waste places of this island can do so without let or hindrance from anyone'. Over the next 30 years, there were a further nine attempts to bring in new access legislation, all largely based on Bryce's bill and all equally unsuccessful.

To see how far, and how fast, things then changed, it's instructive to take a closer look at two pieces of legislation enacted just a decade apart: the Access to Mountains Act of 1939 and the National Parks and Access to the Countryside Act of 1949. The 1939 Act was brought in as a bill the previous year by the Labour MP for Shipley, Arthur Creech-Jones. All through the 1930s, the public mood for greater access had been building up steam, galvanised by the Kinder protest of 1932 and its controversial aftermath. The idea of a first national long-distance path, the Pennine Way, had been floated by Tom Stephenson in a 1935 *Daily Herald* article, entitled 'Wanted – A Long Green Trail'; support for the idea was instantaneous and massive. The annual Winnats Pass access demonstrations grew every year. Rambling groups had mushroomed everywhere, and were confident that their time had finally come.

On the morning of 2 December 1938, Creech-Jones rose in the Commons to launch his bill, substantially the same measure that had been rejected or filibustered out well over a dozen times throughout the previous half century. He outlined the well-worn grievances, particularly in the north, and left it to the bill's seconder, Nuneaton Labour MP Reginald Fletcher, to expound more philosophically, and humorously, upon the principles at stake. Fletcher talked of his own lifetime's love of walking: 'I myself in the Lake District have watched trousers giving way to knickerbockers, knickerbockers giving way to shorts, and shorts in their turn giving way to shorter shorts. Looking at some of those shorter shorts, I have smiled to remember that my father walked and scrambled over every fell in the Lakes wearing a bowler hat and clasping an umbrella as firmly as any British Prime Minister being taken for a walk up the Berchtesgaden path.'

The last reference is a reminder that this debate was taking place only two months after Neville Chamberlain had returned from Munich waving his little piece of paper and declaring that he had secured 'peace for our time'. Fletcher's dig was very well aimed, for it was rapidly becoming evident that Hitler's assurances counted for nothing; the country was in a highly restive mood and could see a war fast approaching. To that end, supporters of the bill made much of the need to ensure that the nation's youth were as fit as possible, and in what better way could that be achieved than by granting them access to the hills, mountains and moors of upland Britain? There were explicit appeals too about helping to foster a new sense of patriotism in the land by giving people the chance to experience its finest bits for themselves. 'How can you expect some people to feel patriotic about the rookeries in which they have to live?' demanded Fletcher.

The patriotic case was expounded with most passion by Fred Marshall, Labour MP for Sheffield Brightside and a longstanding supporter of ramblers. 'Beautiful and lovely scenery has not only an aesthetic value,' he insisted. 'It has a definite spiritual and moral value. One who is in the habit of contemplating England's natural beauty is a better man and citizen for doing it.' Drawing in the spectre of rearmament for war, he brilliantly conjured up the image of his Sheffield constituents: 'men who stand and toil before the vast furnaces in blinding heat, smelt and pour the steel, fashion, hammer, and roll it into all kinds of useful articles, from the tiny razor blades to the great blocks of armour which line the sides of the great Leviathans of war, are absolutely precious to this country. The service they have given to it is incalculable. These men stand behind this Bill. They are the men who will carry on that wonderful craftsmanship and they are not content to spend their week-ends in places where they can see nothing but the belching smoke of factory chimneys. They ask for the national right to see the lovely spots of our land.'

'What has this House said to them?' Marshall continued, on something of a rhetorical roll. 'With incredible ingratitude this House has said, "No, you will disturb the grouse." The House has mumbled something about private property and the damage they will do to the gritstone rocks. And the owners have said "No". They have said, in effect, "We are having a few gentlemen from London for a shooting party for a day or two for the glorious twelfth, and therefore we must close the moors for twelve months, and anyone found on them will be summoned for trespassing." They have put up their miserable little boards "Trespassers will be prosecuted" which really deface the eternal hills, and are at once an insult and a challenge to the youth of these great industrial centres.'

To most of their Conservative opponents, these arguments were nigh-on irrelevant, for they detected something far worse lurking within them. 'The Bill really aims at the nationalisation of property,' boomed Captain Frank Heilgers, the MP for Bury St

Edmunds and the government's chief spokesman in the debate. 'There is more behind it than one imagines,' he continued in the tones of a gumshoe sleuth, 'because I notice that the names of three Front Bench Members of the Socialist party are on this Private Members Bill.' Oh, well spotted, sir. Other Tory Knights of the Shires smelled the same rat. Brigadier General Douglas Clifton Brown (Hexham) 'began to feel that the principles underlying the Bill were to down private property and to nationalise the land'. Robin Turton (Thirsk & Malton) thought that if the bill was successful 'we shall be going very far towards Marxian Socialism.'

Sir Patrick Donner (Basingstoke) apocalyptically warned that 'unless the Bill receives the drastic amendment which, in my opinion, it will require, it will have unjust and lamentable results. I do not want to base my objections on any ludicrous argument,' he stated, before going on to do just that: 'it might be said that, while Scott, the explorer, crowned the South Pole with the Union Jack, we may witness every mountain top in the United Kingdom crowned with a bin placed there under the auspices of the anti-litter league.' He also demanded financial compensation for landowners, should the bill become law.

Not all of the Tories were quite so lacking in any appreciation of the way the world was changing. Within the party, there was – the likes of Clifton-Brown and Turton excepted – a pretty stark north–south split, as there was in practically every interest group concerned with the bill, the ramblers' movement included. The Conservative MP for Leeds West, Vyvyan Adams, stated firmly 'that the broad principle of the Bill is incontestable', before going on to slyly chide his colleague Captain Heilgers for the 'extraordinary intellectual agility' he had displayed in the debate. 'He made a speech,' Adams continued, 'which, with great respect, I would say would have been substantially out of date when this question was last discussed in the year of our Lord 1908 [it had in fact been discussed since]. He said, for example, that there is no public demand for the principle of this Bill. There may not be any public demand from Bury St Edmunds, that hive of industry. My honourable and gallant Friend represents a part of East Anglia in which, incidentally, I was born; but let him go north and then he may be able more accurately to assess the need for fresh air in those densely populated areas . . . My honourable and gallant Friend sets up the shooting interests against the need of millions of industrial workers to escape from drabness, monotony and gloom and to realise the natural treasures of our country. Never have I heard such an audacious, or witnessed so unblushing, an opposition of sectional interest to the general good.'

With only 154 MPs in the parliamentary Labour party, the bill's sponsors knew that they would have to rely on Liberal and Conservative votes to get the legislation enacted. For all the har-rumphing, most Tories seemed to realise that some change was inevitable, and best therefore to manage it as smoothly as possible – and by smoothly, I mean most in their own interest. The bill passed its second reading and was sent off to committee, where it was torn apart by the Conservatives, and reassembled in a way that bore practically no resemblance to the original. Limited access would be granted, but only after a tortuous, and potentially expensive, process of permission was applied for. The most controversial addition, however, was to make trespass a criminal offence for the first time in British history, with a fixed fine attached to it of anything up to £2.

'Trespassers Will Be Prosecuted' is a phrase embedded in our national DNA, for it is a perfectly British blend of archaic pomposity and empty threat. Like most people, I grew up all too aware of the menacing signs that frowned across gateways and fences, and could recite the words long before understanding what they actually meant. After all, the only other time I ever heard the word 'trespass' was when mumbling the Lord's Prayer in church or school assembly – 'forgive us our trespasses, as we forgive those who trespass against us.' Even that changed when they brought in the trendy new Lord's Prayer in the 1970s, the one that made older relatives tut with bewildered disapproval. In that, 'trespasses' became 'sins', and we knew all too well what those were. Stealing, lying, swearing, eating too many sweets, cheeking your parents, hitting your sister, rummaging around in your classmates' pants – they were all sins, and so, apparently, was going into a forbidden field or wood. Everything that was fun seemed to be a trespass.

Yet the signs are a nonsense; 'wooden liars' as they became widely known. Unless you have caused actual damage, you cannot be prosecuted for trespassing; it is a civil matter, not a criminal one. The Limitation Act of 1623 made this very clear: 'if the defendant disclaims any title to the land and proves that the trespass was negligent or involuntary and that he has tendered sufficient amends before the action was brought, the plaintiff will be non-suited.' This gave rise to the long-held belief that, if you were challenged by a farmer or landowner, you should offer a couple of pennies in recompense of any damage, declare that you make no claim upon the land and no trouble would ensue. It didn't always work out quite that simply.

Even with no basis in law, 'Trespassers Will Be Prosecuted' signs usually achieved their aim simply by scaring people off. This was a point frequently pondered upon in the many access debates in Parliament. In 1908, the Edinburgh Liberal MP Arthur Dewar said that the phrase was a 'terminological inexactitude if ever there was one', but that 'it was quite enough to frighten away perfectly innocent people, because they did not know the law.' In the 1938 debate, Labour and Liberal MPs, and even the odd Tory, confessed that they had knowingly trespassed on their walks, and would happily do so again. The soggy legal position was perhaps best illustrated by James Chuter-Ede, the Labour MP for South Shields and future Home Secretary in the Attlee government. He described a personal experience: 'I recall walking along a footpath and being stopped by a gamekeeper who asked me if I knew that I was on private land, and I said "Yes, what about it?" He said, "My only instructions are to ask you if you know that you are on private land." I said, "Does it not occur to you that we should not call it a public footpath unless it was on private land?" and he replied, "I know nothing about that, Sir. My job is to ask the people who come here, do they know that they are on private land." I said, "I suppose that every one of them has turned back," and he replied, "Yes, every one except you, Sir." That kind of spirit is not the way to secure good feeling between the general public and the landowner. It is an abuse of the ignorance of the person who is legitimately using the footpath, and I am quite sure it would not be defended in public by any landowner.' Not defended perhaps, but extensively employed nonetheless.

For the well-to-do rambler, confident of his rights, the signs acted not as a deterrent, but as a magnet. Sir Leslie Stephen, Victorian writer and father of Virginia Woolf and Vanessa Bell, founded the supremely well-heeled, all-male Sunday Tramps walking club (every member in *Who's Who* and, as Stephen himself put it, 'precisely the kind of person who writes articles for newspapers'. So cocksure of their own importance were they that one of their number, novelist George Meredith, suggested that the conversations on their walks 'would have made the presence of a shorthand-writer a benefaction for the country'. On their fortnightly tramps in the green lanes and byways of the Home Counties, the appearance of a 'wooden liar' would be the perfect spur for exploration: 'they gave a strong presumption that the trespass must have some attraction,' Stephen explained. 'To me it was a reminder of the many delicious bits of walking which, even in the neighbourhood of London, await the man who has no superstitious reverence for legal rights.' They even devised a chant about their legal rights that they would perform in unison should they be challenged for trespass, and after blasting it at the startled keeper or farmer, would force a shilling on to him. They might just as well have sung in close part harmony, 'Look here, my man, don't you know who we a-aaare?'

To those lower down the social pecking order – in other words, practically everyone else – the signs, and the gamekeepers, ghillies and guns that backed them up, worked very effectively indeed. But by the time of the 1938 debate, knowledge of the fundamental loopholes in the law of trespass was no longer confined to those in the upper echelons. The staggering upsurge in working-class walking organisations, together with the thirst for knowledge that accompanied it, meant that the implicit threat was no longer enough. Arthur Creech-Jones's bill returned from committee to the Commons bearing almost no resemblance to its former self. The advantages it now contained were almost all for the landowner, and chief amongst these was the criminalising of trespass.

Labour and Liberal MPs were horrified by the idea, and it is interesting to note how many impassioned contributions came from some of the most impressive of their number, the free-thinking men of cast-iron conviction whose reputations have only grown with time, rather than being utterly forgotten like so many colleagues, their own colourless yes-men and the baying public-school twits on the Tory benches alike. The Liberal MP for East Wolverhampton, enlightened industrialist Sir Geoffrey Mander, described it as 'almost equivalent to a new Enclosure Act'. Joshua Ritson, a Durham miner turned Labour MP for the city, strode energetically up on to the moral high ground, saying: 'I am anxious lest people whom I have known all my life should now be restricted and be fined for wandering about on the moor, and if that should happen, I say that it would be not only serious, but a very wicked thing.'

Philip Noel-Baker, the hugely impressive Labour MP for Derby, war hero, Olympic medallist, co-founder of both the League of Nations and the United Nations and winner of the 1959 Nobel Peace Prize (and who also found time to have a 20-year affair with Megan Lloyd George) stated that the bill was fatally poisoned, should be dropped and that he regarded 'this incursion into the law of trespass as a restrictive evil'. Sidney Silverman, the pocket-sized Dennis Skinner of his day (he even sat in the same place in the chamber now occupied by the Beast of Bolsover), drew himself up to his full five feet nothing as he declared that criminalising 'merely to be upon the land' was 'doing something so dangerous as to outweigh any of the other advantages that remain in the Bill'.

James Chuter-Ede put it into historical perspective with the observation that 'by this so-called compromise, the landowning classes are getting with respect to their land a thing that the old landlords' Parliaments would never have given them in the eighteenth century.' He continued: 'Surely so fundamental an alteration in the law of England as this ought not to be slipped in as a final Amendment into a Private Member's Bill as a result of some compromise arrived at, not upstairs, but mainly between the various landowners' associations and the Commons and Footpaths Preservation Society (CFPS). This is an Amendment which we ought not to pass.' Here was a nod to the internecine battle that was also raging within the rambling movement at the time. It was widely held by many, particularly in the Ramblers' Association, that the CFPS, as the main negotiating organisation with the government, had sold them all out with their acceptance of the reworked bill. The CFPS is now the Open Spaces Society, and there are many diehard ramblers who have still not forgiven them.

The amendment to nullify the trespass clause was narrowly defeated, and the Access to Mountains Act – the title was pretty much the only thing that had survived intact – became law on New Year's Day 1940, by which time the country was at war and not much thinking about a Sunday stroll. Amongst those on the losing side were many who, five and a half years later, would find themselves as Cabinet ministers following Labour's post-war landslide election victory. They too would neither forgive, nor forget.

To my generation, it's all too tempting to imagine that the country marched in solidarity into a bright new dawn with the 1945–51 Labour government. In truth, following Attlee's thumping victory, public enthusiasm for their new masters ebbed away with alarming rapidity. Rations became ever tighter, the economy was in tatters and life failed to improve at all for the vast majority of people. Even landmark legislation such as the creation of the National Health Service and the nationalisation of the mines and the railways was beset with unforeseen difficulty. Britain was broke, knackered, cold, hungry and deeply gloomy (quite literally; power supplies were restricted and countless overseas visitors remarked on how ill-lit and smoggy were the streets of our major cities). The worst winter of the twentieth century crippled the country even further in early 1947, leading to death threats aimed at Mannie Shinwell, the Minister of Power. The Labour government was desperately in need of some feelgood headlines, and these they hoped to get from the National Parks and Access to the Countryside Bill, outlined in the King's Speech of 26 October 1948. The thrust of it was to create 12 National Parks, an unspecified number of Areas of Natural Beauty (AONBs) and Britain's first official Long Distance Paths (LDPs). It also aimed to tidy up the chaos around footpath law, by making every local authority draw up a definitive map of its rights of way network. Included within it too was the repeal of the much-hated 1939 Act.

The tone of the debate, starting on 31 March 1949, was a world away from that of a decade earlier. There was no doubting that real change was going to happen, and for a Commons more used to dealing with an apparently never-ending sequence of hardship and difficulty, much underscored by vicious class and political rivalry, the degree of consensus around the topic, and the feeling that it was good news all round, produced something of a carnival atmosphere in the chamber.

The bill was introduced by the Minister of Town & Country Planning, Lewis Silkin, who attempted to turn the bleak national mood to its advantage, in stating that 'with the increasing nervous strain of life, it makes it all the more necessary that we should be able to enjoy the peace and spiritual refreshment which only contact with nature can give.' There was none of the circumscribed language of earlier debates, when access campaigners had had to tiptoe deftly around the Sir Bufton Tuftons on the Tory benches. Silkin rose to unaccustomed powers of oratory in summing up what the bill meant: 'Now at last we shall be able to see that the mountains of Snowdonia, the Lakes, and the waters of the Broads, the moors and dales of the Peak, the South Downs and the tors of the West Country belong to the people as a right and not as a concession. This is not just a Bill. It is a people's charter – a people's charter for the open air, for the hikers and the ramblers, for everyone who loves to get out into the open air and enjoy the countryside. Without it they are fettered, deprived of their powers of access and facilities needed to make holidays enjoyable. With it the countryside is theirs to preserve, to cherish, to enjoy and to make their own.'

Conservative opposition was muted, and where it came, it sounded by contrast like the mumblings of some bespittled old buffers in a dark corner of the Athenaeum. A few made reference to the fact that they dreaded rural areas of Britain becoming like 'Mr Butlin's holiday parks', a name that they could barely say without a shudder. Sir Edward Keeling, MP for Twickenham, talked about England's highest peak, Scafell Pike, and felt obliged to point out that 'there is nothing in the Bill to prevent the local planning authority from acquiring that summit and erecting on the top a Tea Kiosk – with one capital K – or a Kozy Kafe – with two capital K's and a z.' Colonel Sir Ralph Clarke, MP for East Grinstead, worried that, with the trespass law gone, ramblers who were accidentally shot by grouse-hunting parties might now feel emboldened to take legal action. Major Tufton Beamish, who'd inherited his safe seat of Lewes from his father, Rear Admiral Tufton Beamish, snorted that great danger came from 'townsmen who probably did not know the difference between a badger and a fox or, at any rate, not the difference between their smells'.

A small number of Tories stayed obstinately off-message, and could raise no enthusiasm for the measure at all. The Lonsdale MP, Sir Ian Fraser, declared that 'it is unthinkable that a farmer should bring his horse into one's back garden in the suburbs, but it is not unthinkable that one should take one's clumsy ignorance into his farm yard and let his beasts stray. Indeed, the people in the towns demand the right to go and harm the countryside because they do not understand it.' Osbert Peake, a Leeds MP, voiced his suspicion that Labour sympathisers were temperamentally unable to enjoy the places they were planning to free, telling the chamber how 'I remember during the war giving a night's hospitality to a war-time colleague, who now occupies an important position on the Government Front Bench, and taking him for what I thought would be a treat for him. It was a drive through one of the most beautiful parts of Yorkshire. I must say that he did not seem very interested, and spent the drive reading in *Lloyds Weekly News* and the *Sunday Dispatch* the accounts of a speech he had made the day before.'

Not for the first time, and certainly not for the last, the greatest opposition to the measures being proposed by a Labour minister came from behind him on his own benches. To some of the new intake of Labour MPs, whose election had surprised everyone, themselves included, it gave them a chance to roar out a few of their most cherished radical tenets. One such came from the veteran Suffragette Barbara Ayrton Gould, who had snuck an unexpected election victory in Hendon North on her eighth attempt at getting into Parliament. The 1945 *Times Guide to the General Election* had certainly been caught on the hop: her defeated Conservative opponent, Brigadier E. W. C. Flavell, was given a fulsome biography, including the fact that he 'formed and commanded the first Paratroop Brigade, and on D-Day was the first brigadier to drop with his troops', whereas all they could find to say about the new MP was that she was 'a journalist'.

Her beef was that Silkin proposed to give much of the power of administration of the new National Parks to members of the local county councils. 'I ask myself,' she posited imperiously, 'what is the personnel of a great many of these county councils? Many of these councils are reactionary. Unfortunately, there are still plenty of reactionary councils today, largely composed of the descendants of men who originally enclosed beauty spots for their own convenience . . . Frankly, I do not trust them.'

She had a point. Under this legislation, it was up to the county councils to draw up definitive maps of the rights of way under their jurisdiction. As most of the cities operated as county boroughs of their own, the elected representatives of Manchester or Liverpool, for instance, had no say in the definitive maps of Lancashire; this was a job solely for the rural authority, despite the fact that the majority of walkers likely to benefit from the legislation would be people from the nearby big towns and cities. With the rural councils heavily weighted towards the landowning squire, both politically and in terms of actual membership, it was inevitable that the definitive maps, when they finally came, would significantly under-represent just how many well-used paths there were on their patch. The rights of way that still shudder to an inexplicable halt at old county or parish boundaries demonstrate the point.

Another new female Labour MP, whose victory in Blackburn had also not been widely predicted, made a huge mark on the debate. Unlike Mrs Ayrton Gould, past retirement age and shortly to lose her seat and die soon after, Barbara Castle was one of the brightest young things of the new Parliament and went on to become the foremost Labour matriarch of the twentieth century. Even into her nineties, she was vocal in needling Tony Blair's government into remembering its heritage; Gordon Brown called her 'my mentor and my tormentor'. To her, the bill was a major factor 'in the social revolution that is now taking place', for it 'marks the end of the disinheritance of the people of this country from enjoyment of the countryside'.

Mrs Castle was particularly excited about the new Long Distance Paths (LDPs) that would arise from the legislation. The previous year, she had been one of a group of Labour MPs (Hugh Dalton, the ex-Chancellor of the Exchequer, was another) to walk sections of the proposed Pennine Way, in the company of its creator, Tom Stephenson. They became a regular walking group under Stephenson's tutelage, and explored many of his putative new paths, in Pembrokeshire, the Lake District, the Cheviots and the Brecon Beacons. 'I should like to think that some of the foot-slogging the Chancellor of the Duchy of Lancaster [Dalton] and some of my honourable friends and I did last May has blazed the trail in that regard,' she announced triumphantly.

Good-natured references to Tom Stephenson's walking group cropped up repeatedly throughout the debate. Fred Willey, another of their number, said that he'd found it rather less 'blazing the trail', as Barbara Castle had put it, but that 'personally I found it more like a forced route march, and I understand that we are still remembered in the locality as members of "Dalton's Circus".' The patrician Westmorland Tory William Fletcher-Vane laconically described it as 'that deplorable event . . . when the Chancellor of the Duchy of Lancaster, waving, I believe, a red silk handkerchief, and followed by about half a dozen admirers, trooped all along the Pennines . . . what my constituents said, particularly about the troop of photographers who followed them, is nobody's business.'

Reading the debate made me think how much we could do with a few more politicians pulling on their walking boots today. In the past 20 years, we've heard of very few, or at least any that have continued walking once the press photographers have left. On the Labour benches there have been former leader John Smith, ex-Foreign Secretary Robin Cook, Chris Smith and Dennis Canavan, a salutary roll call when you remember that half of that group died of massive heart attacks in their fifties (Cook while walking in the Scottish mountains). On the Conservative side, there's former MP turned *Times* columnist Matthew Parris and, always looking like a slightly melted Action Man, William Hague. In the 2010 election, the Tory ranks were swollen by the arrival of a real live Action Man, über-yomper Rory Stewart, as the new MP for Penrith and the Border in Cumbria. As part of his *Boy's Own* pedigree of soldier, diplomat, writer and adventurer, he spent nearly two years walking 6,000 miles from Iran to Nepal, via Afghanistan, Pakistan and India, and, on being selected as candidate for the 1,200-square-mile constituency in late 2009, spent much of that winter getting to know the patch by walking around it, something that he said 'allows me to capture the spirit of a place in a way that I could not by car'. As you might expect, most Liberal Democrat MPs claim to be fond of walking, even the ones who look as if they would drop dead if they tried, but none really spring to mind as hardcore ramblers. Or anything else, for that matter.

To today's politicians, walking is not the *hobby du jour* that quite projects the image that they are so eager to cultivate. It's all a bit too frumpy and slow for the insatiable demands of the 24-hour news media. So instead, they must go jogging, for that is far more in keeping with our adrenaline-fuelled, go-getting culture. Jogging is macho and sweaty, and allows them to look as if they are sponsored by Nike (hey, the youth vote!) as they manfully grunt and tug on a water bottle helpfully carried by their private detective. Like so many elements of our modern political system, it is a direct import from the USA, where no self-respecting presidential hopeful fails to take a well-photographed jog or two just prior to an essential vote. It's a high-risk strategy, though. In May 1991, George Bush senior collapsed while jogging and, for one awful day, the world contemplated the possibility of President Dan Quayle. Even Bill Clinton had a go, when you'd think that footage of him all pink and panting would have been the last thing the spin doctors would want to remind us of. It was, of course, Tony Blair who first brought the habit to our shores, but even Gordon Brown – looking like a sack of coal in trainers – was seen tottering around St James's Park, no doubt in a vain attempt to outdo serial jogger David Cameron. I suppose that at least we should be thankful that our politicians have looked west for inspiration, rather than east, or we'd have Nick Clegg wrestling bears on the *Six O'Clock News* or a bare-chested Boris Johnson harpooning carp in the Serpentine.

The National Parks and Access to the Countryside Act came into law two weeks short of the end of the 1940s. The decade had been brutal, bloody and difficult, but there was a sense that better times were on the way, and that the new provisions of the act would be a significant contribution towards that. Bizarrely, however, driving through the creation of ten new National Parks proved to be a whole lot easier than establishing a handful of official Long Distance Paths. While provision for the National Parks could be somewhat vague and general, with extensive exemption from planning restrictions for farming and forestry, the establishment of footpaths was far more specific. Each one needed to be precisely measured, mapped, signed and publicised, and every landowner on its route could – and often did – object. Establishing exactly where public rights of way existed was the major problem, for these were not yet mapped by Ordnance Survey, who were concerned only with the existence on the ground of tracks and paths, and not their legal status as public or private routes. The official OS *Instructions to Field Examiners* of 1905 had stated their case with characteristic baldness: 'the Ordnance Survey does not concern itself with rights of way, and Survey employees are not to enquire into them.' It was not until 1958 that the Ramblers' Association finally persuaded OS to mark them on their maps.

Neither were rights of way generally mapped by local authorities. Just as general access legislation had taken tortuous decades to be enacted, and only then once it had been almost entirely castrated by landowners, the course of footpath legislation was similarly rutted. The first attempts to bring in simpler rules to identify and map public footpaths, based largely on a certain number of years of continuous use, were made in 1906, but despite general support in Parliament and amongst the public, the bill was sidelined. So were the next ten attempts over nearly 30 years, and it was not until 1932 that the Rights of Way act was finally passed. Once again, unwelcome alterations were forced into the act by the Lords at the very last minute, but at least it gave a legally defined notion of a public right of way as being a footpath, even across private land, that had been in continuous use for 20 years.

Every inch of access to land and the use of footpaths has depended – and continues to depend – on tiny nuances of law, common practice and precedent, all sifted and nitpicked over in countless court cases. In 1905, a judge had succeeded in declaring that the tracks used since time immemorial by visitors to Stonehenge were not public footpaths, and it was against this kind of backdrop that the much-emasculated 1932 Act finally limped on to the statute book. It also included the idea of councils holding maps of rights of way within their remit (although this had been included in the measure as a way for landowners to document that disputed routes were *not* public, by doing so they had to show which were), and it was hoped that these would gradually coalesce into definitive maps of the rights of way network. The 1949 Act enshrined this as a legal requirement, and every council had now to map its paths. Some urban authorities, such as Cardiff, Ipswich, Norwich, Plymouth and various London boroughs, have still not managed it 60 years later.

The new Long Distance Paths were, for the most part, carved out of existing rights of way as mapped throughout the 1950s. That in itself was difficult enough, for there was considerable opposition in many places, but when trying to forge a new link path, the problems were massive. For the Pennine Way, the highly charged totem of the new policy as it crested the backbone of England through some of the most hotly contested areas of all, 70 miles of new path were needed, and there were numerous local enquiries stuffed full of the area's many vested interests. The usual crew of grouse shooters muttered their opposition, but the lion's share came from water boards, who insisted that walkers would pollute the gathering grounds of municipal supplies. Bearing in mind that the path would take the high ground along the watershed of northern England, this was an argument that ran and ran, even though it was dismissed by expert opinion time and again. And what of other users of the land? As an editorial in the *Manchester Guardian* put it, 'does the minister now intend . . . to close all those paths, roads and railways over [the water authority's] gathering grounds, and if not, why not?'

On Saturday, 24 April 1965, after 14 years of enquiries and a full 30 years since he had first floated the idea in the *Daily Herald*, Tom Stephenson was the guest of honour at the ceremony in Malham to open the Pennine Way. By now the secretary of the Ramblers' Association, Stephenson was justly thrilled with his achievement, realised exactly as he visualised it three long decades earlier, as 'a long green trail from the Peak to the Cheviots . . . just a faint line on the Ordnance Maps which the feet of grateful pilgrims would, with the passing years, engrave on the face of the land'. Strangely enough, Stephenson himself never did the walk in one go; neither did Alfred Wainwright, who produced one of his celebrated guidebooks of the route in 1968. His promise to stand everyone who finished the walk half of bitter in the Border Hotel at Kirk Yetholm is said to have cost him £15,000 in the 23 years from then until his death. Wainwright's book ends with the weary promise that 'you won't come across me anywhere along the Pennine Way. I've had enough of it.' This might be related to the fact that he famously sank to his waist in a peat bog on the Dark Peak, and had to be rescued by a National Park warden. The many boggy mishaps aside, the path even spawned its own bespoke injury, Pennine Way Knee, specifically affecting the left leg and caused by the fact that the path most often took the westerly route around peaks, thus stretching the left side more than the right.

Even with the hundreds of named trails that we have these days, the Pennine Way, the one that started it all, remains the undoubted alpha male of the pack, the toughest, hardest bastard there is: 268 miles from Edale to Kirk Yetholm (plus however many you have to add to reach your accommodation or because you got lost), a total of 32,000 feet climbed, and all invariably in shocking conditions. Most people take between two and three weeks, although the 20-year-old record stands at two days, 17 hours, 20 minutes and 15 seconds, with no sleep at all.

The 'faint line on the Ordnance Maps' became scored rather deeper than Tom Stephenson had anticipated, for Britain's first National Trail struck an instant chord, and tens of thousands came to sample it. By the mid-1970s, large sections were a squelchy morass, and others so wide from the feet of hikers walking abreast that they were likened to a six-lane motorway, three tracks going north, three south. With two school friends in 1982, I walked the Dales Way from Ilkley to Windermere, the last (and only) time I'd ever walked a long-distance path. There's a section north of Horton-in-Ribblesdale where it joins the Pennine Way for a mile or two, and I can still remember the shock when we hit it, for it was like stepping off a country lane on to a busy, wide highway. On the worst-affected stretches, plastic netting and mats were laid, which were later replaced with flagstones salvaged from the floors of demolished cotton mills, which seems entirely fitting when you remember the Winter Hill and Kinder protestors, the spiritual ancestors of the route. Many people hate the flagstones, but as I trekked along them on top of Kinder Scout, the thin grey ribbon of pavement stretched off over the black peat as if in a monochrome *Wizard of Oz*, and I was strangely charmed. But then, I wasn't carrying a 25lb backpack and with 270 miles to go.

I knew that I had to walk at least one of the National Trails for this book, but the more I read of the Pennine Way, the surer I felt that it wasn't going to be this one. Although the grand-daddy of British LDPs, it has been comprehensively eclipsed by other routes, most notably Wainwright's Coast to Coast walk, and it's now estimated that fewer than 2,000 people complete it every year. More than that, though, the route itself didn't much appeal to me, for it is always portrayed as relentlessly dour and dirty, mile upon mile upon bloody mile of bog, moor and driving rain. I could imagine all too easily the kind of misanthropes that such bleakness would appeal to. And always has: in the 1971 Countryside Commission report on the route, when hundreds of walkers were counted and surveyed, reasons given for doing the Pennine Way included that it is 'the furthest thing from so-called civilisation', 'remote from crowds, motor vehicles and the destructive influences of modern life' and 'to get away from the prying eyes of bureaucracy'. Wouldn't you love a night in a remote moorland pub with that lot?

For a couple of highly entertaining days, I became slightly obsessed with reading the dozens of online diaries by folk who had managed the Pennine Way. They all shared a relentlessly upbeat tone, speckled with more revealing (and always funnier) moments of either coruscating agony or withering bathos.

Folk put their every odd thought and muscular twinge into these diaries. One man detailed his pre-trail training regime, which involved taking daily walks with a cheap rucksack that he'd filled full of 23lb of potatoes. The rucksack makes his back ache and then break out in spots, but it only gets worse: 'The training received a setback when I realised that the family had robbed some of the potatoes from my pack and the 23 lbs I thought I was carrying was in fact only 17 lbs. A further setback came when I realised that the potatoes were sweating and sprouting, so I had to find an alternative and turned to newspapers, bringing the pack back up to 23 lbs.' You see? It's better than *Emmerdale*. Things started to improve for our intrepid hero, but then pack-related disaster strikes again: 'Another setback to the training occurred when I took out the newspapers from the rucksack in order to sew on some new closure straps. The newspapers were taken off for recycling and I had to look for something else to carry. I tried a 12 pack of Tetley's bitter, but it was rather uncomfortable and not very well balanced, and ran the risk of becoming depleted in training! I therefore reverted to carrying some A level physics books which somebody was throwing out – just the thing for a bit of light reading en route!'

And off he goes, doubtless to the considerable relief of his family. Meticulously cataloguing the real ales on offer in every pub, he gradually heads north, but is not happy on reaching the youth hostel at Haworth, which is 'in a fine old mansion with much more room than most. However, my dormitory was filled with a coachload of German teenage boys and the floor was littered with empty beer cans (despite this not being allowed by the YHA).' Youths in a youth hostel; whatever next? To escape, he heads to a nearby pub 'where I met a Cornish chap from the same dormitory and was bored to tears by his rambling tales, so only stayed for a pint and escaped for an early night.' The paths, the hostels, the portions of apple crumble and the pints of Theakston's all tumble by, until the heart-stopping climax is reached at Kirk Yetholm: 'I finished with a meal at the Border Hotel of steak and kidney pie and chips for £3.50 and 5 pints of the local bitter.'

Such painstaking accounts are not even just products of the incontinence of the blogging age, for if you poke around in the dusty corners of most local reference libraries, you'll find much the same sort of stuff in print form. Neatly typed, with grainy pictures, an unflagging monotone and a haphazard approach to punctuation (few commas, lots of exclamation marks), they are the proud, self-published records of men – always men – taking themselves right to the edge and facing their inner demons, before overcoming them with a dry pair of socks or a decent pint of Pilkington's Old Scrote. One such marvel that I unearthed in a Lancashire library is the 1985 logbook of a man who did the Pennine Way, while his wife and her cousin drove each day's leg of the route in a temperamental 'Volkswagen caravanette'. This doubled up as their nightly accommodation, the ladies sharing the bed while Rambling Man kips in a bunk he has rigged up in the front. He's not at all keen on paying good money to park up in caravan sites, when there are so many lay-bys to be had for free. The ladies are 'none too pleased at the lack of toilet facilities on these moorland night stops', he reports. 'Still – the cows and sheep manage – so what's the difference?'

At Malham, the gang stumble across a big ramblers' rally to mark the 20th anniversary of the Pennine Way's opening. Seemingly imagining himself as a reporter on the regional teatime news, he tells us: 'Today, Mr Tom Stephenson, now 92 years of age, is guest of honour at Malham House where select guests are meeting for dinner, amongst them are Barbara Castle (Politician) and Mike Harding (Joker), but I am not invited!' Further north, he gets lost one day in the mist, and although he reaches that evening's appointed destination anyway, the fact that he went 'wrong' worries him all the way to Scotland. His poor wife is forced on the next bank holiday weekend to drive him back to the same place, just so that he can re-walk the 'correct' bit of route. That she didn't take advantage of the situation and bury him on a lonely peat moor is a mystery.

Both of these scribes from the Pennine frontline have dabbled with the other National Trails, as well as numerous other long-distance paths. For our online correspondent, this was the first of his three trips along the Pennine Way, each recorded in microscopic detail. He also repeats Wainwright's Coast to Coast and the Cambrian Way, from the top to the bottom of Wales. The reason for reprising his steps, he says, is that he has 'exhausted the walks around Britain that particularly interest me and are of a suitable length'. Aside from the fact that none of his trips take him any further north than the Lowlands of Scotland, I find the idea quite astounding that you've walked everywhere you could possibly wish to have walked. What of the hundreds of thousands of miles of other rights of way? The 1,200 or so named long-distance paths? It's a hoary cliché, but the variety of landscapes in Britain and Ireland is way out of proportion to the size of our islands. There is surely enough to keep anyone busy and fascinated for life – except, it seems, for Mr Sack O'Spuds.

Five other National Trails were created at the same time as the Pennine Way, though they took even longer to become reality. The Cleveland Way, a horseshoe around the North York Moors National Park, opened in 1969, the Pembrokeshire Coast Path a year later, and a year after that the Offa's Dyke Path through the Marcher borderlands of England and Wales. By far the longest was the 630-mile South West Coast Path, a series of old coastguard tracks that hug the cliffs and shore from Minehead in Somerset, all the way around Devon and Cornwall and to Poole in Dorset; the last section of this monster was finally opened in 1978. And in 1972, the South Downs Way opened, unique amongst the early National Trails in that it is a bridle-way throughout, thus open to horse-riders as well as walkers. Cyclists too, of course, a constituency that didn't feature much in the early days, but since the arrival of the mountain bike have loomed ever larger, faster and bolshier along its hundred-mile route, much to the chagrin of the ramblers.

Nine more National Trails have been added since then, as well as something over a thousand other named long-distance routes and who knows how many unofficial ones, all the slow-release legacy of the 1949 Act. Not until Tony Blair's govern-ment was elected in 1997 did the Cabinet again contain so many enthusiastic walkers, a fact undoubtedly linked to the next big leap forward in access legislation, the 2000 Countryside and Rights of Way (CROW) Act for England and Wales, and the 2003 Land Reform (Scotland) Act. Labour's hill-walking leader John Smith, the first to promise a 'right to roam', had died just three years earlier, something that focused minds and intent enorm-ously; in some ways, the legislation is his legacy. They might have failed us on so much, but it has been almost entirely thanks to the Labour Party that we have the freedom to walk as much as we do. It almost makes me wish that I'd voted for them. Almost.

In the footsteps of the ancestors on the Ridgeway, in the Vale of White Horse, Oxfordshire

4. THE OLD WAYS

The choice of which National Trail to tackle pretty much decided itself. The chippy pride of the northern rambling tradition had been a joyous eye-opener, but I fancied seeing how the booted brigade slotted in somewhere softer and more southerly. I also wanted to go as far back in time as possible, to walk a route that way pre-dated the Gore-Tex age. The Ridgeway had long fascinated me, the idea of a prehistoric M1 through some of the most intensely cultivated and inhabited parts of the country. I'd walked a couple of small stretches years earlier, and remembered them with huge affection; since then, the idea of doing the whole route had lodged firmly in my mind. Amongst pagan mates, walking the Ridgeway was a must, a rite of passage and pilgrimage to burrow you deep into the ancient rhythm of the land. Not many of them had actually done it, but they could all talk for Albion about it. It was time to stop talking, and start walking.

There was the added bonus that it looked really quite easy, especially after the peat hags and knife-sharp winds of the north, and even more so when compared with some of the other National Trails. Up against the Pennine Way or the South West

Coast Path, the 90-mile Ridgeway is a Sunday stroll of a path, ideal for someone still struggling to kick the fags and get into shape. The trail's highpoint is less than 900 feet, a figure I'll regularly top at home in Wales, and its route through the generous belly of southern England surely meant that I'd never be too far from a microbrewery and a Thai restaurant.

Vague timelines are something of an occupational hazard whenever we wind the clock back beyond the Romans, but there's no doubting that the Ridgeway, or parts of it at least, have been used for as long as people have roamed across our landscape. Nearly all of the route lies 300–800 feet above sea level, higher than the swampy forests that once occupied most of the lower ground. The swift-draining chalk would have provided the ideal texture underfoot, its baked-white surface visible for miles in all weathers and times of day or night. Over five or six millennia, usage of the track waxed and waned, for trade, transhumance, droving and driving. No driving any more, though: a byway open to all traffic (a B.O.A.T.) it may be for large sections of its route, but after fierce and bitter battles, the Ridgeway has now been declared officially motor-free, and concrete blocks have been placed along its length to enforce this. It survived 6,000 years open to all for every purpose, but only when it became a route solely for our leisure have we had to block and police it.

The official National Trail is only around a quarter of a longer prehistoric route stretching from the Wash to the south coast. The 1940s committee charged with establishing our first long-distance paths suggested that a Ridgeway trail should go from the Chilterns to Seaton, in east Devon. The irrepressible Tom Stephenson spent long, happy hours with his pencils and his Ordnance Surveys and came up with an idea to extend this proposed path northwards to Cambridge. But it was the section from the Chilterns to Avebury that was the first to be designated as the Ridgeway, and although it was suggested in the 1940s, it wasn't until July 1972 that the Environment Secretary gave his assent. Unlike the Pennine Way, whose route had taken 14 years of difficult negotiation to sort out, the Ridgeway took just 14 months, the opening ceremony taking place on Coombe Hill, above Wendover, on 29 September 1973. It was much shorter, of course, and needed very few new paths, but there was also a far greater acceptance of public access along its route than in the Pennines. Furthermore, the opening of the first few National Trails had been hugely popular; momentum was on its side. Since then, paths extending it at both ends have been created, and it is possible – though not for me this time, thank you – to follow what has become known as the Greater Ridgeway, 363 miles from Lyme Regis to Hunstanton.

The lesser Ridgeway path is neatly divided into two halves, with the River Thames between Streatley and Goring as its mid-point. The eastern half, from Ivinghoe Beacon, near Tring, trills up and down the northern edge of the Chiltern escarpment, often parallel to or following the prehistoric track known as the Icknield Way. West from the Thames, the route to Avebury has always been known as the Ridgeway: it is a distinct, wide track that scorches its ghostly way across the upland plains of Berkshire, Oxfordshire and Wiltshire.

Since the official path's inception in 1973, all the guidebooks have recommended that you walk it from west to east, Avebury to Tring. The only reason given is that this will prevent you having to stride into the teeth of the prevailing westerly winds, but it was hard to imagine that that was likely to be a massive consideration on the outskirts of Aylesbury. Not once did it occur to me that I should follow the route this way: walking our oldest track is a pilgrimage, and who the hell ever went on a pilgrimage to Tring? Looking at the maps too, it was obvious that the eastern half of the Ridgeway through the Chilterns was far comfier than the windswept heights of the west. It seemed more logical, and a far more rewarding experience, to edge myself out of civilisation little by little, not start with a crash amidst the crop circles and henges of Wiltshire before heading like a spellbound commuter further and further into the orange-skied *banlieue* of London. And then there was the simple equation that it made most sense, logistically and cosmically, to go east to west, from the rising of the sun to its setting. Ivinghoe to Avebury it was.

So close is the Ridgeway to London that you can more or less take the Tube to it. Chesham, the last outpost of the Metropolitan Line, lies less than ten miles south of Ivinghoe Beacon, but no buses connect the two, and it would take for ever, and cost a small fortune, getting out from London early enough to tube it to Chesham and then taxi it from there. Until 1961, Metroland had pushed deep into the Chilterns, with Tube trains going as far as Aylesbury, Princes Risborough and rustic Quainton Road. Buses would connect from Aylesbury, but the shortest and easiest route was a train from Euston to Tring, and then a cab to the Beacon and the beginning of the adventure, my first attempt at completing a long-distance path since 1982.

'You walking the Ridgeway then?' said the Turkish cab driver as I swung my rucksack on to the cream leatherette back seat of his Merc. Resisting sarcasm (who else is going to be wearing a rucksack, leaping into a cab at 8 a.m. in Tring station, and demanding to be taken to Ivinghoe Beacon?), I admitted that, yes, I was. 'How long you taking to do it, then?' asked the driver, staring at me in the rear-view mirror. 'Eight days,' I replied. 'Pfffft,' he retorted, letting his eyes roll theatrically in the rear-view mirror. 'Some people do it in five. Where you staying tonight?' 'Wendover,' I replied. Another eye roll. 'Most people make it to Princes Risborough on the first night.' Just over an hour and a half later, I saw him again, as the path had its first humiliation in store by leading me straight back to Tring station. He waved, looked at his watch and shouted, 'Hey! Two hours! That's too long, my friend.' He was licensed, I noticed, by the Dacorum Council: the local authority hereabouts, and clearly not, as its soundalike namesake might suggest, the national arbiter of politeness.

That first day, on an admittedly easy little woodland canter into Wendover, I learned two new things. First, some people in the Chilterns so hate the metric system, and I would surmise virtually everything else European (save perhaps for the wine), that they are quite prepared systematically to scratch the paint out of the grooved figures showing distances in kilometres on almost every Ridgeway wooden fingerpost (both miles and kilometres were given). Take that, Johnny Eurocrat! Second, I learned that trying to walk any distance while desperately needing a crap is no fun whatsoever, and will mean that you are rendered utterly incapable of enjoying the lovely views, the budding leaves or the birdsong. At least, there were no sewage-filled farm yards to go through, reminding me of what I was needing most. Throughout the whole first day, the path brushed past only one farm that smelled even slightly agricultural. The rest just reeked of money.

Within an hour of clearing Tring station for the second time, I'd succumbed to the pull of The Trail. It is amazing how quickly you tumble into this, the feeling that your feet are grooved into the earth, that only the next mile, the next village, the next junction matters. All else quietly melts away. After an hour or so of swishing through beech woods, suddenly coming across a road or a car park was a shock, the cars looking even more brutal than before. There was always time to prepare, though: an imminent road crossing or beauty-spot car park invariably announced itself, as the take-away wrappers, empty cans of Stella and Tesco bags grew in number until it swung into view.

Being so used to the lackadaisical signposting of footpaths in Wales, the ruthless efficiency of the Ridgeway's waymarking staggered me. Aside from the scratched-out kilometre figures, nothing was left to chance – you could easily walk the entire trail without any kind of map, and you can imagine how hard that is for me to say. Any junction, be it of paths, or of paths and roads, was signed, the black-armed wooden Ridgeway signs efficiently directing you from one encounter to the next, augmented by finger posts and even the odd daubed tree adorned with the trail's acorn symbol and a reassuring arrow to keep you going in the right direction. Every kind of path was also colour-coded on the signs and laminated maps that appeared every few miles, for even the Ridgeway itself is a succession of different kinds of path welded together into one. The colour scheme quickly gets absorbed into the brain:

> **white** for permissive paths, not actual rights of way. This didn't apply to any of the Ridgeway trail itself, just some of the side routes branching off.

> **yellow** for a footpath, the bedrock of the trail. Two feet good, four feet (or two wheels) bad.

blue for a bridleway, a track usable by horses and push-bikes too. Bikes far outnumber horses these days, and I can well imagine that there are frantic meetings in council offices up and down the land as to what new name they can come up with for a bridleway to indicate this.

maroon for a restricted byway, a new category introduced by the 2000 Countryside and Rights of Way Act and enthu-siastically taken up on the Ridgeway. This enabled local authorities to keep a route's age-old byway status, while banning the quad-bikers and off-roaders who were enrag-ing the ramblers and horsey types.

a **fiery orange** for a B.O.A.T. (Byway open to all traffic), sub-divided yet again into B.O.A.T.s seasonally closed to motor traffic and those open all year.

So swiftly absorbed are these different categories, so often do you see visual reminders of what category you are currently walking and what category are the many side routes, and so much time do you have to ponder these as you go, that they soon burrow deep down into your thinking and break out in one of the many symptoms of Trail Fascism, an affliction it is almost impossible to resist. Yet resist it you really should, because it is an ugly side-effect of a good walk, and likely indeed to ruin it if you let it.

On the Ridgeway, this particular symptom broke out in me most virulently on the four-mile section known as Grim's Ditch that takes you off the Chilterns and down to the River Thames near Wallingford. On a narrowish strip marked firmly in yellow as a footpath only, I suddenly saw two cyclists snaking their way through the woods towards me. Righteous ramblers' fury bubbled up inside me and threatened to blow like the Icelandic volcano that had cleared the skies of aircraft so thoroughly for the duration of my walk. Should I stand, Amazon-like, in the middle of the path and force them off their bikes? Or let them pass, but with a stern 'You really shouldn't be cycling here, you know' as they sped by? Or, trickling down the scale of bravery, would a filthy look and a low mutter perhaps suffice? Fortunately, the sun came out at precisely that moment and I suddenly realised that we were just three people harmlessly enjoying ourselves on a spring day in a lovely old English wood, and perhaps it was entirely possible that we could all continue that way, with no need for pomposity or tantrums. I stepped aside, admired the bluebells, and wished them a cheerful good morning as they cycled carefully by. They thanked me and went on their way. It was all very easy.

Not so for some ramblers. So intoxicated are they by the rightness of their pastime, and so sure are they that the world would be a wonderful place *if only everyone acted exactly as they do*, that ticking off cyclists and horse-riders, or loudly demanding their rights of way becomes a major component in the make-up of their fondest-remembered walks. And having scrutinised the OS map at five-minute intervals throughout, they know with cold certainty precisely where the footpath becomes a bridle-way becomes a byway, that they are Right and you are Wrong. Nothing gets the thin blood of this sort of rambler coursing so vigorously as that; it is the nearest to an al fresco orgasm he will have had since that view of Helvellyn one late summer day 30 years ago, the one that caused him such swooning delight he ended up masturbating guiltily into the heather. Just don't ask him what he thinks of off-roaders.

Then there is the fascism of the trail itself. You become flanged to it like a rusty old steam train on ancient rails, unable to branch off in any direction, or for any reason. I first became aware of this when phoning to book B&Bs in advance of the walk. When I said that I wanted to stay because I was walking the Ridgeway to the landlord of a place about two or three miles off the path, he sighed and said, 'Well, I'll come and pick you up in Nuffield, then.' 'But I'm walking,' I said. 'I can just walk to yours instead.' He seemed surprised. I asked him if a lot of Ridgeway walkers insisted on being picked up from the side of the trail. 'Yes, and taken back there the next morning,' he said.

To many, walking a long-distance path, especially one that has been officially stamped as a National Trail, is even more like a heritage steam-train trip than I realised. Instead of seeing the path as an integral part of a much greater network, it is just a pretty, but pointless, thing in itself, a truncated chuff from nowhere to nowhere, and connected at either end to the wider world, the real world, by the inevitable car. In between, there are the official stops or stations, and there's no deviation allowed from the one route. Nor can you skip any part of the official path: every last inch has to be religiously trudged, as if in penance. While I can just about understand this completist rationale on the wide, ancient track of the Wessex Ridgeway itself, I fail to get it at all on the eastern half of the National Trail, much of which dates back only as far as a Thursday in the 1970s when some county council twonk drew it on the map. It is quite some achievement to transform something so inherently joyous and liberating into something so tediously anal.

Conscious of having to carry everything on my back, I'd ditched all my beloved Ordnance Surveys and had invested a tenner in a kind of map I'd never used before, one of the specialist walker's maps, made of 'strong durable waterproof polyethylene' and produced by Harvey's of Perthshire. It's very good and does everything it claims to do, but it wasn't helping to assuage the nagging feeling that walking a National Trail was a fixed, unmovable exercise. The path is portrayed in varying shaped chunks and perfectly adequate detail, but oftentimes it's cut off only a mile or so either side. It was a map of the trail, for sure, but with absolutely no context of the land through which it progressed. It was like having a plan of a 90-mile corridor, but with no idea of what was in the rooms that led off it.

Edging past Chiltern pony paddocks and golf courses, it was hard to conjure up images of any ancestors stomping this way. Only the gigantic beech trees, and the chalk and flint mix of the soil in which they sit, hinted at anything much beyond last month. I'd purposely decided to walk the Ridgeway in mid-April, hoping to catch that magical week when the beech leaves first open into a canopy of feathery, lime-green iridescence, before they quickly darken and harden into their summer wear. After the coldest winter in 30 years, however, nature was behind schedule, and, with a few unexpected exceptions, the entire walk was done against a stentorian backdrop of skeletal trees and bare branches. Not that it made the Chilterns' legendary trees any less impressive: perhaps more so, in that all there was to look at were their trunks, bark, labyrinthine roots and branches, rather than the sweeter, but far more ephemeral, pleasures of buds and blossom.

Even more pleasurable was the ground underfoot, for chalk is always a treat and a novelty to me. Not knowing its lands too well, I constantly marvel at its desiccation, its dazzling Wensleydale whiteness and texture, its quiet sense of style and playfulness. A well-worn path through chalk is doubly enchanting, for there is no better surface on which to recall the words of Edwardian poet Edward Thomas: 'And the prettiest things on ground are the paths / With morning and evening hobnails dinted / With foot and wing-tip overprinted.' Not so many hobnails these days, but the galloping horseshoe-prints, mountain-bike tyre tracks and the stomp of a thousand walking boots etched into the ashen track gave it the look of a massive, elemental work of art.

Where the Ridgeway burrows under the M40, near Lewknor, there are countless graffiti messages scrawled on the walls of the tunnel. None are in paint or pen: all are in chalk just picked up off the path, and where words have got too nasty or offensive, people have simply rubbed them out. As a result, there's a lightness of touch and a sense of humorous interplay in the graffiti that you don't normally find in an underpass, and I spent a very happy ten minutes chuckling at it as the lorries thundered by overhead.

With two such distinct and different halves, it is the chalk that defines and unites the Ridgeway path, for this was the dry, high route along the top of the scarp that runs diagonally across England from Norfolk to the south-west coast. It's no coincidence that this is roughly also the country's dividing line between the wealthier bottom-right corner and the more spartan north and west. The Ridgeway runs along this cusp, something of a last hurrah for the money as it looks down, quite literally, on its muddy, lowland neighbours.

As the miles squeaked by, and the soles of my boots whitened up, I began to love the chalk and flint beneath my feet. Together, these equal-and-opposite twins represent a much-cherished version of fantasy England. Chalk is soft, yielding, clean, pure, white, strangely coquettish and makes us think of Vera Lynn, the white cliffs of Dover and Mr Chips scribbling on a school blackboard. Flint is dark, unfathomable, unyielding, rock hard and brings to mind ancient arrowheads, rudimentary blades, the plucky underdog and some of the loveliest, yet simplest, architecture of the Church of England. Softness and toughness, purity and resolve, education and warfare, Sir and God: our favourite combinations, and those that we rather like to think define us as a nation.

Of all the chalk-and-flint districts, there's nowhere quite as rhapsodic as the Chilterns, particularly to Londoners of a certain standing. This modest range of woods and hills shields the capital from the dirt and dullness of the provinces; its flinty little villages, topped with their red tile roofs, are the England of a painted pantomime backdrop. This is a land of chivalrous knights, swooning maidens, magical forests and lusty greensward – even the reintroduced red kites, swirling overhead in vast numbers these days, fuel the Tudorbethan fantasy. It's Betjeman's 'Beechy Bucks', the Grand Duchy of Metroland, bulwark and avatar for all manner of medievalists, nostalgists and fantasists: Stanley Spencer, Enid Blyton, Roald Dahl, Eric Gill, the Shelleys, John Piper, G. K. Chesterton and Sir Francis Dashwood. It's where you'll find *The Wind in the Willows* and *The Vicar of Dibley*, Gray's *Elegy Written in a Country Churchyard* and Bunyan's *The Pilgrim's Progress*, *Three Men in a Boat*, *Chitty Chitty Bang Bang* and the Bekonscot model village. And acknowledging the sinister shadow at the heart of the suburban idyll, it's also where you'll find *The Avengers*, *The Saint*, *Midsomer Murders* and Miss Marple. Darkest of all, most weekends since 1921, you might also find the British prime minister of the day, kicking back at Chequers.

The Ridgeway path makes great play with Chequers, flirting with it from all angles. Coming from Wendover, it's a steady slog up to the Boer War memorial on the top of Coombe Hill, at 853ft almost the highpoint of the entire Chiltern range (Haddington Hill, on the other side of Wendover, is 23ft higher). Another good reason for walking the Ridgeway east-west is that this affords, as you reach the monument, a magnificent first view of the mansion, sat far below on a platform flanked between Coombe Hill and another outstretched ridge, Beacon Hill. Like the two arms of a Brobdingnagian armchair, the hills thrust out into the Vale of Aylesbury, with Chequers as the well-upholstered seat between, peering over the lip and down into a world it will never have cause to know. The next minute, the mansion looked as if it were the prow of a ship, ploughing through the waves of flint and chalk in its wake towards the calmer waters of the Vale ahead.

Huge leather armchair or ship of state, the position made perfect sense; a redoubt firmly bedded in fantasy England, yet looking out, a little shyly, a little haughtily, on to the plains of the real world. It hit me suddenly that, over the last 90 years, events of probably far greater political significance had been ignited here, where the men of power gather and relax over croquet and a vintage burgundy, than ever occur in the daily hurlyburly of Westminster and Whitehall. It was from Chequers, usually after a well-lubricated dinner, that Churchill made many of his most celebrated wartime radio broadcasts. According to Margaret Thatcher's autobiography, this was where she decided to torpedo the *Belgrano*, dreamt up the poll tax and first realised she 'could do business' with Mikhail Gorbachev. The Chilterns are our locum capital.

When Lord Lee decided to give Chequers to the nation, specifically to the prime minister of the day as a weekend retreat, there was much debate in Parliament and the country. Liberal peer Lord Haldane warned that the trappings of an English country house existence could prove far too distracting to chaps from the middle classes, for, after all, it could no longer be assumed that PMs these days would come to office with their own estate. The PM since 1916, David Lloyd George, was just such a middle-class occupier of the office, and he was passionately in favour of the idea, even if he never much took to the place as its first prime ministerial occupant.

The last Liberal PM might not have been a huge fan of Chequers, but his Labour successors most certainly have been, more so even than most of their Tory counterparts. Ramsay MacDonald delighted in playing the country gent: Harold Nicolson recorded in his diaries turning up to Chequers to find Britain's first socialist prime minister sporting a full set of tweeds, plus-fours and a fob watch, while carrying a log in one hand and an axe in the other. The house and estate, said the Cabinet Secretary of the time, was having 'a marvellous effect on these Labour people'.

Three Labour PMs have loved the place so much that, on leaving office, they've bought nearby properties to prolong the dream. Telling us all that we need to know about the progress of the Labour Party since the war, these have gone from Clement Attlee (left office 1951, bought Cherry Tree Cottage on the outskirts of nearby Great Missenden), to Harold Wilson (1976, bought Grange Farm on the other side of Great Missenden) and Tony Blair (2007, bought the stately baroque pavilion of Wotton House, just north of Thame. To complete the illusion, the Blairs even employed the housekeeper from Chequers in their new home, and completed the double by buying a London home in Connaught Square, which bears more than a passing resemblance to Number 10).

In an even more stunningly accurate metaphor for his entire premiership, Blair's successor Gordon Brown finally creaked into office having made loud protestations that, as the fabled son of the manse and cheerleader for prudence, he would be the first prime minister since Andrew Bonar Law in 1923 to forgo the delights of Chequers. This was intended to underline the difference between himself and the Prince Regent excesses of the Blair regime, under which Chequers was regularly used for get-togethers with casts drawn from all sections of politics, the media and showbiz. Like so many other of his gruffly shouted Puritan principles, it didn't hold for long, and Brown became a passionate convert to the place, going there most weekends and holidays, and hosting parties every bit as lavish as his predecessor's.

From Coombe Hill, the path descends to skirt around Chequers, passing through the grounds. Of course there are CCTV cameras everywhere and signs warning that you mustn't stray from the right of way, but in fact it was all a great deal less hysterical than you'd expect. These days, when you have to go through everything but a strip search just to get into a local BBC studio or the offices of a minor insurance company, it was a reassuring and quite charming surprise to find that the prime minister's country residence was behind a fence that consisted of wooden posts and a bit of wire strung between them. Once you cross the drive of beech trees planted by Churchill, the fence becomes even more cheerily rustic, in that it is made of old railway tracks chopped and upended into the soil.

When the PM's in residence, however, security is far tighter and has been so since the early days. The handover of the house finally happened in 1921, just as the partition of Ireland was taking place. When Lloyd George was occupying the house, IRA graffiti was found just down the road and a group of Irish students walking nearby were arrested and held in police cells. When the Ulster Troubles re-ignited in the late 1960s, a footpath across the estate was deemed to be too close for comfort and an application made for its closure. According to Norma Major, who wrote a book about Chequers while husband John was its prime occupant, this resulted in an 'inevitable public enquiry' and 'four years of wrangling before the footpath was moved'. All the more amazing, perhaps, that the Ridgeway still passes through the grounds, clipping across the main drive just inside the gates. Mrs Major's purse-lipped opinions on the world are unintentionally hilarious, and none more so than when she tells of her husband's surprise elevation to the top job: 'To become Prime Minister just a few weeks before Christmas, as John did in 1990, was not ideal timing. For one thing, it threw the Christmas cards into chaos . . .'

On the desk in the prime minister's study at Chequers sits a silver inkwell designed and inscribed by Lord Lee, the benefactor of the house. Its Latin motto ('Stare Super Antiquas Vias; Videre Quænam sit Via Recta et Bona, et Ambulare in Eá') is helpfully translated and inscribed into English, presumably for those very same PMs from the middle classes who not only failed to have a country estate to call their own but who may even have lacked a classical education. It's a lovely motto, one that seemed to sum up even my small effort in ambling the Ridgeway, and it echoed through my head as I skirted the estate: 'To stand on the ancient ways, to see which is the right and the good way, and in that to walk.'

There were three weeks to go to a general election and, as it was to turn out, a new resident at Chequers. Despite the profound effect the house seemed to have on its Labour inhabitants, you couldn't help but feel that a Tory, especially a patrician posh one like David Cameron, would be far more suited to the area. I walked past dozens of vast 'Vote Conservative' hoardings in lush paddocks, and even more of their smaller brethren on little posts in people's front gardens. The only other party that seemed to be gaining local support was UKIP, whose posters could often be seen peering out from behind fake mullioned windows, just beneath the three burglar alarms. One sign was entirely new to me: warnings of the use of 'Concealed CCTV', which seemed to crop up particularly in pub gardens. One of the great joys of doing a trail is the way in which normal life and its tedious rules just evaporate away, and that includes the feeling that if you pass a pub, you are duty bound to stop for a pint, regardless of the time of day. Most were horrible. If there's a part of the world that screams cosy rustic pub, it's the Chilterns, but gastro-greed had overwhelmed them and they were nearly all pretentious restaurants or cheerless food barns. On the second day of the walk, one foot had really started to hurt, so I hobbled into a pub that looked like something out of 'Dick Whittington' from the outside, but turned out to be a glossy pine and chrome wannabe within. As I entered and ordered a quick fortifying brandy, the unwelcome sound of Dire Straits was oozing out of the CD player. Ten minutes later, visiting the gents, it was Phil Collins and, when I came out, Simply Red: surely the musical equivalent of 'three strikes and you're out', and all I needed to know that I'll never return.

The B&Bs I stayed in were run by ferociously efficient ladies of a certain age, who managed to welcome me in, get me out of my boots, rustle up a pot of tea, bake a light sponge, order the kids to piano practice, saddle a couple of horses and hoover the Labradors, all without pausing for breath. They reminded me of a great routine I saw once in Glasgow by American comedian Scott Capurro. He'd been touring England for weeks, and had garnered a wealth of material about how mad the English were, a sure-fire winner of a topic in Glasgow. He wondered aloud why Britain needed an army, as all we had to do, he said, was position on the white cliffs of Dover a few battalions of upper-middle-class English ladies, their arms folded and one eyebrow raised menacingly. No-one would dare invade.

I'd rather them any time, though, than their husbands, who were either golfers in loafers or tweedy types in regimental ties. In one guest house, I was grilled by an ex-army chap, who, his wife whispered to me, had already had three heart bypass operations. It quickly became obvious why: he was permanently on the verge of scarlet-faced apoplexy. His wife invited me in to watch the early evening news with them, which was accompanied by a constant barrage of heckling from him. During one story, they took vox pops in the street, one coming from a young male student with shoulder-length hair. 'Get a bloody haircut!' he kept shouting at the screen; we never got to hear what the student had to say. His wife, doing her best to keep the mood sweet, asked me if I had a wife or children. 'No, I live with my partner,' I replied, provoking a snort of derision from the corner as he plunged back into the pages of the *Telegraph*. At breakfast he told me, at some length, about the organised holidays that he leads to the Second World War battlefields of northern France, 'though never to the American beaches in Normandy – what bloody good were the Yanks? Too little, too late.' Despite my still-painful foot, I fair danced out of there and back on to the trail.

The Chilterns must be up there as having perhaps the best signposted footpaths in the country. It wasn't just the Ridgeway that was waymarked with such colour co-ordinated vigour, but so was every single footpath, bridleway and byway that either led off it or connected to it. And I never came across a single broken stile or gate. The Chiltern Society, run with the same brisk efficiency as the area's B&Bs (and probably by the same formidable ladies), is largely responsible for this laudable state of affairs. Not only do they have a Rights of Way group to browbeat any recalcitrant local government worker into submission ('Come on now, chop chop!'), they also publish and sell their own footpath maps, some 28 of them, which will set you back £70 for the whole pack. They're at the same scale as an OS Explorer, though each covers only a small area as it is designed to be more portable than a sometimes bulky OS. They're very beautiful as well, emphasising not just the paths, statutory and permissive, but pubs, car parks and Anglican churches too, a set of features that makes as good a definition of the Chilterns as any. This is, you surmise, a supremely map-literate part of the world. I was tickled to see on the Chiltern Society website a button haughtily labelled 'Report Something', which sounded like one of the buttons in longstanding Chilternite Roald Dahl's great glass elevator. Report Something – anything: stray sheep, hoodies, drug dens, inconsiderate parking, a porch with no planning permission, late-night noise, smoking on an open-air station platform, bad highlights, suspected Labour tendencies, wearing something that's *so* last year. On the report form, you are politely asked to nail the location of your grievance with an OS grid reference, the inference being that anyone wanting a proper moan would, of course, know both what that meant and how to do it.

After four days, I reached the Thames at the Goring Gap. It's one of those names that I'd seen on the map, but had rather dismissed as a classic piece of British landscape over-exaggeration. Rural Oxfordshire is hardly the Alps, I thought, and having driven this way a few times, I'd not had cause to change that opinion. Dipping down to it on foot from the ridge of the Chilterns, however, gave me a completely different angle on the landscape, and suddenly, the name made perfect sense, for the Thames slicing through the hills really does create a notable gap. Only by walking slowly into it, with the Wessex Downs (and the cooling towers of Didcot power station) rising up ahead, could I see it, for it is subtle and needs a similarly subtle approach to be appreciated.

Until 1837, Goring, on the eastern bank of the river in Oxfordshire, had nothing much to do with the larger, more important Streatley, over on the western side in Berkshire. Then a toll bridge was built connecting them, and three years later, the railway came, but only to Goring. That then became the major settlement, and so it is today. The twin villages are exactly half-way along the Ridgeway path, and provide a much-needed splash of semi-urban glitz – a cashpoint, a shop that's open past five o'clock, a choice of places to eat, that sort of thing.

Earlier on the Trail, near Watlington, I'd bumped into a party of four Americans walking the other way. They'd decided to do the Ridgeway after reading about it in *The New York Times* a few months earlier. I later found the article online, its opening words stealth-bombed to excite any historically minded New Worlder: 'The Ridgeway is the oldest continuously used road in Europe, dating back to the Stone Age.' A grand supposition, but it had done its job. My American friends had had two nights and a day's rest in Goring, which seemed to be stretching a good thing to possible breaking point, but they'd *loved* the place. Cute, quaint, cheerful, old, so very *old*; all the things that do it for a party of enthusiastic Ohioans. They were loving it all in fact, including – and this may come as a shock – the 'amazing B&Bs and brilliant food in the pubs'. I crossed my fingers, and hoped they weren't booked in at Colonel Shouty's.

My B&B at Streatley was in the home of a delightful lady, a retired school geography teacher. We sat for hours in her conservatory, drinking tea, watching the sun go down and chatting about life and, more importantly, maps. She told me that she once taught Clare Balding, the jolly-hockey-sticks TV presenter. When she got the class to draw maps of their home area, Clare's was nearly all pubs. I was proper excited by now, for the following morning I was being joined by an old college mate and his wife, to do the long stretch up on to the Ridgeway proper, that great chalk highway and bulwark, that liminal border between worlds, that self-declared 'oldest road in Europe'.

It was great to see Jon and Helen, even more so because they had come equipped with the right OS for our day's 16-plus mile walk to Letcombe Regis. God, I'd missed a decent map. My Harvey's trail plan had been doing its job with perfunctory precision, but I fell on their Explorer map like a starving man on a plate of chips. And just in time too: the section we walked was the first stretch along the Wessex Downs, where you needed to see the Ridgeway in its far wider topographic context. From here to the path's end at Avebury, the landscape is strewn with ancient relics, all painstakingly mapped: other tracks, hill forts, tumuli, ditches, temples, sarsens, standing stones and circles, field systems, deserted villages, barrows, enclosures and earthworks. It's OS at its best, the image on the map demanding closer inspection and intimating huge rewards.

There was much else to learn about the area from the map. In stark contrast to the popular image of southern England, the names of Starveall and Skeleton Farm hinted darkly that these downs are a barren prairie, where little would ever grow. And so it is: the fields we passed looked like ethereal installations at the Tate, so full were they of flinty rubble. As a result, much of the area has been given over to horse gallops and, over the next few days, it was a pleasure to watch them flying by, the horses sleek and sinewy, their riders red-cheeked and intent. On the map, it looks as if the day's walk would be entirely dominated by the great hulk of Didcot power station, sat belching in the Thames valley below. On the ground though, it doesn't much intrude, at least not in the foreground. I'd caught my first glimpse of the cooling towers two days earlier as I was crossing a field just south of Watlington, and they remained part of my horizon for four days, eventually vanishing in a blue-sky haze near Uffington. They never offended me, though; quite the opposite. It was good to see real life chugging onwards as I glided indulgently across the landscape, and better still, the power station, and its changing position from my viewpoint, gave me a powerful sense of my own locomotion.

The Streatley to Letcombe Regis stretch, where there really is nothing to break the flow, was my longest day's walk, and it was great to have such good company. I love walking alone, going at exactly the pace that suits only me, but it is quite possible to have too much of your own company. It was a blazing spring Saturday, and the chalk track dazzled phosphorescently. You could often see it miles ahead or behind, a pale corduroy ribbon across the green swells of downland. Far below to our right, the vale shimmered in a gentle heat haze. In the fields at our side, skylarks trilled and hares squared up to each other as we strode by, laughing and gulping lungfuls of freedom.

Up here, it was far easier to raise the spirits of long-gone farmers and drovers, merchants and messengers. Walking ancient paths is hugely powerful, for it places us directly in touch with our ancestors ('Foot of Briton, formal Roman/Saxon, Dane and Sussex yeoman', as Andrew Young had it on the South Downs Way). This is very much part of their magic, for we share these ways with the pounding feet of countless unknown others. It is a sensation that we will only ever get on foot, for not only are we on exactly the same routes as our forefathers, we are also travelling in precisely the same way and at the same speed as them. And it is the perfect speed for contemplation and revelation.

Along this prehistoric motorway that winds its way through the voluptuous curves and swells of the downs, great hill forts punctuate the way like ancient service stations. Segsbury, Uffington, Liddington and Barbury are all on the lip itself of the ridge, while the track generally held back in its lee, unseen from below. There's little evidence that they were ever used defensively, and it was far more pleasant to imagine them as gathering places for travellers and pilgrims, somewhere to refuel, stock up, pay respects and swap news or gossip. Uffington is the overlord of the clan, the mighty ridges of its fort visible for miles either side, and its indeterminately ancient chalk 'horse' (or dragon, or cat, or serpent) a fine example of early advertising to the lowland tribes.

A mile or so beyond Uffington is Wayland's Smithy, the most powerfully atmospheric neolithic relic on the entire Ridgeway. Usually described only as a burial chamber, it is so much more than that. People may indeed have been buried there, but it is no municipal graveyard, for this has long been a place of celebration and ceremonial focus, a point of power for all time. Look at it on Google Earth, and two fields further along the Ridgeway you'll see another of Wiltshire's famous features, a crop circle. This one is in the shape of a gorgeously geometric jellyfish, pertly swimming its way upfield. I just love Wiltshire, and it was such a pleasure to be back there and, even more so, to have walked there from suburban Hertfordshire. Crop circles and UFOs, tumps and relics, crazy pagans and beer that can fell a frisky bullock all make it one of our most exhilarating counties to visit. Even in the trim little towns, where posters advertise tennis tournaments and whist drives at the Conservative Club, there's the sense that, just beneath the sensible frocks and comfy jumpers, there are tattooed warriors waiting to burst out.

One of my favourite photos of my dear departed dog Patsy was taken as we walked this bit of the Ridgeway on a similarly bright spring day in 1999. As I passed the spot where I had taken the photo, a little vortex of wind suddenly whipped up on the path just in front of me. Chalk dust and a couple of leaves spun round and round in a perfect circle about 18 inches high, and

I just knew it was her. She spent hours of her life spinning in circles, chasing her tail; virtually anything would set her off. 'Hello Pats,' I whispered, my eyes prickling. The vortex vanished, a solitary leaf floating out of it and off up the path. I followed it up into Wayland's Smithy, settled against the trunk of a massive beech tree, and fell into a deep, contented sleep.

Prior to doing the Ridgeway, people had warned me that the most knackering part of it was dropping down to your overnight stop in the villages below, and climbing back up again the next morning. The same is said of the South Downs Way, a similar chalk ridge route. I found it a wonderful aspect of the walk, a kind of daily decompression and chance to contextualise the high way within its wider geography, to head off the bone dry tops down to the welcome springs, brooks and streams below. Watering was very much the theme, for there are some marvellous pubs in those villages too; a world away, thankfully, from the overbaked fakes of the Chilterns.

These were journeys between seasons too. The vale is only 300-400 feet beneath the ridge, yet it was weeks ahead in its spring plumage. Up on the Ridgeway, hawthorn blossom was tight and tentative, budding leaves looked delicate enough to be blown away with one gust, excitable daffodils waved in the breeze. Down below, cherry and apple blossom frothed lustily, magnolias swung in pendulous bloom, the leaves on the trees danced full and crunchy, tulips and bluebells lit up gardens and verges. I never tired of walking slowly up and down through this progression, one of English nature's finest shows, and I couldn't quite believe how many B&B owners told me they usually had to drive their Ridgeway walkers back up on to the trail in the morning. Being a puritan at heart, I was keen not to get into a car for the duration of the walk, not to break the spell and bring myself crashing back to normality. That could wait.

Loveliest of all the ascents from the vale back up to the Ridgeway came one sunny Sunday morning. I left the village in which I'd stayed just as the four-bell peal of the medieval church was repeating its call, over and over, to morning service. The only other sound was the excitable twittering of birds in the blossom-heavy trees. Sunday mornings have always been my favourite time of the week, their atmosphere like no other. Time hangs more languidly, and there is an indefinable sense of freedom and possibility stretching far into the distance. It was there in my childhood when my dad would drive us through empty streets to be the first at the doors of the swimming baths. It thrilled me in my Brum dancing years, catching the first bus of the morning back from some city-centre club or squat party, the bizarre mix of passengers – us hollow-eyed ravers and a gaggle of Jamaican ladies in fabulous hats on their way to church – only making it more special. Nor is the sensation confined to still-slumbering urban streets. Even in my tiny Welsh village, where, to the untrained eye, a Sunday morning looks much the same as any other, there is something sweeter and less hurried in the air, and it was there in bucketfuls as I marched and sang my way back up to the path, the church bells ringing and my mind as playful as a box of kittens.

If Didcot power station is the elephant in the room on the eastern section of the trail, then Swindon is its westerly equivalent. Wiltshire's largest town, more than three times the size of Salisbury, struggles to shake off its image as a corpulent, corporate nowheresville, fed by the intravenous drips of the Great Western Railway and M4. Famous for producing trains, pneumatic blondes – Diana Dors, Melinda Messenger and Billie Piper – and having the most terrifying roundabout in the land, the massive sarsen stone chip on its shoulder is periodically polished every time there's one of those competitions for city status between the usual municipally desperate suspects. In 1999, the town council made one of its regular requests for an upgrade, only to be told by the Home Office that its bid was 'too materialistic'. As both rebuff and proof of the charge, Swindon did, however, win the competition to become the UK's first official twin town to Walt Disney World in Florida.

More fittingly perhaps, Swindon's real twin town was revealed to be Slough, in Ricky Gervais's excruciating series *The Office*, when the decision was taken to consolidate both branches of the Wernham Hogg paper company in the same place. Both towns evoke exactly the right image of open-plan tedium, of designated parking space one-upmanship on grey industrial estates and instantly regretted fumbles at the Christmas party. It was some surprise, therefore, when the National Trust relocated their headquarters to Swindon in 2005. Not everyone was happy: one manager confided to the *Financial Times* that 'I can't think of anywhere worse.'

The arrival of the NT in town caused some significant ripples in the local property market, if not on the new estates that make up the bulk of Swindon itself. Period properties in nearby villages were snapped up as soon as they landed on the market, and it only served to widen the suspicious divide between town and country. From the Iron Age hill fort at Liddington, just off the Ridgeway, I gazed down on the motorway and the massive town still spreading like a stain beyond it. Though if you look on the toposcope there, erected as a millennium project by Liddington parish council, you'd be hard pressed to work out quite what you were looking at. The arrow pointing towards the town is marked as to Cirencester, nearly 15 miles beyond. London, Oxford and Marlborough – none of which you can see – are marked. Swindon, which you cannot miss, is not. If Liddingtonians had their way, you feel, the mile (and several grand) gap between their village and the outer reaches of the eternal city-in-waiting would be landmined.

The trail was drawing to a close. As I marched like a centurion across the Marlborough Downs towards Avebury, the feeling of regret about finishing became stronger with every step. During my week on the Ridgway, the niggles and frets of daily life had been replaced with a calm certainty that my only goal was the next mile and the next view. Everything suddenly seemed so absurdly simple, that love and landscape were all that I needed. As I walked: I inhaled the words of Richard Jefferies, that great Victorian worshipper of these Wiltshire paths and downs: 'It is eternity now. I am in the midst of it. It is about me in the sunshine; I am in it, as the butterfly floats in the light-laden air. Nothing has to come; it is now.'

With only about half a mile to go, I saw a slight figure coming along the track towards me, under a rucksack much the same size. It was obviously a fellow Ridgeway walker, but one who was only just setting out. Most unexpectedly, I felt such a surge of jealousy towards her, of all the wonderful things she was going to see, smell, hear, think and feel over the next week. We chatted like long-lost cousins, and I lapped up her excitement. A nurse near Sheffield, she'd decided a couple of years ago to do an annual solo walk on a long-distance path; this was her third after the Dales Way from Yorkshire to Cumbria and the West Highland Way in Scotland. Strangely, my only previous LDP walk had also been along the Dales Way, though I was 15 at the time and it was more of a long pub crawl, interspersed with some walking and the odd bus trip when we were too hungover to move unaided. I told her – possibly with a little too much evangelistic zeal – that I was sure it was better to finish at Avebury, rather than Ivinghoe, despite what all the guidebooks said. Coming into Avebury really did feel like the right conclusion, the end of a pastoral symphony that had been almost imperceptibly swelling to a glorious climax. Either way, she was going to have a great time, and we hugged each other goodbye, two complete strangers united for just a few minutes, but in the same cause. I crossed the line, if there had been a line, one week and two hours after leaving Ivinghoe Beacon, and a new addiction had begun.

To walk an ancient path, you probably need to go no further than a couple of miles from your front door. Although headline grabbers like the Ridgeway, the Icknield Way, the Sweet Track on the Somerset Levels or the Golden Road in the Preseli Mountains of Pembrokeshire make much of their undoubted antiquity, the footpath network everywhere takes you straight back deep into history, for they are some of the oldest features in our landscape. If you're in the right frame of mind, you can feel it, those moments when suddenly you're walking where thousands have gone before you, passing the same trees, fording the same streams and breathing the same champagne air. There are tell-tale signs on the map and ground alike: odd dog-leg routes edging around long-vanished boundaries, holloways and green lanes sunk like pensioners into comfy armchairs, smugglers and drovers routes heading high over the hills, church ways, pilgrimage routes, monks' trods, herepaths, salt ways, drift ways and portways.

Into the higgledy-piggledy ancient British network of tracks and paths came the methodical Romans, who sliced their roads through the old ways in much the same way that we do with motorways now. In some parts of the country, the pattern left by the Romans endures still: where I live in mid-Wales, for instance, almost all of our market towns are between 15 and 18 miles apart, a day's march. Many of the Roman roads are now tarmaced and integrated into the modern network, some as great trunk roads such as Watling Street (the A2 from London to Dover and the A5 from London to Wroxeter, near Shrewsbury), Icknield Street (the A38 in the Midlands) and the Fosse Way (the A46 from Leicester to Lincoln and the A37 and A429 in the south-west). Perhaps the most thrilling is the A68 north of Corbridge in Northumberland, the Roman Dere Street. So empty is the landscape and so straight the road, that it is all too possible to lose any sense of perspective and speed, as the many warning signs make clear. Other Roman ways are much-loved B-roads and country lanes, but many were never aggrandised by tarmac and provide some of our most striking bridleways and byways. And they almost always are bridleways or byways, rather than mere footpaths: proof that a route's historic use, however far back it may date, is still generally used to determine its contemporary status.

Two of the most evocative paths I've ever walked have been over some of the best extant stretches of Roman road, both on bleak moorland. One sits high on Blackstone Edge above Rochdale, its tight cobbles and grooved channel like an illustration from a school textbook about the marvels of Roman engineering. Odd, therefore, that there is much academic debate as to whether the track is genuinely Roman or later. No such arguments at the other, north of Ystradfellte in the Fforest Fawr, the splendidly gloomy western part of the Brecon Beacons National Park. There, the cobbles are not quite so intact, but they still impress as the track runs up through a conifer forest in a perfect straight line, before cresting the hill by the ten-foot stone blade of Maen Madoc, its rough Latin inscription still faintly legible on the side. This is part of Sarn Helen, the great legionary causeway from Carmarthen to Conwy, often said to be the last time anyone successfully managed to build a road that unites north and south Wales. There's some truth in the bitterness: the building of a decent north–south road in Wales has been a stated priority of government since the 1920s. It still is.

Britain's most celebrated Roman remain, Hadrian's Wall, is also the site of what is commonly said to be the country's most expensive footpath. The 84-mile Hadrian's Wall National Trail was first proposed in 1984, given approval by the government in 1994 and finally opened in 2003. By the standards of the early Long Distance Paths, 19 years might seem a reasonable average from idea to inception, although it should perhaps be remembered that the Wall itself – 80 Roman miles long, and with forts every mile – took only six years to construct. The National Trail's budget of six million pounds was also rather bigger than Hadrian's.

Most of the money was spent on compensating landowners for the 30 miles of new path that were needed to drive the project from Wallsend, now swallowed by Newcastle, to Bowness-on-Solway, on the Cumbrian coast; it took a dedicated team of

11 officers seven years to sort out the hundreds of claims and complications. The Lonely Planet guide *Walking in Britain* called it a 'latter-day battle between the Wall's guardians and the restless natives hereabouts', the latest in a very long line. In one instance, in order to create a path where none existed near the village of Banks in Cumbria, a compulsory order had to be made – not because the landowner objected, but because, as the council's own minutes put it, 'she has an aversion in general to signing legal documents'. No such reticence at the other end of the trail, around the village of Heddon-on-the-Wall, near Newcastle. Despite being one of the least attractive parts of the route, it was here that the bulk of the compensation money was spent. Heddon's other recent claim to fame was as the epicentre of the 2001 foot-and-mouth outbreak – another bumper year for the compo.

Some of my favourite old paths are those that were used to go to market. These I imagine to have been supremely sociable ways, alive with chatter and laughter, flirting and gossip. Trouble too at times, of course: the sheer physical graft of shifting goods through muddy ruts, exhaustion and disappointment at a poor day's trading, even theft and harassment. After finishing the Ridgeway at Avebury, I wanted to go and walk another of Wiltshire's finest, Maud Heath's Causeway: not just any old path to market, but quite possibly the grandest in the country. Maud Heath was a fifteenth-century widow from Bremhill, between Calne and Chippenham. Every Wednesday, she walked four miles to market in Chippenham to sell her eggs and poultry, down into the valley of the River Avon and back up the other side into town. The river was notorious for frequent flooding, and in those conditions, the path was treacherous.

She fell on numerous occasions, breaking her eggs and ruining her clothes.

On her death in 1474, she left a bequest 'in land and houses, about Eight Pounds a year, forever to be laid out, in the Highways and Causey leading from Wick Hill to Chippenham Clift', according to the inscription on a memorial pillar erected in 1698 by the Kellaways bridge over the Avon. This was plenty enough to build a raised walkway across the marshy valley and for it to be maintained by a trust. Not only is the causeway still there, so is the trust, who still meet and pay out grants from the initial investments, more than 500 years later.

Maud Heath's Causeway is at its most impressive where it soars over the river, elevated on 64 arches above the modern lane by its side. At other places, you'd barely notice it if you didn't know it was there, a cobbled pavement, home to the same wheelie bins and fag ends you'd find anywhere. What is most touching about the story, though, is that Maud Heath herself never benefited from this most gracious act of generosity, for she was long dead by the time it was constructed. That her name lives on, and is thanked daily, is as fine a legacy as anyone could hope for. The memorial pillar by the bridge ends with the most sweet and enigmatic of inscriptions: 'Injure me not.' Is this a prayer for passers-by, a plea to highway engineers, a warning to would-be vandals or a message from beyond the grave from Maud herself?

These paths to market are a far cry from their contemporary equivalents. Rights of way in our city centres have been comprehensively wiped from the map, as whole swathes of shopping districts become privatised and policed by surly young men in polyester uniforms. Signs reminding us that this is not a public right of way are welded to every CCTV post, and there are always plenty of those. For the first time in our history, we have granted wholesale ownership of huge chunks of our mercantile centres to fast-buck developers and their shadowy mates, and it is they who decide who goes, and who does not.

If transporting a basket of eggs a few miles in the Middle Ages was a formidable challenge, it's hard to imagine the logistics for the drovers, as they steered whole herds of sheep and cattle hundreds of miles across the country. From at least the Norman age well into the twentieth century, hundreds of beasts at a time, in columns anything up to half a mile long, were moved at a steady two miles an hour from the wilder country of the north and west to the merchants and markets of the south and east. Some of the old drovers' roads were tarmaced, but the majority were left to green over and sink gradually into the landscape, as paths official and not. A straggly line of hawthorns, sheep fleece fluttering in its lower limbs, alongside just a hint of a dip in the field, gives the gentlest of nods to its former life.

Walking or driving in rural Wales (or in parts of Scotland, northern England and the West Country), you are regularly reminded of the drovers and their impact on the landscape. Isolated pubs high in the hills often point to their overnight stops, as do small clusters of three Scots pines. When the drovers reached England, they would swap pine for yew trees to identify the inns and farms where they could shelter. Even in some of the most quintessentially English parts of the country, there are tangible reminders of the noisy cavalcades of Welshmen and their beasts that used to bustle through. A line of country lanes east of Leamington Spa is still known today, and marked on OS maps, as the Welsh Road, as is the Welsh Way near Cirencester in the Cotswolds. In true-blue Stockbridge, a Hampshire town of handsome Georgian houses and fine trout fishing, there's an old drovers' inn whose frontage is painted with the Welsh slogan *Gwair Tymherus, Porfa Flasus, Cwrw Da a Gwal Cyserus* ('seasoned hay, sweet pasture, good beer and comfortable beds'). It's as good a motto as any for a long walk, with or without the livestock.

Framfield path number 9 and Nicholas van Hoogstraten's half-built Hamilton Palace, near Uckfield, East Sussex

5. ON THE WARPATH (SOUTH)

OS Landranger, number 187. My dog-eared old copy, pre-dating the imposition of front-cover photos, is named Dorking, Reigate & Crawley, which sounds like a firm of solicitors you might find on one of the handsome high streets on this sheet. Brass name plaque, established 1894, although there's only one Mr Crawley there now, and he's dreaming of the day when he can take early retirement and move permanently to his Executive Plus apartment in an Andalucian golf resort. The map cost £1.40, although chances are I nicked it during my teenage carto-heist years. 'Selected roads revised 1975' is its most up-to-date legend, so it's no wonder that the M25 is shown mostly as a theoretical light-blue dashed line, nudging its way across woods and fields, and looking about as disruptive as a gentle stream.

Map spread, I'm on the hunt for the homes and stomping grounds of some typically enthusiastic ramblers. This Surrey hinterland is a good place to look. Despite the motorways, the rat runs and the commuting hordes, there are plenty of green corners, wooded hills and bits tightly policed by the National Trust and their ilk. Footpaths too: not just the regular rights of way threading between villages and through copses and paddocks, but a wealth of named long-distance paths as well. On my older map, there's the Pilgrim's Way in Olde English typeface, an early medieval track from Winchester to Thomas à Becket's shrine at Canterbury, and the North Downs Way National Trail, opened in 1978 and making its cartographic debut. Frequently, the two form the same route.

Thirty odd years on, and the modern Landranger 187, as well as showing the brutal reality of the M25, is crawling with named LDPs. On the cover map, now relegated to the back, the North Downs Way is shown, but the ever-obedient OS also remind us that it is part of the E2 European Long Distance Path – not that any Surrey stalwart would ever refer to it as such, or at least not without a few choice expletives attached. Handy, though, for those occasions when the urge grips you to walk from Leatherhead to Luxembourg, and who hasn't had one of those? Inside the map, the keen rambler is spoilt for choice: there's the Eden Valley Walk, the Forest Way, the Greensand Way, the Downs Link, the Sussex Border Path, the Way South Path (or was it the Path South Way?), the High Weald Landscape Trail, the Sussex Ouse Valley Way and the West Sussex Literary Trail. There's a corner of the London Loop, for those Hoxton hipsters who will exhaustively blog about their trundle through Cheam, Carshalton Beeches and the outer reaches of Purley. Most irresistible of all is the Vanguard Way, with the tough choice of which glittering trailhead to aim for, Croydon or Newhaven.

I'll call my mythical rambler from Landranger 187 Dave. He lives in one of the villages south of Weybridge, and walks every morning to the station (Effingham Junction perhaps, if only for the comedy value of the name), where he catches a train to work, at the University of Surrey in Guildford. Dave came to Guildford as one of its earliest intake of students, back in that apocalyptic year of 1968. Originally from the Potteries, he's never felt much at home in Surrey, but his degree became an MA, then a PhD, then a lecturer's post and, for the last 12 years, he's been head of department, so although he likes to keep his vowels as flat and northern as possible, he's lived in chi-chi Surrey for well over two-thirds of his life. Dave's north Staffs tones get even stronger when he's had a pint or two (real ale only; lager is the devil's work), as does his absentee devotion to Port Vale FC.

To be honest, Dave hates his job, but he's far too near retirement to think about quitting. As someone who came to a university that was forged brand new in the white heat of technology and the blazing flames of potential revolution, he just wants to slap the pallid little remote-controlled excuses for students that file through his seminars these days. Not that he ever would, of course. Dave is a lifelong pacifist and socialist, though he voted Lib Dem last time round, as the Labour vote in Surrey had shrunk to Monster Raving Loony proportions, and he quite liked their stance on Iraq and tuition fees. He's kept very quiet about the latter since. His most radical daily activity is buying the *Guardian* from the tiny pile at the station newsagents, dwarfed beneath tottering mountains of *Daily Mails* and *Telegraphs*. Even that just makes him feel worse, though. He hates the *Guardian*'s incessant wittering about Twitter and Facebook and Borough bloody Market, and would, if truth be told, rather have the *Telegraph*, because the crossword's better.

Dave and his wife Maureen have never made great friends locally. When the kids were growing up, they were pals with other nearby couples from the school run, but most of these have since upgraded to Richmond or retired to the coast. They have the immediate neighbours round every Christmas for a stilted hour or two of sloe gin and avoiding contentious topics. That aside, cats are fed, cars waved at, parcels looked after and residents' association meetings occasionally patronised. Dave hates those meetings, the golf club Hitlers and their Neighbourhood Snoop schemes, but 40 years in Surrey has taught him that it's best to show your face once in a while, or who knows what whispers might fill the vacuum.

Walking came to Dave's rescue 15 years ago, when the kids were leaving home and barely a week went by without some new named path being unveiled in the local paper. Age and a grumbling knee had put paid to his squash playing, so he took to heading out into the hills most weekends, usually alone but sometimes with Maureen or his colleague Roger, and had soon walked most of the waymarked routes in Surrey, Sussex and Kent. He tried joining the local Ramblers' Association group, but it was just the residents' association in gaiters. Twice now, he's had week-long walking holidays in the Peak District, which brought back fond – and some difficult – memories of his childhood; he was surprised to find himself quite so glad to be going back to the Hornby train-set prettiness of the North Downs. Walking became not just a hobby, but an ideological passion, a one-man crusade to reclaim his land, his history. He's read up on the Diggers and the Levellers, on enclosures and Kinder, and the knowledge gives a spring to his every step.

Politics used to be so straightforward for Dave, but all the black-and-white certainties of the seventies social revolution and the them-and-us Thatcher years had long since dissolved into a murky grey soup. He'd been briefly excited, and not a little

amazed, by the strength of local feeling against the 2003 invasion of Iraq, and had helped organise a coach from the area to
the huge march in London, but then spent all day praying that he
wouldn't bump into anyone he knew, lest they saw him march-
ing under placards saying 'Dorking Churches Say It's Not On,
Mr Blair!' and, worse, thanks to its witheringly posh sentiment
and even posher rhyme, 'We Don't Want a War in Iraq, We Just
Want a Walk in the Park.'

Dave writes a good letter; over the years, he's had a few
printed in the *Guardian*, the *Independent*, *Private Eye* and the
Surrey Advertiser. He'd become an active member of the Ramblers'
and the Open Spaces Society, and diligently lobbied politicians
and council officials about blocked paths and the debate over
the right to roam. One case had excited him over all others, had
reminded him of his red-hot, long-lost beliefs. He wrote letters to
MPs, councillors and one terribly wry one that he was thrilled to
see printed in the *Observer*. He'd even driven down to Sussex, in
his and Maureen's tiny Fiat, to join a demonstration of ramblers,
under police protection, as they attempted to walk the notorious
path that had been blocked by the man Dave hated more than
any other on Earth. More than Jeremy Clarkson. More even than
Thatcher.

Every pantomime needs its villain, and in the long-running
Cinderella that is the story of the rambling movement, no rap-
scallion ever came with a more dastardly swank and hollower
cackle than Nicholas van Hoogstraten. The battle over the Sussex
footpath past his home near Uckfield occupied more column
inches, drew more protestors and caused more fury than any
since Kinder Scout. There were a lot of Daves out there, and they
rose as one. To the local authority, East Sussex County Council,

the Hoogstraten path is known as Framfield 9 – even the name sounded like a gang of imprisoned hostages or victims of a miscarriage of justice. *Free the Framfield 9!*

Where do you start with Hoogstraten? The name, perhaps, for the 'van' is, of course, pure affectation. And that's not his only name, for he has admitted to using up to 20 aliases, reportedly including Nicholas Hamilton, Dr Karl Brunner, Paul Clark and Reza Ghadamian. According to a 2009 report in *The Times*, when Hoogstraten was cleared, on technicalities, of charges in Harare of illegal currency dealing and possession of pornography (many of the images included Old Nick himself with his latest Zimbabwean squeeze), he changed his name by deed poll. Changed it to – cue blanket green lighting and a thunderclap – Adolph von Hessen. He's behind you!

Perhaps I should let him paint his own portrait, for he's not been shy of speaking up. On his upbringing: 'My mother was just an object, something I inherited. She used to wind my father up by telling him what a bastard I was. The only relationship I had with her was: "Give me some money."' Or that of his own five children, by three different mothers ('Once you've had black, you never go back'), none of whom were deemed suitable Mrs van H material ('Do I look stupid?'). One of his broodmares said that when her waters broke on a valuable carpet, he ordered her to clean it immediately: 'Of course. It was a blooming twelve thousand pound Persian silk carpet. When one owns art one has to be a custodian of it. She was only the carrier of my child. Anyway, the baby didn't come for ages.'

His business methods are even less savoury. At its height, his empire included 2,000 properties, mainly in London and Brighton, and thousands of tenants, or 'riff-raff' as he preferred

ON THE WARPATH (SOUTH)

to call them. Evicting a tenant once, he allegedly assisted in hurling their furniture out of the window, describing it as 'the best bit of fun I've had in ages'. Others were beaten up, or came home to find staircases and roofs removed: 'That was just amusement,' he explains. 'Entertainment. Of course I threaten tenants on a daily basis. It's perfectly legal; people have got to pay their rent.' In 1968, he was imprisoned for ordering the firebombing of one of his tenants, a Jewish holy man. When he came out of prison, he allegedly kidnapped his own accountant, who he claimed had stolen £140,000 from him: 'Look, I was justified. I took him to Paris and locked him in a property I own there for two years. I fed him on sardines and biscuits and he worked for me until he'd repaid the debt.' The properties with which he was linked were often in a shocking state of disrepair. Five people died in an arson attack on a third-floor flat in Hove in 1992. There was no fire escape, a fact that the council had repeatedly reported, although they had found it nigh on impossible to prove actual ownership of the property, as, true to form, this was vested in a labyrinthine network of stooges and paper companies. He wasted no time in mourning the dead, however, describing them as 'lowlife, drug dealers, drug takers and queers – scum'.

Previous convictions included demanding money with menaces, forcible entry, bribery, handling stolen goods, assault and contempt of court. In 2002, he was convicted of the manslaughter of a business associate, Mohammed Raja, who was stabbed and then shot in the face by hired hitmen in front of his grandchildren. He was sentenced to ten years, but freed on appeal after a year in Belmarsh. 'Raja was nothing,' he said then. 'If I had a list of people I wanted executed that maggot wouldn't even have figured.' He was contemptuous of the dead man's family for seeking compensation from him ('They're a bunch of shit-bags, they always were'), and the way that he had been brought to trial ('The police and judiciary are dishonest and incompetent. They fitted me up. I had to keep my mouth shut during the trial but now I'm going to fuck the lot of them').

In 1985, he began building a lavish mansion on a site he – or rather, an opaque network of companies – owned near Uckfield. The largest private house to be built in Britain in the twentieth century was to be his mausoleum and the home for his art collection. Rumours swirled that it was a retirement home for Robert Mugabe, whom Hoogstraten had described as 'a hundred per cent decent and incorruptible'. Planning permission was only granted a decade later, not that such civic niceties ever made much difference to Hoogstraten. And as for a public footpath running through the estate, well, that was beyond irrelevant. He blocked it with a padlocked fence, two lines of barbed wire, a vast shed built right across it, and a stack of old refrigerator units piled high.

A seemingly unassuming, if steely, woman called Kate Ashbrook was to be his nemesis. She has been perhaps the most dogged of all access campaigners in the last 30 years, as full-time General Secretary of the Open Spaces Society since 1984, trustee and twice national Chairman of the Ramblers' Association, and with her fingers in the wholemeal pies of almost every other organisation involved in access to the countryside. It was Kate who, on 10 February 2003, wielded the bolt clippers that first freed the Framfield 9, some 13 years after it had been so thoroughly blocked off. It had been a long, expensive, explosive saga.

I invited Kate to come and walk Britain's most notorious footpath with me. It was her first visit since those heady days of

2003, and the pride was still etched on her face as she showed me the various flashpoints. She had taken the action personally against Hoogstraten, and then against East Sussex County Council when they cravenly caved into him and agreed to divert the path, ploughing tens of thousands of pounds of her own money into the fight. It was worth every penny. 'The Hoogstraten case was brilliant,' she said, 'because he was just *evil*. You need people like that, because then you can explain the issues to folk really clearly.'

If it sounds unwise to be speaking so ill of the undead, then she probably need not worry, for Hoogstraten seems to have disappeared from the Sussex landscape. His unfinished monster mansion, its copper domes glinting over the hedgerows, sits gathering dust and damp, and the black-suited security guards that used to surround both him and the estate have vanished. I'm excited – hugely so – to see it for myself, for villainous bling on a scale this monumental is a rare commodity in our modest little land. The mansion reminds me of somewhere I've seen recently, and then I remember. It's the Trafford Centre, but as built by Nicolae Ceaușescu. Fantasic. I mean, awful. Terrible. But, gosh, absolutely fascinating.

Once the footpath battle started raging, Hoogstraten ploughed into ramblers with the same panto gusto as every other opponent he'd ever faced. 'What kind of people go rambling? Perverts,' he declaimed to Lynn Barber in the *Observer*. It was a theme he returned to regularly, telling a journalist from the *Independent*, 'You ask any policeman, he'll tell you. They're what we call the dirty mac brigade. Flashers. Very few decent upright citizens, people who pay their rates, taxes and have a house they own, are anything to do with the Ramblers' Association.'

It sure did the trick. That outraged letter from my mythical Dave would have been one of the 5,000 that poured in to the Lewes headquarters of East Sussex County Council, although only 166 of these came from residents of the county itself. It could be seen, I say to Kate, as the ramblers' jungle-drum beating, the indignant rent-a-rant of people who probably write a couple of letters of complaint every week about something or other. She's not having that. Locals were terrified to speak out, she says, and indeed one official at the county council, which was supposed to enforce the right of way, said that his officers were 'scared to death' of Hoogstraten. You would be, I'm sure. But no local residents, not one from Palehouse Common, the hamlet by the path's blocked entrance, or Framfield or Uckfield, came out in support of the ramblers. In fact, as Kate admits, they 'rather hated us. They didn't like the intrusion, or the parking problems, or the press.'

Much as he would be loath to admit it, Hoogstraten was a pawn in a game whose rules were set by Kate and the Ramblers' Association. They were every bit as ruthless as him, but considerably smarter (not that it's much of a competition; read a few interviews with Hoogstraten, and intellectual capacity is not what springs to mind). The path was first reported as blocked to East Sussex County Council in 1989 by a local RA member. Despite his repeated protestations, nothing was done. It was only in December 1998 that the national RA realised that it was Hoogstraten's land that this path ran across; his growing notoriety (and growing mansion) meant that they had found their perfect poster boy. They invited campaigning journalist John Sweeney (he who lost it with the Scientologists on *Panorama*) to come and see for himself; he wrote up his experience in the

Observer of climbing the fence and being told again and again to 'fuck off' by a security guard. It was good timing: the piece appeared on Sunday, 3 January 1999, just as thousands were strapping on their boots and heading out for a muddy New Year country walk. The story spread like wildfire, in the liberal and conservative press alike. The debate around the Countryside and Rights of Way Bill was going on in Parliament, and occupying much space in the media too. Landowners were being lined up by various countryside organisations to splutter indignantly about the iniquities of the planned legislation, but nothing they could come up with could compete with the 'Evil Monster of Uckfield' and his downtrodden ramblers. Hoogstraten was the best weapon the RA could have prayed for, and they deployed him with strategic precision. When Mohammed Raja was murdered in July 1999, and Hoogstraten's collar felt in response, the RA, while doubtless mumbling all the right noises of sympathy, must have thought that all their Christmases had come at once.

Kate and I set out to walk Framfield 9. It's about a mile long, disgorging on to the A22 after crossing through the grounds of a country hotel and equestrian centre. Ironically, four years after Kate had victoriously snipped through the barbed wire at the other end, the hotel blocked the path with a dung heap and a fenced-off car park, and the Ramblers were off again. Today, it's a clear run through, if a little ambiguously waymarked in the hotel grounds. I have to say, though, it's not the greatest of walks. Press reports back at the height of Hoogstratenmania made it sound like an Elysian paradise, a gentle canter through Merrie England, with skies unbounded and glorious views over the Downs. In truth, the path crosses a couple of scratty fields, a claustrophobic little wood, a slippy footbridge in a thicket of weeds and the truly uninspiring grounds of the hotel. The only thing that makes it even slightly interesting is the occasional view of Château Hoogstraten.

That's not the point, I know. It's the principle of the thing. Which is why the diversion, as proposed by Hoogstraten's proxy company, and eagerly accepted by terrified county council officials, was never going to be acceptable to Kate and the thousands that cheered her on. 'It's not the proper route,' she tells me firmly. 'The proper route is the original route that generations of people have used. It should be a lovely straight walk from Framfield to . . . to wherever it was going, but you can see here that it wouldn't have been.' So does that mean that all footpath diversions should be so stoutly resisted? She thinks for a moment and is prepared to concede that the only diversions that might possibly be justified are those that re-route some footpaths out of farm yards. A little later, over a pint in a particularly nasty nearby pub, she elaborates on the point. 'Paths are our history; they're absolutely fascinating. They show where people used to walk and ride, and the great thing is that, in most cases, they are undisturbed, so that even if they don't make much sense today, they're there for a reason – which is why I don't like paths being mucked about with, just for the benefit of some private person.'

Her passion is astonishing. Her bravado too, when you consider how Hoogstraten was inclined to treat his adversaries. She's been doing this for three decades and more, and travels thousands of miles every year to support local campaigns, speak at meetings, lobby councils, gee up the troops, confront recalcitrant landowners and be the public face of an issue that's both deeply complicated yet barely flickers across the radar of most people. I ask her if she thinks things have improved during her span. 'It has changed,' she replies. 'It used to be very, very negative, but after the CROW Act, landowners saw that actually public access to land didn't cause the kind of damage they thought it would, so they have moved a bit, and they also recognise the benefits to the economy that accrues. They can't rely on farming any more; they have to diversify, so they do see that it may be quite a good thing. They have moved a bit, I think.' She tails off, and I detect something almost regretful in her tone. 'The battle's much harder to fight now,' she continues, carefully measuring out her words, 'because it's nothing like as black and white these days. Landowners used to be really quite evil. I was always going on the *Today* programme and having a real knockabout with the president of the CLA [the Country Land & Business Association, formerly the Country Landowners' Association], but it just doesn't work like that any more. They've moved more in our direction.' 'And maybe you've moved a little in theirs too,' I suggest. 'I don't know about that. I hope not.'

Luckily for Kate, before we leave Framfield 9, I ask if we can go and have a little wander along the footpath's continuation to the north of the lane. It's a mess. Broken stiles with vicious-looking electric cabling pinned to them, and the path forced into an almost impenetrable nettle-and-bramble-filled ditch. Kate whips out her camera and snaps away, her eyes gleaming. Two days later, she sends me copies of emails between her and the Rights of Way officer at East Sussex County Council in which she is demanding action, and he is promising it. You would, you really would.

As we walk back to her car, she positively scurries past a nearby farm. 'They're not friendly at all,' she sidemouths to me. When we get to a safer distance away, she turns back and points out the paddock jumps and overdone hanging baskets. 'See, horsey types. Nouveau riche. It's them that are the trouble, it's always them. They just think that if they spend enough money, they can buy their privacy. Well, they can't.'

It's not a unique – nor indeed a new – observation. I heard it countless times from the footpath and access activists that I met, the strident belief that it's the nouveau riche that are ruining the countryside. It's why Nick van Hoogstraten became such a pin-up for them, for he was the physical manifestation of all the avarice and arrogance that so many ramblers are certain lurk beneath every sharp suit and brassy hairdo. They point at the garish gates, mock the mock-Tudor treble garage and raise their eyes in horror at the security cameras, blacked-out SUVs and leylandii.

I sympathise, of course I do. I'm as much of a snob as the next *Archers* listener, but it's something I do try and rein in a little, for I'm frankly quite scared of what lies a bit further down that particular path. Whereas the great access battles around the northern cities were driven by a highly ideological class war, almost everywhere else – here in southern England in particular – they seem to have been powered by regular surges of good old British snobbery; one, furthermore, that tends to come from both sides of the political spectrum. Left-leaning access campaigners and bluff old right-wing landowners are as one on the subject, as they put aside their differences and gang up instead on those in between.

Was it ever thus. I remembered the nouveau riche rage of

Ralph 'Vegetable' Wright in Flixton, a fit of pique that had proved to be the inadvertent midwife of the rights of way campaign movement. And I was reminded of the 1938 Commons debate on the Access to Mountains Bill, when the 'person in the motor car', the Rolls-Royce in particular, had become the bogey figure of the day and all-purpose cipher for flash, brash and thoroughly reprehensible. Joshua Ritson, the ex-miner turned Labour MP for Durham, started it off with: 'There are landlords and landlords, but we are getting now a new class of landlord. I have always paid and shall always pay tribute to the old aristocratic families, who never bothered at all about these matters, but now we are getting some new ones, the quick-rich gentlemen, who can afford to have more gamekeepers than there is game on the job. As I said upstairs, we have some Americans now, and they are as boisterous as they always are . . . I agree that it is the people with motor cars whom we are up against most of all and that they are the people who do the damage, but is that any reason why we should punish the poor people who never get a breath of fresh air, but whom we are now beginning to allow to do so? They always behave themselves, and I think the people in the motor cars are more dangerous than anything else by breaking bottles on the roadside and dropping their cigarettes and other things that are more dangerous than cigarettes. They are a danger to the country generally, and they should be taught decent manners when they are out in the country places. They go and tear up wild flowers, and yet our people have to suffer because these other people cannot behave themselves.'

Robin Turton, the Tory squire who had inherited both his country pile and parliamentary seat of Thirsk and Malton from his uncle, boomed in agreement: 'Like the honourable member for Durham, we do not always like the man in the Rolls-Royce who wants to transport home most of the countryside, whether poaching for grouse or taking wild plants . . . The honourable member for Durham talked about new landlords, but there are also new people coming to the countryside, who would not come there but for the motors, who do not behave as the people who walked to the countryside behaved in the old days. We must deal with the man who comes in his Rolls-Royce and thinks he owns the countryside. People in the country want protection from that type of man.'

In the Lords debate on the same bill, the point was spelled out with even greater disdain. Viscount Swinton: 'The man who really does the damage is a much fatter and more prosperous kind of person, who comes in a closed motor car, who takes what he is pleased to call, and what we used to call, carriage exercise, and then, having sat with the windows tight shut smoking a very fat cigar, he emerges with an equally fat partner and probably sets alight to your moor, having first picked anything which is within range.'

To some eyes, there are the noble poor, those grateful saints who, in Ritson's words, 'never get a breath of fresh air' but 'always behave themselves' (really?). They're fine, but it's the others, you see, who are the problem. Came from the gutter, but instead of having the good grace to stay there, they've gone and got themselves some cash, and the airs and graces to go with it. Fur coat and no knickers, don't you know. It's John Betjeman's residents of Slough who 'talk of sport and makes of cars / In various bogus-Tudor bars / And daren't look up and see the stars'. And according to Alfred Wainwright, their offspring are even more hideous: 'The worst offenders [at trashing paths] are parties of school children, often too many in number to keep under control, who treat the paths as playgrounds, kicking and throwing stones, romping over the verges and generally having fun.' Playgrounds? *Fun?* In the hallowed cathedral of the countryside? How dare they.

So much the worse, therefore, when these parvenu hooligans start to look at the countryside not just as somewhere to go and ruin on a Sunday afternoon, but as a place in which they'd quite like to live. Then the collective shudder passes through not just the old landowners, but the liberal ramblers as well. Many of them – us, sorry – have also relocated to the country, but of course, *we* did it for all the right reasons. We are sympathetic, have bought a few books on local history, and even read some of them, have chuckled delightedly at the picaresque habits of our new neighbours and hardly ever grumbled out loud that Ocado doesn't yet deliver to our postcode district. We respect old country ways, although we are a mite choosy as to which ones we like to uphold. Not so keen on the caged dogs, prying eyes and earthy racism that we pretend not to hear in the pub. But we do adore the sense of community, the fields and fresh air and, most of all, the ancient right to wander down people's drives and through their gardens or fields, just because the postman used to do it a hundred years ago.

The idea of the immutability and immovability of a footpath is the holy grail for many, and it underpinned the Hoogstraten case and many others. Generations have gone that way, then so must we. There's great romantic appeal in the notion, of course, for the most beautiful paths are usually those that are as ancient and integral a part of the landscape as the trees and streams. But it presupposes that we, indulging ourselves at our considerable leisure, are the rightful, natural successors to those who had no alternative but to trudge this way through the hail, mud and rain every sodding day of their entire lives, and I'm not sure that we really are. Surely too the biggest threat to rural Britain is the gallop towards turning it into one huge museum, clapped in the aspic of our national insecurities. If the paths and tracks, the veins and arteries of the countryside, are frozen for ever, how can we expect the body that they feed to maintain a pulse?

There's the same judgemental selectivity about farmers. We like the ones that come and sell their cheeses and lamb shanks at the farmers' market, with their rosy cheeks, salty language and eye-watering prices. We admire the enterprise of those who let out charming barn conversions as eco-friendly holiday lets or who turn their farm yards into petting zoos come lambing time (even if we mutter about yet more eye-watering prices on the way home). Most of the rest of them terrify us, though, with their monobrows and monosyllables, shit-spattered pick-ups and sheepdogs that go mad at the sound of a twig snapping two fields away. Yet it's from them that you'll learn more about the land, and all that is woven into it, than from any number of interpretation boards, downloadable leaflets or rambling club leaders.

Joseph Ritson's quaking horror about the behaviour of 'boisterous' (read flash and uncultured) Americans provides another of the most dependable leitmotifs in our much-cherished hauteur. However much we can look down on our home-grown nouveau riche, we can always find a bit extra for our Stateside cousins. It gave the nineteenth-century story of the 'Pet Lamb Case' in the Highlands its necessary dynamite, and it surfaced again rather more recently, in the most controversial access battle since Hoogstraten: Madonna versus the Ramblers.

The Queen of Pop's brief embrace of the English Dream seems like just that now: did it really happen? Or did we all collectively hallucinate that the world's biggest music icon attempted, as one of her regular makeovers, to pass muster as a Wiltshire gentlewoman? The story unfolded in much the same way as ever: loud-mouthed Yank comes to our shores, throws on the tweed, has a crack at hunting and shooting, but doesn't really understand how we do things here and thinks it can all be solved by throwing money at it. Once we've got over preening and flattering ourselves with their presence ('Gosh, you want to come and live with little old *us*?'), the knives come out and we lacerate them.

With her then new (and now ex) husband, Guy Ritchie, Madonna bought the Ashcombe Estate, on the Wiltshire–Dorset border a few miles east of Shaftesbury, in 2001. She plunged enthusiastically into English country life, being snapped quaffing bitter in local pubs, wearing caps and going on the odd game shoot. The newspapers could hardly get enough of it, but before long, they were bored with happy and needed a new angle, preferably one that would enable them to start sticking the boot in. It first came in the shape of some new gates erected at Ashcombe in 2002. Not realising that they needed planning permission, it wasn't initially obtained (although retrospective permission was soon granted), and the papers gratefully fell on the story, bloating it out of all recognition. A pair of stone columns with two wrought-iron gates became 'twelve-foot security barriers', if you believed the endless stories in the *Mail* or the *Telegraph*, neither of whom could leave the story alone.

It was the same two papers that cranked the tale up another level, by filling their pages with speculation that the new CROW

Act could see some of the Ashcombe estate downland classified as 'open access', and scaremongering that this could result in ramblers picnicking on Her Madge's front lawn. Most of the stories were handfed to journalists by campaigners against the right to roam, who correctly thought that the best way to do that was by dangling the juicy carrot of celebrity under the snouts of the press. Madonna was, according to the same two papers, incandescent. In the *Mail*, she was quoted as describing ramblers as 'Satan's children' and 'those fuckers', and that 'she has even written to Tony Blair to complain about the forthcoming "right to roam" legislation, which she sees as a stalker's charter.'

Except, it seemed, she hadn't. No letter was received in Downing Street, and Madonna herself, in an interview with *Q* magazine, laughed off the words placed in her mouth by an overeager journalist. 'I haven't got anything bad to say about the ramblers,' she declared. The only truth in the report was that once the maps were published showing all the proposed open-access areas, there were seventeen parcels of the Ashcombe estate marked as such, which the Ritchies decided to appeal against. But then so did 3,173 other landowners, though they'd not gone on stage in a conical bra, so they barely scraped a mention. The hearing was held in the spring of 2004, and concluded that fifteen of the seventeen pockets of land should remain private, while the remaining two - those furthest from the house - would become open access. To *The Times*, the *Independent* and the *Daily Mail*, Madonna won. She lost, according to the *Guardian*, while the BBC and the *Telegraph* called it a 'partial victory' for the superstar. The press coverage was dreadful. Celeb-sniping swept away the facts, and the few that did make it through were often contradicted within the same article. Did the job, though. The mud stuck.

Madonna responded with an interview in *Vogue* designed to show that she was as much a part of the Wessex landscape as Stonehenge or discarded bottles of White Lightning. The pictures of her sporting jodhpurs and feeding chickens didn't quite persuade us, and neither did her zealous protestations of how much she now loved England, and felt that it was truly her natural home. Her fate was sealed, perhaps, with her enthusiastic account of a recent weekend at Ashcombe. Cecil Beaton had been a previous inhabitant of the estate, and to celebrate their fourth wedding anniversary, the Ritchies had set out to re-create a Beatonesque weekend of folly and frolics, culminating in a show where all their A-list friends were obliged to do a turn. Gwyneth Paltrow, Chris Martin and Stella McCartney sang a spoof version of Madonna's hit 'American Life', which they rebranded 'American Wife'. Artist Tracey Emin and former model Zoe Manzi wrote and recited a poem. Interior designer David Collins spoofed Noël Coward's famous song with a rendition of 'Don't Put Your Daughter on the Stage, Mrs Ritchie' (accompanied by Madonna's eldest, Lourdes), while the Ritchies themselves performed a raunchy pastiche of a Restoration comedy that had first appeared at one of Beaton's Ashcombe *fêtes champêtres* in the 1930s. As if all that wasn't enough, 'Sting played the lute, and Trudie read some sonnets.'

Although, of course, Madonna herself has long gone from Ashcombe (the *Vogue* interview alone must have ensured that), I had to go and see what all the fuss had been about. I stayed the night in a nearby village pub, where the landlady airily told me over breakfast, 'Oh yes, Madonna came in here once. No-one was much impressed.' I can believe it. I felt like a cosmopolitan ponce there, amongst the red faces and Wurzel accents; quite how Madonna thought she might fit in is anyone's guess.

The press coverage during the battle made it sound as though the Ritchies were holed up in their compound, having landmined the footpaths. In fact, the public rights of way across the estate – including a decent stretch of the Wessex Ridgeway – were never closed, or even slightly threatened: the whole episode had only been about the access land brought in by the CROW Act. If anything, the paths are in far better nick than most others, and they were a joy to walk.

This is Cranborne Chase, a lofty chalk ridge that looks down towards Salisbury Plain. For an all-too-brief few years at the beginning of the nineteenth century, the view would have included the three hundred-foot-high tower of William Beckford's Gothic extravaganza, Fonthill Abbey, until it collapsed for the third, and final, time in 1825. The Ashcombe estate is down in a smooth valley that looks as if it has been gouged out of the chalk by a giant ice-cream scoop. I took the path down into it from Win Green, the highest point on Cranborne Chase. Nothing was left to chance: the estate signposting of its paths was efficient, unfailingly polite and tastefully retro in its uniform shade of British racing green. It was a warm summer's day, with bees humming, cuckoos singing, and perfect little cotton-wool clouds tripping lazily across a cornflower sky. 'We just fell in love with it,' said Madonna about their first visit to Ashcombe. 'In the summertime it's the most beautiful place in the world. It just stayed with us, haunted us for a really long time.' Me too: this was possibly the single most idyllic walk that I had all year, and writing about it months later brings it all back and makes me smile wistfully. For the first, and quite probably the last, time in my life, I suddenly felt sorry for Madonna, for what she'd had and then lost – and not even the image of Sting plucking his lute could make me hate her.

Many of the access or footpath battles you hear about these days involve celebrities, for the tales fit so well with our need to trash the upstarts and, in particular, the always reliable narrative of building 'em up to dash 'em back down again. Jeremy Clarkson, Keith Richards, Ashley and Cheryl Cole, Claudia Schiffer, John le Carré, Eric Clapton, Gary Barlow, David Puttnam, Peter Gabriel and Andrew Lloyd Webber have all had their skirmishes. With the proposals for universal coastal access still being hotly argued over, it is likely that there will be many more. Sometimes the threat of stalkers and paparazzi is deployed, usually to a chorus of scoffing from the very papers that pay top dollar for shaky telephoto lens shots through the same people's herbaceous borders. Sometimes it's their human rights, which only brings on a burlesque crescendo of 'poor diddums'. And, touching another nerve of the moment, sometimes it's health and safety, things such as the possibility of lawsuits from injury on their land. That goes down worst of all: two obsessions of the tabloid tubthumpers in one fell swoop, and they almost knock themselves out with their own sarcasm and sanctimony. Turn over a few more pages, though, and there'll be the ads: 'Tripped Over a Paving Stone? MAKE THAT CLAIM!'. The only other grouping that regularly makes it into the papers over footpath battles on their land are bankers, and they get even less sympathy.

The politics of the footpath and access movements has always been a strange mix of old Right and firebrand Left. I've not made it into the former category quite yet, but I have spent most of my adult life in the latter – at least by my own definition; many of my friends and family would probably disagree, once they'd stopped laughing. In truth, I've been a shameless political slapper, having voted, at one time or another, for six different parties: Liberal, Labour, Communist, Green, Lib Dem and Plaid Cymru. No Tory or UKIP, though; not yet, anyway. On any conventional scale, my views have definitely slidden rightwards, and it's in this area of land ownership and custodianship that I can see it most glaringly.

Growing up in 1970s Worcestershire, by far my favourite outing was to Witley Court, a few miles south-west of Stourport. Originally a medieval manor, it had been added to by successive owners, eventually becoming one of England's most extravagant stately homes by the late Victorian age, when it was owned by the Ward family, the Earls of Dudley. Witley was famous for lavish living, for parties where royalty, aristocracy, politicians and celebrities mixed in the orangery, the parterre gardens or draped themselves over the sides of the massive ornamental fountains. Two hundred staff oiled its wheels, and it took 50 tons of coal a day to keep the monster warm.

Even more than with most stately homes, Witley's progress mirrors that of the country at large. The Wards' fortune was eaten by its opulence, and after the Great War, the much-battered family put the estate up for sale. It was bought by the epitome of new money, Kidderminster carpet baron Sir Herbert Smith. From humble beginnings, he'd risen to become the most powerful man in the town, where he was known as

'Piggy', thanks to his portly stature and shaved head. Though he loved life as lord of the manor, he was ill-prepared for the costs, and ran the house and estate into the ground, skimping on maintenance and keeping only a skeleton staff. Like an earlier Hoogstraten, he caused fury by blockading all the footpaths that ran across the estate.

On 7 September 1937, a fire broke out in the basement of the court, quickly spreading to the ballroom above. Thanks to Sir Herbert's economies, the fountains lay unused, and the reservoir that fed them was almost empty. Not that it would have helped had they been full, for the water-pumping equipment had rusted up. The staff battled valiantly to save furniture and pictures, but it was too late. In 1939, with the country on the brink of war, Smith sold the house to a demolition contractor, who stripped it of all its finery, leaving it as a roofless shell.

It was in this state that I first encountered Witley Court, with a few further decades of plundering and weather-beaten decay etched into its gaunt frame. It excited me like nowhere else, from the moment you passed one of the lodge houses on the main road and bumped your way up the rutted track, the skeletal ruin growing ever larger on the skyline. Back then, you just nipped over the fence and had free run of the place, up crumbling staircases into the bedrooms, down into the dark, mouldy cellars, galloping along the broken balustrade of the grand terrace steps, even jumping into the vast, wrecked fountains. And there always seemed to be crows.

One day, at the age of about 12, I had persuaded my dad to take me there, ostensibly to walk the dog. Standing in the ruins was an elderly lady, muffled up against the cold. We got chatting to her, and it transpired that she had grown up in Great Witley, the nearby village where most of the house's army of staff had lived. On the night of the fire, she said, villagers – few of whom would still have been employed at the Court, thanks to Sir Herbert Smith's swingeing economies – came out into the street to watch the flames dancing in the sky. They cracked open bottles of beer, and chanted 'Burn, you bastard, burn!'

She said it in such a deadpan way, a look of resigned indifference on her face, but the shock electrified me. It was partly hearing a little old granny swear, but there was more to it than that. To the 12-year-old me, history was dates and kings and battles and the invention of the spinning jenny. It was cause and effect, question and answer, a smooth, smug progress through the ages to the zenith of civilisation that was late 1970s Britain. For the first time, I got a glimpse of the real story behind the textbook, and it both confused and thrilled me.

'Burn, you bastard, burn!' soon became my aggregate philosophy towards the landed gentry, and when I brought friends home from university and beyond, I'd always take them to Witley Court, to demonstrate my firm belief that the best stately homes are those that lie roofless and abandoned. To my junior socialist self, everything the ruling classes had done was evil, while the working classes could do no wrong. Being stuck in the middle, I was taking the traditional route of trying to slum it downwards, massive over-compensation springing from the bottomless well of middle-class guilt. 'The land is ours!', I hollered to anyone who would listen, which was mainly other self-lacerating folk from comfortable backgrounds.

Writing guidebooks in my twenties and early thirties, I trotted around plenty of stately piles, a sneer etched on my lips as I went. In the late 1990s, the *Guardian* ran a regular feature where they would invite two people of diametrically opposing views to correspond on a common issue, and they would then print the letters that had winged their way back and forward (by fax, if I remember rightly). Some report had come out saying that the number of people visiting stately homes had dropped quite considerably, and they wanted to explore the issue through the medium of a contrived dust-up between an aristo and a self-appointed Robespierre. I was asked to do it, and pitched against James Hervey-Bathurst, owner of Eastnor Castle in Herefordshire. No wonder you're losing visitors, I told him gleefully. You're stuffy, pompous and 'make the average visitor feel like an unwelcome oik'. Where, I demanded, was the history of the 'folk who built [the stately homes], skivvied and cooked and cleaned and curtseyed'? The Saturday this appeared in the paper, I fantasised that I was being cheered over toast and marmalade up and down the land. Dave and Maureen in Surrey, I'm sure, were doing so. If only they'd actually existed.

As you'd expect, Mr Hervey-Bathurst (you can imagine how pleased I was that he was called that) proved to be the very model of affable politeness in his responses. He finished with a point that was an almost perfect counterfoil to my Witley-shaped fixation: 'When my wife and I were hesitating about moving into Eastnor, we were encouraged to do so by the local community. People do not want a derelict ruin at the centre of the estate; by developing and maintaining the property we, and similar houses, generate needed income for the rural community. Most historic houses now rightly play a useful role in their communities. This input must be maintained and improved.'

I could see even then a glimmer of truth in what he said, but I was still busy fighting the class war from the comfort of the pub, and it took until a year or two later, when I moved from urban Brum to rustic mid-Wales, for his words to begin to sink in properly. A decade of rural life since then has almost obliterated my old beliefs. The rural economy is such a fragile and inter-dependent entity, and a well-run country estate or major farm is its beating heart. Most importantly, those running such places are playing a very long game, their motivation above all others not to drop the baton that has been passed to them down the generations. The vast majority take their centuries-old responsibilities, to footpaths and bridleways as much as their tenants and neighbours, very seriously indeed. You'll never get such abiding consistency from politically motivated landlords, and having seen what a fist of a job the men from the ministry did in set-ups such as the Forestry Commission and the MoD, I'm regularly grateful that no government, of any persuasion, has ever managed to nick any more of the land. As John Ruskin put it: 'No man is so free as a beggar, and no man more solemnly a servant than an honest landowner.'

None of this is clear cut, and it never will be. The history of our land, ties, access and identity is riddled with contradiction and ideologically square pegs that, however hard we try, we cannot bash into the round holes we've so lovingly fashioned. Even a case as apparently crisp and clear-cut as the Hoogstraten battle has irony laced through it. One of the most quoted facts about the Framfield 9 footpath was that it dated back, in Kate Ashbrook's words, to '1862, and is thus at least 140 years old. It was shown on the county council's composite map prepared under the Rights of Way Act 1932 as a public footpath admitted by the landowner, and it has been shown on every draft and revised definitive map since then. Few paths are better documented.'

Indeed it is, but the fact that it was definitively recorded in 1862 is due solely to the fact that this was part of the documentation of an enclosure order, in this case for the 'remaining wastes' of Framfield Manor. Proof that we should be allowed to walk the path today is therefore based on what historian and writer W. G. Hoskins called 'the legalised theft' of the enclosures.

Although the process dates back to medieval times, the ongoing enclosure of huge tracts of British land accelerated dramatically through the eighteenth and nineteenth centuries. According to the venerable environmentalist Marion Shoard, in her classic book *This Land Is Our Land*, there were in England during those two centuries 5,400 individual enclosures under 4,200 private Acts and various general Enclosure Acts, which resulted in the privatisation of more than seven million acres of land. This is, as she puts it, 'more than the total area of the following ten contemporary English counties: Derbyshire, Nottinghamshire, Northamptonshire, Buckinghamshire, Bedfordshire, Hertfordshire, Cambridgeshire, Essex, Norfolk and Suffolk'.

For the finest, most righteous howl of anger at this land grab that changed our relationship with the land for ever, it is best to spend some time in the company of John Clare (1793–1864). The greatest nature poet England has ever produced, his prodigious talent combined with the era of Enclosure Acts, leaving us with thousands of perfectly crafted observations from the frontline of breakneck rural change.

To Clare, the enclosures brought:

> *Fence meeting fence in owner's little bounds*
> *Of field and meadow, large as garden-grounds.*
> *In little parcels little minds to please,*
> *With men and flocks imprisoned, ill at ease.*

The right time, the right talent, but also very much the right place. John Clare was born and raised in the village of Helpston, one of thirty or so parishes that make up the Soke of Peterborough, a curious cul-de-sac of history. Historically, the Soke was a semi-detached enclave at the northern end of Northamptonshire, so that Clare was known from the very beginning of his poetic career as the 'Northamptonshire Peasant Poet', a label that quickly became yet another stifling enclosure to him. When the creation of the first county councils was being debated in Parliament in 1888, the Marquis of Exeter, lord of the manor of one of the Soke's great houses, Burghley, bored his fellow lords rigid with lengthy demands that his little fiefdom be granted its own county status. It is said that members of the House of Lords nodded this odd arrangement through just to shut Exeter up. This lasted until 1965, when the Soke of Peterborough was amalgamated with Huntingdonshire to the immediate south. Just nine years later, Ted Heath's great local authority shake-up resulted in the absorption of the entire authority into neighbouring Cambridgeshire, and there it remains today. Nominally, at least: people there still identify far more readily with Northamptonshire, if anywhere.

To have stayed stock still, yet see four different counties drift by within a century fits this quite beguilingly odd part of eastern

England. It feels apart and beyond, yet deeply rooted into its fertile soil, while straddling the border where the limestone belt dissolves into the ethereal weirdness of the Fens. Despite being foursquare Middle England, it is an area on the cusp, somewhere in which it is monumentally easy to get lost and disoriented, and entirely the right place to have produced rural England's most heartfelt, heartbreaking battle-cry.

Most of his early poems, those that made him a near overnight sensation in Georgian literary society, were passionate evocations of his native landscape, in its diverse moods and detail. Like many young boys before and since, Clare had combed his own back yard with reckless glee, in the company of friends and alone, always watching, always noticing. His poetic account of the freedom of an English rural childhood set the bar for every dirt-poor-but-'appy saga since, from *My Fair Lady* to *The X-Factor*. And like them, Clare's sudden success, when everybody wanted a piece of him, was painfully short-lived. The instant spotlight rarely lingers long.

Clare loved his paths, and knew them intimately. In his childhood, Helpston was encircled by three great fields, each divided into strips for cultivation by all landowners and tenants of the village. To the south of the village lay Royce Wood (Rice Wood, as the OS has it), and beyond that, Emmonsales Heath, a massive wide-skied common used by all for rough grazing. Clare and his boyhood mates had the run of it all, 'roaming about on rapture's easy wing'. They knew every furlong, strip, copse, heath, pond and wood, and exactly which path would take them where. But a path was more, far more, than a means to an end: it was a world of its own, with its own lore and mood, somewhere to be relished not just for what it did, in taking you from A to B, but for what it was. Nearly two centuries on, we are by his side, smelling the earth and air, as in *The Flitting* he extols the

> *Green lanes that shut out burning skies*
> *And old crooked stiles to rest upon.*
> *Above them hangs a maple tree,*
> *Below grass swells a velvet hill,*
> *And little footpaths sweet to see*
> *Goes seeking sweeter places still.*

It was losing the paths that focused them so sharply into Clare's mind and poetry. His childhood and adolescence coincided exactly with the time that the enclosures reached his part of the world. When he was six, the nearby village of Bainton became the first in the area to be enclosed. A decade later, an Enclosure Act was passed in Parliament for Helpston and all its surrounding parishes, and over the next few years the young John watched with mounting horror as favourite trees and copses were ripped out, streams blocked and diverted, and fences and gates thrown up across the fields and heaths in which he had wandered freely, developing an intimacy with every leaf, flower, insect and bird. As a graphic reminder, 'On paths to freedom and to childhood dear / A board sticks up to notice "no road here"': a punishment almost impossible to bear for one so sensitive.

He railed with increasing bellicosity about the injustices of enclosure, which brought him into direct conflict with some of his wealthy patrons, who had, on his initial success, been delighted to be seen publicly supporting the nation's new favourite peasant. After the dizzying sales of his first collection, which needed reprinting four times within the first year, the pressure was on for a swift and successful sequel. The title poem of the collection, *The Village Minstrel*, did not beat about the bush:

> There once were lanes in nature's freedom dropt,
> There once were paths that every valley wound, –
> Inclosure came, and every path was stopt;
> Each tyrant fix'd his sign where paths were found,
> To hint a trespass now who cross'd the ground:
> Justice is made to speak as they command
> The high road now must be each stinted bound:
> – Inclosure, thou'rt curse upon the land,
> And tasteless was the wretch who thy existence plann'd.

Such bald sentiment brought immediate use of his red pen by one of Clare's most effusive supporters, Lord Radstock. 'This is Radical Slang' he scrawled across the lines when given a proof copy of the collection to see. Radstock's unbending attitudes – he had already objected to a line about a baby 'all beshit' – can perhaps best be seen in the titles of his own most successful books, *The British Flag Triumphant!*, a collection of naval tales about us whupping the French, and *The Cottager's Friend; Or, a Word in Season to Him who is so Fortunate as to possess a Bible or New Testament, And a Book of Common Prayer*.

Looking at poems such as this one, it's easy to be lulled into a belief that Clare was some early The Land Is Ours propagandist, who would have been at the forefront of any protest smashing down the iniquitous gates and fences. In truth, the new order terrified him, and he cowed before it, as his celebrated sonnet on the topic so forensically demonstrates:

I dreaded walking where there was no path
And pressed with cautious tread the meadow swath
And always turned to look with wary eye
And always feared the owner coming by;
Yet everything about where I had gone
Appeared so beautiful I ventured on
And when I gained the road where all are free
I fancied every stranger frowned at me
And every kinder look appeared to say
'You've been on trespass in your walk today'.

Caution, dread, wary, fear, frown, trespass: words with which any modern walker is all too familiar. But there are signs already that Clare's mind is troubled way more than it should be by such matters. 'I fancied every stranger frowned at me' (even as he walks on the open road) is the key line here: most people he passed by would surely have been wrapped up in their own minds and worlds, scarcely even acknowledging the furtive poet skittering by, muttering to himself. And this is why we remember John Clare today, not just for his lyrical power, but for the delusions and mental decline that eventually sent him to the madhouse.

For someone who never had much to begin with, it was Clare's extreme sense of loss that defined his life, informed his poetry and ultimately destroyed his sanity. His first-hand witness of the effects of enclosure both confirmed and exacerbated this, but it was by no means a unique example. The lost figure of Mary Joyce, his first love at school, haunts his work throughout. She came from a smarter background than him, so her father forbade any further alliance and, although she remained unmarried in the neighbouring village of Glinton for the rest of her life, it is not believed that they ever spoke again. Even when the sad news of her death in a house fire in 1838 reached him, he continued to think and write of her as his second wife and pine for her by name in poems and diary entries for the rest of his days. She had long since transcended from being a flesh-and-blood Northamptonshire wench into a totem for all that had gone: not just first love, nor the commons and paths, but childhood, innocence, comradeship, freedom, easy sexuality, his status as pin-up of the chattering classes. Family too. John was born a twin, but his sister – a far stronger baby than him – died after a few days. Surprisingly little is made of this in Clare's numerous biographies, but it must have set in stone the heart-breaking emptiness and perhaps his sense of viewing life from the sidelines that stalked him for ever.

With some irony, if you care to visit Clare's native country today (and you should), it is its sense of openness that first strikes. Big-sky country, it's a place of cornfields and cornflow-ers, poppies and skylarks, languorous clouds, good pubs, woods and furzey commons (at least in early summer, when I was there. Heavy, sodden soils and vicious north-easterly fronts – 'Flood bellowing rivers and wind roaring woods' – are its lot come the winter). Church spires are still the tallest things for miles around. Many of the natural (and indeed man-made) features of Clare's tender verse can still be found, and there are innumerable good paths and open spaces binding them together. Compared with many other rural parts of the country, this seems to be an unsung walkers' paradise. But then, unlike Clare, we have no intimate knowledge of just how much more free it once was, for we are measuring our sense of its accessibility from a very dif-ferent base. On top of that, Clare was witnessing the area as it hurtled into the modern age: enclosures, breakneck industriali-sation in the limestone quarries and finally the coming of the railways, all events that traumatised him. Now the spent quar-ries are designated nature reserves, many of the former railways signposted wildlife corridors or cycle paths and, to the amateur eye, the fields look reassuringly timeless. The leisure age has spun its illusion, and we tumble for it. I don't suppose Clare would have done.

The Soke is a surprising understudy for the Cotswolds. Shown a picture of villages such as Castor or Barnack, many would guess that they were looking at Something-on-the-Wold or Somewhere-on-the-Water. They share the same geological bedrock of mellow limestone, the same fleshy productivity and easy nature, and are full of similar honey-coloured Georgian piles that set the property sections of the weekend papers ablaze with desire. Yet there are no tourist coach parks here, no flocks of Japanese snappers, no antique emporia, no artisan patisseries flogging cupcakes at two quid a bite. There are barely any places to stay, and none at all in Helpston itself. As I wanted a night in the village, I kipped in the back of my van parked on the verge of what I thought would be a quiet country lane, but which instead proved to be a major route for tractors, muck-spreaders, hay-balers and even a few enthusiastic members of the local dogging fraternity. John Clare would be proud, on all counts.

As with most poets, Clare's popularity has waxed and waned according to changing fashion and prevailing moods. Because of the acute sense of loss that permeates his poetry, he seems to swim back into view whenever times get rough, which may partly account for his growing popularity these days. Writers, composers and artists seem eternally fascinated by him: Edward

Thomas, Iain Sinclair, R. S. Thomas, Benjamin Britten, John McKenna, Geoffrey Grigson, Adam Foulds and Edward Bond have all produced major Clare-inspired works, and there have been paintings and exhibitions, radio plays, TV documentaries, dramas and readings galore. One event in Clare's life seems to capture the artistic imagination far more than any other, and that is the longest walk that he ever undertook, 80 miles in July 1841.

This was no loving, leisurely nature ramble. Clare was escaping an asylum, at High Beach in Epping Forest, to which he had been committed four years earlier. Over four days, with no money or food, and in already ruined shoes, he hobbled from Epping Forest back to Helpston, sticking mostly to the route of the Great North Road, what we now know as the A1. Clare's journey has enthralled us ever since, and many have felt moved to follow in his fevered footsteps. In the visitors' book of Helpston parish church, numerous modern-day pilgrims record that they have walked there from Epping, and when recent fundraising efforts were going on to help convert Clare's birthplace cottage into a museum, the central event was a sponsored walk from High Beach to Helpston, albeit not clinging quite so closely to the thundering Great North Road as had Clare nearly 170 considerably quieter years earlier.

A few days walking his landscape, with a book of his poetry in my satchel, was an absolute pleasure of the purest kind (save for a field of frisky bullocks), but I was starting to feel quite bonkers by the end of it. On some of the walks, I found that I was reheating arguments in my head as I was pushing along paths chemically scythed through fields of corn or stamped through woods. The realisation dawned that this was not a unique occurrence, either. I thought back to my daily walks at home. Many of them inspire me and help produce and foment ideas, but all too many get used to rehearse barbs that I'll never actually have the guts to use, or to chew over long-flavourless gobbets of ancient grievances. Walking with Clare brought a stark understanding that down that road does lie an unnecessary madness, a raging fury and unspecific, unfillable sense of loss, and it brought me up sharp.

One way to quieten such nonsense is to physically stop walking, and focus instead on something very small and specific: a bud, a hedgerow flower, a leaf, an insect, a fern, the bark of a tree, the play of light on water or of water on rock (this is one of the reasons that picking blackberries, bilberries or mushrooms is so therapeutic). Mentally note down every detail of it and be prepared to wonder at its perfect design. Spend as much time as you dare in the pursuit. The eye and the brain are refocused, and you can continue in a far humbler frame of mind. Doing this also seems entirely appropriate in the company of John Clare, for it is his unerring instinct for the tiny details of the natural cycle that marks him out from a slew of contemporary nature poets, usually men of means, as they wandered and declaimed through the countryside.

Perhaps though, it only leads to another kind of madness, one in which the perfection of nature only sharpens in relief the dreary mess that we tend to make of it. All I can tell you is the answer that came as I put flowers on John Clare's grave in Helpston churchyard. They were a gorgeous bunch of pungent Sweet Williams, a pound in the honesty box – well, honesty Asda bag – at the farm opposite his birthplace. It seemed thrillingly appropriate, for William was the name of his penultimate son; William Parker, in fact, for Parker was John's father's first name and grandfather's surname. I smiled at a small link cemented, for William Parker was my grandfather's name too, a man I knew only briefly. Another twinge of loss fluttered by.

Clare's grave is a low slab of local stone, with his details on one side and a defiant motto on the other. Only, the final letter of the sentence, an 'E', temporarily disappeared from my sight – and indeed, lichen seems to be doing its best quietly to obliterate it.

'A POET IS BORN NOT MAD,' it said.

The calm before the storm: Wainwright's Coast to Coast path, at Ennerdale Water, Cumbria

6. ... NOW WALK THE WALK

Stuff. More Stuff than can possibly be good for you. Do I really need quite so much Stuff just to go for a walk? And does that Stuff really need to be quite so hi-tech, streamlined, lightweight, ergonomic, as-tested-by-NASA and so witheringly expensive? Ah yes, sir, you could compromise your safety, your health, your comfort and quite possibly YOUR LIFE by using some old crap from the Army & Navy store, but is it really worth the risk? Gosh, I never knew that a pair of socks could make that much difference.

But I fall for it, hook, line and very costly sinker. Of course I do. I'll sit through an advert break on the television and shout abuse at the stupid bints who are prepared to pay 60 quid for a tub of cream because it's rammed full of made-up science as demonstrated by jiggly graphics, but now I'm standing in the outdoor shop, wallet prised open ready to be raped, and I'm willing myself to believe the exact same guff about rucksacks, bivvy bags, waterproofs, tents, camping mats, cookers, fleeces, trousers, T-shirts, boots and whatever other exorbitantly priced nonsense they can persuade me to buy in the next hour.

Before setting out to walk the Ridgeway, I had an image of myself as a gentleman stroller of the old school, and that I was going to remain entirely aloof from the marketing mania that has now eaten the walking industry alive. There I'd be, soaking up the oldest path in the country in dubbined leather boots, cotton, linen, silk and tweed, a direct descendant, both spiritually and sartorially, of the tribes and travellers who had gone before. I'd sniff haughtily at the Gore-Tex-clad masses as they crinkled past, sounding like a thousand crisp packets being opened.

With some glee, I stumbled online across the manifesto of the Band of Historical Hillwalkers, which 'advocates the exploration of the great outdoors wearing attire made by underpaid adult craftsmen in the United Kingdom, as opposed to fashionwear made by underpaid children in the Pacific Rim'. My people! I was almost ready to sign up.

> Tweed, wool and leather boots are worn in preference to inferior man-made materials. The BHHW considers velcro, gortex [sic] and other such imposters objectionable and the wearing thereof is politely discouraged.
>
> Our mandate is to get outside, breath the air and engage with the world for a few moments. Along the way we make pinhole photographs or draw and paint the scenes before us, taking time to be present and amazed by the world. Whether hiking 15 miles or just strolling a few hundred yards onto a salt marsh the Historical Hillwalker pauses and interprets the scene before them, seeing the world rather than merely glancing at it. In this way we engage with the colours, the play of light and the atmosphere and by doing so become whole and happier.

I wanted to believe it; I truly did. But the text just became more and more pompous, and the photos – all fully Fuji digital, rather than pinhole – were mainly of people in jeans and anoraks wandering across the marshes of north Kent, or looking terribly pleased with themselves in various pubs. Artist Billy Childish was one of the founder members, but it seems that he's not much involved these days, and, in an interview in *Time Out* in February 2010, declared that he was forming a new outfit, the Damp Tweed and Hobnails Walking Association, not that there's been any mention of it since. I too would have to find my own style, and my own way.

'All the gear and no idea' has been a phrase that I've bumped up against lots in recent years. I first heard it when interviewing a veteran surfer in Pembrokeshire as he described the urban numpties, whose training mainly consisted of reading the weekend-paper lifestyle sections, and who were turning up in increasing numbers on the beach that he'd surfed for decades. I could see it for myself on a daily basis when they opened up mountain-bike tracks, including a hairy two-mile descent, on the mountain above my house, where I'd walked the dog for years. All too often, the ones being winched off the slopes in a pool of blood and shattered bone were the ones kitted out in the brightest, newest lycra, the flashiest, most aerodynamic helmets and on bikes that cost way more than I'd ever paid for a car.

Popping out for a few essentials for my walk along the Ridgeway, I was soon a good 500 quid down. I say popping out, but in fact it was a highly stressful two-day canter around mid-Wales and the Borders, a breathless race against the clock to snap up that all-important last pair of gloves with essential ThermaLite® technology. I started as I meant to continue, in an old-fashioned gentlemen's outfitters in Ludlow, being soothed

by the sound of the ticking clock and the calm tones of the solici-
tous assistant. In an ideal world, they would have kitted me out
from head to foot, like a Victorian explorer heading off to the
Tropics, but it quickly became apparent that, for all their tweedy
loveliness, it wasn't going to suffice. As the clock ticked down
to retail closing time, I screeched into Shrewsbury and shuttled
frantically between the town's two main outdoor supplies shops.

They are the two chains that you'll find in most medium-
sized British towns: Millets and Blacks. They are also owned
by the same company, and appear to be run in artificial competition with each other, even, as I discovered in Shrewsbury,
to the point where the branches of each are just yards apart on
the same street – all part of the illusion of choice. Blacks like
to aim themselves at the more aspirational outdoorsy type, the
serious sort who truly believes that he'll be bivouacking through
the Pyrenees, even if all the pricey gear he buys in readiness only
ever makes it as far as the camping field behind a pub in the
Malverns. They are big on rugged, ballsy euphemism: a water
bottle is a Complete Integrated Hydration System, and you'll get
withering looks if you're not sure of the difference between a
daysack, a backpack, a rucksack, a ramblesack, a belt pack or a
compression sack. They're big too on must-have, trademarked
technology that you'd never heard of three seconds earlier:
don't even think of buying poles without an integral AntiShock®
system, a GPS with no HotFix™ satellite technology, or a pack
that's lacking an Excel® 300D Ripstop polyester contrast, let
alone a Self Adjust carry system and Bi-Radial® chassis. I have
made none of those up. Looking you straight in the eye while
they reel off these fantastical technologies will be earnest young
men in branded fleeces and bum-fluff beards, who promise you

that that particular bit of kit saved their bacon last year when they were yomping across the Faroe Islands. Cowed into submission, you buy it all.

Across the street in Millets, it was all aimed at a far camper camper. The shop assistants were mumsy types and chatty fat lads with highlights, and while Blacks had been an ocean of khaki and frowning colours, Millets were a party of dayglo in multiple plastics. If Blacks were for gadget freaks and wannabe survivalists, Millets were unashamedly pitched at claques of lasses wanting all the gear for a totally wazzed-up weekend at some festival off the M4. Once the 40 quid Cath Kidstonesque tent had been erected, pissed and puked out of, shagged in and tripped over, it would be blearily abandoned, along with a thousand sagging compatriots, to the primordial ooze.

The Ridgeway walk, though, had been a hop from one prebooked B&B to the next, but to do the Coast to Coast, I was notching it up a couple of gears. I'd loved the walk, the idea of the trail and the stately progress across the landscape, but I'd ended up in the B&B routine of having breakfast around eight and then being back on the path and walking from about nine. Most days, I seem to reach my destination for that evening's stop between five and six. It was like going to the office, a proper 9 to 5, more so than my normal life has been for 20 years, and it had begun to piss me royally off. For starters, I was only ever seeing the landscape and the wildlife at exactly the same time every day, and was missing the two best bits – sunrise and sunset, when so much of the world, both this one and the ones beyond, come dazzlingly to life. For my last day's Ridgeway walk down into Avebury, I'd asked the B&B if I could forgo the breakfast, get a packed lunch instead, and headed out of there at six, just as the sun was inching up and casting its buttery light over the dewy slopes. I saw more wildlife in those first few hours than I had throughout the previous week.

For the Coast to Coast therefore, I was going to mix it up: stay at some B&Bs, pubs and maybe the odd hotel as a treat, but also perhaps take a tent and a bivouac (bivvy) bag, so that I could camp or sleep rough as the mood took me. Neither was I going to pre-book anything except the first night's accommodation, so that I could wing it, both in terms of daily distance travelled and even in terms of my chosen route. Freedom on the trail. I would need, therefore, a great deal more Stuff.

Mindful of the stress and expense of that pre-Ridgeway shopping crawl, I went online. Hours later, with my eyes and brain nearly bleeding, I wrenched myself away from my laptop, way more confused than I'd been beforehand. And I'd bought nothing. Instead, I'd devoured scores of angry and illiterate reviews, worried just how great was the difference between a three-star- and a four-star-rated camping mat, watched a few YouTube videos of shaven-headed Americans cooking survivalist rations in the woods and read endless autistic lists of kit posted on forums by lads called JungleWarrior and BornSurvivor (a.k.a. Kevin of South Shields and Darren of Biggleswade). In short, I'd been scared silly. Even more so by a forum dedicated solely to the Coast to Coast path, where I'd read a portentous thread that started with a warning, posted in March, that thanks to Julia Bradbury's television series about the route that had been aired the previous year, accommodation was fast being snapped up, especially for the peak months of May, June and September. I was walking it in May, and reading this, with only the first night's accommodation booked, just three days before setting off.

Visions of limping my way across England, kipping in hedgerows like an old tramp and hanging round the bins at the back of chippies and pubs began to swim before my bloodshot eyes.

To get any idea of the place that walking holds within the modern British psyche, you have to do the Coast to Coast. Officially, it's not *The* Coast to Coast, but *A* Coast to Coast walk, as detailed in his obsessively fastidious manner by Alfred Wainwright, the undisputed god of the rambling curmudgeon. That subtle difference between the definite and indefinite articles is crucial. Wainwright wanted to prove that you could stitch together your own long-distance path out of existing rights of way, and first published his account of doing just that in 1972. In his introduction to the book of his walk, he stated that he wanted to 'encourage in others the ambition to devise with the aid of maps their own cross-country marathons and not be merely followers of other people's routes'. Nearly 40 years on, the thousands tramping religiously in his wake, sticking with dog-like devotion to every twist, turn, stile and gate mentioned in his book, would, I suspect, bewilder him and make him despise humanity even more than he already did. For his path, only one of the infinite possible routes to take you from one side to the other, is now Britain's most popular long-distance walk, and the second busiest in the world, with tens of thousands attempting it every year.

To the authorities, Wainwright's CtC is an unending headache. Despite being the nation's favourite, it is not a recognised LDP (Long Distance Path). Within the Lake District National Park, it is official policy not to signpost it at all, while elsewhere waymarking is sporadic and often unofficial, sometimes as vague as a painted arrow on a rock. Meanwhile, other minor footpaths and tourist-oriented circular walks, each with a fraction of the footfall of Wainwright's behemoth, are relentlessly promoted and signed. It's like sticking up a thousand signposts to guide motorists along every B-road and country lane in an area, while studiously ignoring the six-lane motorway that thunders through the middle of them. Even Ordnance Survey, slavish to every diktat of government, be it from Whitehall or the Town Hall, plaster the map with the likes of the Taff Trail and the Barnsley Boundary Walk, while pretending that Britain's most popular path is not there.

As policy, it's probably counter-productive too. The renegade nature of the route surely only boosts its numbers, for many walkers like to feel like outlaws, even when they are locked in a multi-coloured snake of fellow outlaws 200 miles long. As they stride by, the idea that they are cocking a snook at the authorities puts a definite spring in their step, makes them feel young and radical again. And by ignoring the jazzy leaflets in the hotels and the plaintive signs to try the thrills of the officially sanctioned West Ackerdale Way instead, they know that they have chosen the rebel path. It's a tiny victory, and a little hollow when you're fighting over the last teacake in a wayside café crowded with other CtC pilgrims, but it'll have to do.

On the way up to the path's launch pad at St Bees, I read various newspapers, all agog with excitement about the swearing in, the previous day, of Britain's new Conservative Prime Minister and his Liberal Democrat Deputy. David Cameron is two months older than me, Nick Clegg three weeks younger. They were 43-year-olds taking on real responsibility, I couldn't help but think, as the detritus of the West Coast Main Line rolled past the window in a vaguely dispiriting blur. By contrast, I was alone on a train, heading north with a rucksack heavy with Stuff, odd aspirations and a few kilos of mid-life crisis.

An hour between trains at Barrow-in-Furness didn't put me in a better mood. I doubt that it ever would. Lunch options seemed to consist of a large, sweaty outpost of the Wetherspoon empire or the kind of café selling only sandwiches that taste of Tupperware and clingfilm. Diagonally opposite the station was a statue of a footballer in mid-kick. I tried to work out who it was just by looking at him, but no recognition stirred. According to the plaque, it's Emlyn Hughes, Barrow's favourite son and, to my generation, the chirpy, squeaky one opposite Big Bill Beaumont on *A Question of Sport* ('Number six, please Dave!'). The announcement of his death (in 2004, aged 57, from a brain tumour) had been one of those moments that makes a whole generation suddenly feel considerably older and sadder. As was finding yourself the same age as the prime minister. Or going to Barrow-in-Furness.

It's the generational leap that startles the most at these times of gubernatorial baton-passing. My step-mum turned 60 in May 1997, just weeks after Tony Blair's precisely orchestrated sweep into government. Her birthday party still stands tall in my memory as one of the strangest nights I can remember, and not entirely due to the fact that I had necked an 'E' in the erroneous belief that it would help smooth my way through the evening. Given that the party was held on a claustrophobic cruise boat chugging down the River Severn, from which there was no escape for a full four hours, this proved not to be such a great idea. Most of their friends, and most of our family, are old school Tories, but it wasn't the change in political complexion of the government that drove them all to be extra-drunk and extra-maudlin that night. It was the realisation that their generation had, in one fell swoop, been booted from power, and that it was never coming back.

At least on the Coast to Coast walk, it looked as if I would be one of the youngest participants. Even walking down to the beach from St Bees station, I could see various backpacked figures who were obviously on the same mission. There were couples, singles and groups, and they all seemed to be in their fifties and sixties. A gang of four blokes called me over in broad Yorkshire accents. 'Hey fella, culd you tek us picture please?' A camera was waved in my face and I snapped them grinning, full of hope and trepidation, comradeship and excitement, as they performed the traditional launch of the walk by dipping their boots in the Irish Sea and collecting a pebble to take to the other side of the country. We all shook hands and wished each other well.

Half an hour later, I caught up with them on the sandstone cliffs of St Bees Head, Cumbria's most westerly point. It had been a moderately stiff climb up there, but the reward was sweeping views of a freezing grey sea, and an assortment of caravan parks backed by the dark bulk of Sellafield nuclear power station. 'Ye might as well walk wi' us lad,' one of the Yorkshire blokes said, entirely kindly, I know. But I was in a pretty strange mood, and not keen to inflict it on anyone. I thanked him and declined. He wasn't at all pleased, ticking me off with, 'Well, that's not t'spirit of th'Coast to Coast, lad. We're all in this together!' His mates all nodded and smiled at me. I walked on, feeling like a complete shit. Sod's Law, I'd be bumping in to them now at least four times daily for the next fortnight.

After circumnavigating St Bees Head, the path ambles inland through a quarry and down various dusty tracks. For those that think that Cumbria is all tea shops and Beatrix Potter bunnies, have a look around the west of the county, a land forged in rust and pebbledash. That combination of hard-bitten villages, mountains and mines was making me homesick, for it is very much like my part of Wales. Cumbria and Cambria, much though they'd both care not to admit it, are spookily alike, both physically and temperamentally.

Another similarity is that, despite all the obvious natural advantages, they don't always do tourism very well. Brits generally are temperamentally rubbish at the Welcome Host routine, but the more taciturn corners of our island – most of Wales and west Cumbria, for instance – are just useless at it. Even when they're trying to smile, it comes across as slightly defensive, scared or hostile. And sometimes they just can't be arsed even to try. On the second day, I had an early lunch in a village pub-cum-hotel right on the CtC route, somewhere that evidently makes a huge proportion of its income from those walking the path. The interior was brown and faded, the silence hung as heavy as someone standing on your chest and the food barely squeaked across the line marked 'just about acceptable'. The girl behind the bar desperately didn't want to be there and told me how much she hated this time of year, when the walkers starting returning in droves, and keeping her in a bloody job, the bastards. At that point the door swung open, motes of ancient dust swirled around in the watery sunbeams and a middle-aged American couple breezed in, replete in Trail Gear.

'Why, hello there!' the fella opened with. The barmaid grunted in return. 'Do you have a menu please?' She handed one over, plastic and sticky, which they read with lots of forcedly enthusiastic little 'ooh's'. My toes began to curl in embarrassment for them. It was not going to end happily.

'I think I'll have a chicken sandwich,' the man ventured.

'Got no chicken,' replied the barmaid, in a tone that verged on the victorious. 'No tuna either.' He opened his mouth to ask for the next option on his list, but the barmaid cut him dead: 'And duck's off too. So's the gammon.'

'What is the soup of the day?' enquired his lady wife with a dazzling Iowan smile.

'Vegetable,' the barmaid snapped back.

'Oh. And what sort of vegetable would that be?'

'Mixed.'

I met the American couple a little later along the trail, and felt obliged to apologise on behalf of the entire nation for the terrible pub where we'd all suffered lunch in musty silence. They laughed, and told me that it had not been the worst they'd experienced on their British holiday. We got talking about accommodation, and it transpired that they'd booked all of theirs for the entire two weeks of the walk some four months earlier, back in January, and that even then, there were many places that were already full. I'd read online that accommodation was very scarce, but that had been posted by one of the 'sherpa' companies that not only ferry your luggage between guest houses, but offer a bespoke accommodation booking service, for a fairly hefty fee. I'd presumed therefore that they were trying to scare people into using them rather than have to make a stack of their own calls, but it was beginning to look like a royal battle of tenacity to find accommodation for the rest of the trip. If the rubbish places were full night after night, then what chance finding anywhere half-decent?

And the rubbish places seemed to be doing just fine. When I left the sullen pub in which I'd shared lunch with the Americans, that night's bag drop, by one of the many CtC sherpa companies, had just taken place. I had to pick my way through the small hallway of the inn, through a garish sea of hold-alls, rucksacks and suitcases, and an owner quietly swearing under his breath at them all. In an instant, I saw a picture of minibuses full of tat weaving their daily way across the country, scattering bags and belongings to the four winds as their owners tramped inch by inch across the landscape, never deviating from the one decreed route and day-dreaming about being reunited with their trainers. B&Bs, pubs and hotels that, under the normal influence of market forces, would have gone out of business years ago, were being kept alive by this quotidian transfusion. There was something indefinably depressing, and pointlessly Sisyphean, about the whole thing.

As I crossed into the National Park, I noticed a folded piece of paper on the path in front of me. It was an immaculate CtC itinerary, printed off an elaborate spreadsheet and dropped by someone who'd recently passed this way. I half-marvelled, half-shuddered at the level of organisation it demonstrated. Not only did it detail every night's accommodation booked, with con-tact phone numbers and email addresses throughout plus what packed lunch they were or were not supplying, it contained numerous annotated notes, such as the fact that two taxis were booked for 1900 hours next Tuesday to take the happy throng to a pub near Reeth for dinner, and that, on the following Sunday, Trevor, Gordon, Elaine and Terry D had already opted for the lobster at the restaurant in Grosmont, while Peter, Marie and Terry K were having the chicken chasseur.

I didn't even know where I was sleeping that night, let alone what I'd be having for dinner 11 days hence, and as I bumped along the rocky path above Ennerdale Water, I silently congratulated myself on being smart enough to have stepped off this ghastly treadmill, for I was heading instead for a night's wild kip in the woods. My next-door neighbours had lent me their ancient bivvy bag, which I'd tried out one warm night in my garden a week earlier, and had found to be fine for the job. Not for a moment did I consider that a dry night in a lowland garden might be inadequate preparation for wild bivvying in the fells, and not for a moment did I think that it would be – could be, even – anything other than a lovely evening. To that end, I hadn't even gone so far as to check the weather forecast, but, as I'd left my Egremont B&B that Thursday morning, the landlord's last words were, 'Forecast looks good for the weekend.' At the time, that had seemed enough.

At about five o'clock, I breezed past the Ennerdale youth hostel and camping barn, feeling terrifically smug that I was saving myself six or seven quid by going to camp for free in the woods. I say camp: I mean, of course, lie in a large plastic sheath, like some kind of jumbo boil-in-the-bag snack. About two miles further on, I suddenly spied a track that looked interesting, and just up there was a lovely hollow centred on a graceful beech tree in her first flush of the year's leaves. I find that most years, a particular species of tree seems to present itself for my especial consideration, something to sit under, ponder by and read up on. This year's tree, particularly since my Ridgeway walk through 'Beechy Bucks', was unquestionably the magnificent beech. I'd mistimed the Ridgeway trek: in any normal year, my walk in mid-April would have coincided perfectly with the first fluttering of lime-green leaves amongst the legendary beeches of the Chiltern Hills, but this was a year when everything was two or three weeks late, thanks to a sharp winter. Consequently, I'd walked for days through the massive beech woods still in their skeletal winter state: impressive, for sure, but not the breath-taking display I'd been expecting. Since then, I'd seized every chance to hang out with the beech trees and couldn't get enough of their first week or two in leaf. The chance of a night beneath just such a tree seemed like a present from the gods.

Like a little Walt Disney critter, I made camp under that spreading tree, building a fire pit, collecting wood, getting the fire going, even carefully stripping logs in order to build myself a bed of moss. I ignored the ever-greyer clouds whipping in from the west and the freezing – and strengthening – winds. What could possibly hurt you when you're lying on a mossy bed under a quivering beech?

Dinner was a Cup-a-Soup and a few pawfuls of some berry/seed/nut combo from the health-food shop in Barrow. I was still starving, and getting really quite cold, even if the sleeping bag was doing its best. It wasn't dark much before ten; the rain started minutes later. At first, the noise on the bivvy bag was strangely charming, a pitter-patter reminder that I was keeping dry and mainly warm, particularly if I curled up. I imagined drifting off to sleep to its comforting rhythm and waking to a brilliant dawn.

Before long, the pitter-patter went up a few notches and began to physically hurt as the raindrops pelted my head and body. One move – to try and get some air into the bivvy bag – resulted in rivulets of rainwater surging in and drenching me and the sleeping bag. Of all the trees to be sheltered under, a beech in its first few weeks of delicate, feathery leaf, is not high on the list for protection. Despite the fact that I'd had a good four hours of daylight in my little camp, I'd never once thought to go and scan the surroundings for the best places to go in the event of an emergency – I was just too busy being Bambi the forest fawn. There were, I remembered, many conifers and firs in the vicinity, but I had no idea where they were or how much protection they might give.

Whenever you're tempted to think that summer nights are over in a twinkle, think again. This mid-May night went on for bloody ever. I staggered around with a fading headtorch illuminating the branches and rain slicing through the dark in front of me, eventually stumbling on a sizeable fir with what looked like a low, dense canopy. Sure enough, there was barely any rain falling beneath it, and I sank in gratitude against the trunk, huddled in a damp sleeping bag. I could now keep my head out of the bivvy bag and peer through the hood of my cagoule into the dark – encased in the bivvy bag (or, as it was starting to feel like, entombed in the body bag), I'd been hyperventilating and terrified that I was about to have a heart attack. And then up a few more notches the storm went again, and the branches above me were protection no more.

Soaked by now, deafened by the incessant rain and with a freezing wind flaying me, my brain danced with vivid hallucinations. Clearest of them all was a vision of Alfred Wainwright, a man who made Gordon Brown look like Billy Connolly, laughing his scratchy woollen socks off at me. I'd already been fairly rude in print about the cussedly misanthropic Wainwright, and now, here on the path that he created and just below the peak upon which he'd had his ashes scattered, he was exacting a typically well-calibrated revenge. In between panicky hyperventilations that were making my ribcage ache, I blurted out loud an apology to the God of the Lakeland Trail, and begged him for both forgiveness and to let me live, in return for which I would apologise to him in print and promise to keep off both his manor and his legacy in future. He must have listened, for the hallucinations dimmed and into their place swam a plan to gather my stuff and get back, somehow, to the youth hostel I'd passed hours earlier. The forest track was broad, pale and stony, just about traceable in the dark. On the way, I passed gullies, spouts and streams that had been bone dry the previous night, and which were now foaming and roaring with water.

At the youth hostel, I found an open barn, its concrete floor providing little in the way of comfort, but at least its roof worked in keeping the rain off. Hunched on the floor, soaked and freezing, I watched the water splash down off the greenery and drifted into a stiff, uncomfortable doze to its rhythm. Feverish dreams of my own bed skittered across my subconscious, and when I woke up, I knew that I was going home.

The people who worked in the youth hostel thought otherwise. 'No come on, you just need to relax a bit, and you'll be on your way in no time,' I was assured by Susan, an assistant at the hostel, as she cooked breakfast for me and – wouldn't you know it – the two Iowans that I'd met the previous day in that terrible pub. She was quite magnificent, not flinching at all when she came down into the dayroom to find a wet, bedraggled stranger huddled in a chair, whimpering. 'Lots of people have a bit of a shock at the beginning of the Coast to Coast,' she continued. 'It's completely normal. You wouldn't want to give it up so soon, would you?' YES! Yes, I would. From whichever angle the question was posed, only one answer came booming back.

The taxi driver who took me to Whitehaven train station was even nicer. To him, giving up the CtC after two short days and about 20 miles was nothing to be ashamed of. I wasn't, but it was very kind of him to reassure me anyway, telling me how he'd once picked up an American lady who'd given the walk up in Sandwith, the first village on the trail and about a mile inland from its beginning at St Bees Head. 'She said that she hadn't realised there were going to be hills.'

On the eight-hour train journey home, I had plenty of time to mull over my sharp exit from Britain's favourite long-distance path. As per usual, this boiled down to the sticky question of exactly what I was going to tell people, which little excuses I would hide behind. There was the lack of accommodation. The apparently poor standards and high prices of the rooms that remained, and of the food and drink on offer. The zombiefied mass march across the country, a regiment of rambling beards, outdoor OCD and half-a-bitters. The relentlessly upbeat camaraderie of my fellow trailblazers that had succeeded only in making me feel even more alone.

Ah. The real truth.

I was lonely, and envious of those boring beardy bastards, smugly anticipating their chicken chasseur a week on Sunday. However hard I scoff at them, they had got it right and I had got it drastically wrong.

Somewhere past Preston, an idea seeped into my battered brain, and I perked right up. I'd failed to do Wainwright's Coast to Coast, but it would be far truer to his legacy to devise one of my own and walk that instead. And not across northern England, either – this latest sorry saga had been yet one more in a lifetime's litany of unfortunate experiences of the Lake District. I know how passionately many people adore it, and I can absolutely understand why, but it's always seemed alien to me, succeeding in being both surly and twee at the same time. The relentless Outward Bound heartiness, the cagoules and calendars, the fell-bagging one-upmanship – it all left me as cold as a midsummer day in Witherslack. Years ago, I remember hearing a warning broadcast on the radio on some bank holiday Monday that 'the Lake District is full,' roadblocks were in place, the M6 was nose-to-tail and on no account should would-be daytrippers attempt to go there. This made it sound less like an area of stunning natural wonder, and more like an out-of-town retail park. Which, for very many people, it is.

As Cheshire rolled by and the far emptier hills of Wales loomed lovely on the horizon, I remembered Harri Webb's immortal verse: 'What Wales needs, and has always lacked the most / Is, instead of an eastern boundary, an East Coast.' That was it! I would create and walk a Welsh Coast to Coast, starting with my feet in one of the rivers that form the England–Wales border and heading home to cool my toes in the tidal waters of the Dyfi estuary, just three miles from my front door. There was the added advantage that such a route would indeed take me across the entire width of Wales, but at its narrowest point, only 50-odd miles. After days of feeling nothing but vague, creeping dread, excitement pounded through my veins and I couldn't wait to get home and get the maps out.

Better still, I could devise a route that took me across my adopted home county of Montgomeryshire, for it is the only one of the old Welsh thirteen that touches both sides, from the anglicised redbrick of borderland market towns to *Cymraeg* huddles hewn out of sweat and slate. Three days I decided it would take me, and not much wanting another night crying in a wet bivvy bag, I promptly found and booked a couple of B&Bs and set to working out a route that incorporated them. The options were glorious, and limitless.

A few days later, my partner dropped me off early one morning on the border, between Bishop's Castle and Montgomery town. It was the obvious place to start: not only does the modern border run along the Caebitra river, but the spot is perfectly dissected by Offa's Dyke, that mighty eighth-century bulwark between the tribes of Mercia and Wales. I paddled in the river, put my boots back on and set off on my three-day walk homeward. By car, the journey had taken an hour and a quarter.

For the first few miles, I walked along the Offa's Dyke path, one of the loveliest of all our National Trails as it edges its way through the land that is neither England nor Wales, but hovers between them both, a delicious chimera. At this point, the path hugs the dyke itself and exactly straddles the official border. Puddles of bluebells could be seen shimmering in the hollows of the earthwork rampart, orchids in outrageous colours winked from the grass banks, the brand new leaves of oak, ash and beech trees trumpeted their recent return to life. I bumped into two groups of Offa's Dyke walkers in swift succession, and had the same conversation both times. 'Doing the whole thing?' I was asked as I approached. 'No, walking home to the other side of Wales, and making it up as I go along,' I replied smugly.

In Montgomery, I had a pint of local scrumpy, which I fancifully thought might attune me to the rhythm of the place, but which turned out to be vile and left me burping acidically all afternoon. I wouldn't dream of saying that that was the spirit of the place, although there is a culverted stream under the town called the Shitebrook, so maybe it's not quite as Jane Austen as it first looks. Climbing up to the castle, a regular favourite, I spotted a sign for the Montgomeryshire war memorial, which I'd never visited before. It seemed like an appropriate stop on a pilgrimage across the county, so I followed the path high up on to the top of Town Hill, just over a thousand feet above sea level. The monument was soberly impressive, but the view thrilled me viscerally: not only was it an endless panorama of borderland loveliness, but it was the first time I'd seen from the same spot both the Clee Hills in Shropshire, behind which I'd grown up, and Cadair Idris, above the village I now lived in. My whole life in one view: I hadn't realised it was even possible.

Though I say so myself, my invented Welsh Coast to Coast (though I'll settle for the Montgomeryshire Way or, if that's already taken, the Parker Trail) was stunning, and gave me everything that the English one hadn't. I had numerous easy chats, and some great laughs, with people en route: farmers in the fields, old ladies hanging out their washing, workmen on the roads, a shopkeeper or two, landladies and regulars in a few pubs, mothers pushing prams, the mobile librarian, an old boy nailing up the parish notices on a chapel board. Staying with complete strangers in B&Bs quite near home is a novel experience too, giving you unexpected new angles on places you thought were so familiar, and both were great fun as well.

The variety of paths was similarly intoxicating. The most exciting were the sinuous green lanes, winding almost subversively under their leafy canopies around the edges of fields and woods. There were little worn ways grooved into fields, not much more than sheep tracks, a canal towpath and walks along river meadows, glorious strides through the whole landscaped length of the Gregynog estate, sweet little paths that tiptoed through bluebell woods, farm drives, rickety bridges, and zig-zags up and down the many hills. Quite a few country lanes filled in the gaps, and they were some of the best bits of all: high hedgerows bursting with colourful life and sudden views over gates. Not once did I wish I was on a rocky fell.

In one tiny village, there was a nasty blast from the past when I saw a sign hanging on the side of a stile, its lettering faded, but the words still able to burn into my heart:

FOOT AND MOUTH DISEASE
Public Rights of Way are CLOSED in Powys.
Maximum Fine for use £5000.

How quickly, and how sickly, it all came back. The 2001 outbreak of foot-and-mouth had been my baptism of fire to rural life. I'd moved to Wales the previous summer, and had then experienced the wettest, greyest autumn on record (in our local weather station, rain was recorded on every single consecutive day for over three months), followed by a cloudy, damp winter. Just as March – and hope – approached, animals started blistering and footpaths were snapped shut all over the country, even in places miles from any outbreak. Real worry, paranoia and isolation hung over the countryside like a poisonous miasma.

The speed with which these signs had gone up had staggered me at the time – horrified me, if I'm honest. Within just a couple of days, they had turned up on every obscure, forgotten path and bridleway. It was impossible not to compare such brutal efficiency in getting the things closed with the eternally lackadaisical approach to getting blocked ones open. And no path was left unshut. The only place for miles around that I was able to walk the dog was the nearby four-mile beach from Borth to the Dyfi estuary, though there were angry demands in the local paper to close even that, but it was considered logisitically impossible. The boardwalk paths through the dunes were soon taped off, however, as were numerous urban tarmac paths in towns, floodlit cuts behind shops and through housing estates, tracks that hadn't felt a cloven hoof along their length for centuries, if ever. It was a ridiculous over-reaction, and its lingering unease lasted years.

With hindsight, we can see now that the foot-and-mouth crisis of 2001, and the hysterical blanket closure of footpaths that it sparked, ended up doing the cause of public access to the land no end of good. To lose every path in an instant was a wake-up call like no other, and to everyone. It wasn't just the beardies and the hearties moaning, it was the folk who liked a nice run out into the country on a Sunday afternoon, the people wanting to walk their dogs or take the kids somewhere that they could charge around and let off steam. Rural tourism collapsed, the effects rippling through the whole community and alarming even the most loutish of local politicians. It was an apocalyptic vision of what could so easily be, and people didn't like it at all.

It wasn't even an effective way of dealing with the problem. There have been outbreaks of foot-and-mouth since, which have been successfully dealt with in a far more localised way. The 2001 outbreak, and the mass, aggressive closure of all rights of way and most common land, felt like the last stand of an old order, especially as it coincided with the enactment of the Countryside and Rights of Way (CROW) Act 2000, the so-called 'right to roam'. Things would never be the same again.

Researching this book, when I've told English rambling campaigners where I live in Wales, there's been a common response, along the lines of, 'Oh, I don't go walking in Wales. Too many closed paths.' End of. Walking across the width of Wales, I came across only two that were completely inaccessible, each necessitating a bit of a detour, some scrambling over gates and, in one case, an encounter with a farmer that turned into a very enjoyable chat about local history and characters. Only once in 25 years of walking in Wales have I been threatened and forcibly turfed off the land, but I've lost count of the many illuminating and entertaining conversations ignited by having to ask for a little guidance.

It might sound strange to those of an absolutist way of thinking, but the Welsh way has at its core something even more precious, democratic even, than the holy grail of well-waymarked routes for all to march down. There is a danger that, when we walk the prescribed routes, we become stuck in their groove, sometimes at the expense of the wider context of the landscape and its evolution. The boundaries in Wales – physically in this instance, and ethereally in so many others – are more blurred and often more interesting. You have to ask, to engage with the people for whom every lump and seam of the land has a story to tell: they are as intrinsic to the path as the stones underfoot or the flowers in the hedgerow.

This less official, and considerably less officious, Welsh way has a long tradition. As a schoolboy on the run, Thomas de Quincey, later the author of *Confessions of an English Opium-Eater*, wandered as a vagabond through Wales for a couple of months in the summer of 1802. He noted that there was 'no sort of disgrace attached in Wales, as too generally upon the great roads of England, to the pedestrian style of travelling'. From the same era, the less charitable English response to walkers was captured by Pastor Karl Philipp Moritz, a German who set about walking from London to the Peak District. His diary records his amazement at the jeering and abuse he received everywhere, particularly from those on stagecoaches, and the way inn landlords took one look at his pedestrian attire and shunted him immediately into the worst rooms. 'Why do the English disparage walkers so much?' he asked a fellow traveller. 'Because we are too rich, too lazy and too proud,' came the reply.

More than 200 years later, it's a distinction that endures, and, from the Welsh point of view, thank God that it does. In the same way that walking is woven into the natural fabric of life, rather than ring-fenced apart from it, so it is with the Welsh landscape. You can, of course, choose to see it purely as an aesthetic display, a succession of two-dimensional picture postcards; plenty do. But dig just a little deeper into the cultural, social and economic contexts that run through the landscape in recurring leitmotifs, and it comes alive in entirely new, and infinitely richer, ways.

Thank God, too, that the broken stiles, the rights of way that don't translate from the map to the ground and the occasional theatrically surly farmer all combine to put off a certain type of English walker. Sorry, but it has to be said. Were it not for the distinctive Welsh way, in all its bony bloody-mindedness, the beautiful mid-western peninsula of the island of Britain would long ago have been overwhelmed from the east, even more than it already has been. And even nice people, people like us who read the liberal press and recycle every last bit of it, who love the wind on our face and a pint of real ale in our hands, even we can cause untold damage to the fragile fabric of marginalised communities by insisting on our way over theirs. We might not even realise that we are insisting, but we will be.

I've just had a fortnight with the boot on the other foot, and it's been very instructive. There's a tiny cottage that I rent occasionally at the very end of the Llŷn peninsula, that bony arm of north-west Wales pointing at Ireland. In common with the many other little whitewashed stone dwellings dotted around the heathery slopes, the cottage is a *tŷ-unnos*, a 'one-night house'. This refers to an old Welsh tradition that if you started to build a house on common land at sundown and managed to have it roofed and with smoke coming out of its chimney by the following dawn, that house, and the land as far as an axe-throw in four directions, was yours. The little *tŷ-unnos* that I rent sits above the sea on the side of a mountain criss-crossed by paths both official and not. There's no garden as such, just a couple of out-houses (one of which contains the toilet bucket; there's no bath-room, nor indeed running water – you have to collect that from the spring up the hill) so that the house sits squarely as part of the hillside, with no evident boundary.

Since my last visit two years ago, the Llŷn coast path has been cut through on top of the cliffs either side of the cottage, and I saw more people walking up there this time than ever before, I'd guess by a factor of about ten. If I was sitting out-side with my nosy sheepdog, who has a tendency to stand and stare at anything that moves, however far away, then the pattern of behaviour that unfolded when people came past was almost invariably the same every time. I saw them crest the hill that first gave them a view of the cottage and us. They would stop, look a little befuddled, pull into a tight huddle and confer with each other. The walk leader would then very ostentatiously pull out the map, and do a bit of pointing, reassured that they were in the right place, on the official right of way. Visibly bolstered by the knowledge, they would then sail past, heads high and bris-tly chins resolute, not quite near enough to say hello, but never, ever, with so much as a wave or a small detour for a chat.

It reminded me of a passage in a wonderful old book I picked up years ago in the back of some dusty second-hand shop. *The Countryside and How to Enjoy It* was published at the end of the 1940s: it is a splendidly paternalistic instruction manual intended to smooth the way of the great unwashed into their brand new National Parks and designated trails. Amongst chap-ters entitled 'Going on a Journey' and 'What of the Weather?', there is one called 'The Footpath Way', written by S. P. B. (Petre)

Mais, perhaps the author most responsible for educating Britons in the 1930s and 1940s about their landscape and history. 'Never turn aside from an approaching farmer,' he boomed. 'You would consider it a grave discourtesy if you found a caller at your own house turning away when you came out to meet him. The farmer is your host wherever you go in the country and it is necessary to exercise the manners of a guest when you encounter him.' Mind you, he also offers this gem: 'It is quite likely that you may want to call on the farmer either to ask the way or to beg a glass of milk or perhaps a meal. The farmer may be glad to see you in spite of being a very busy man.' Just a hello would have done; I wasn't after rustling up dinner for them.

So inspiring was the experience of being dropped off three days away from home, and then just walking back, taking in familiar sights from wholly new angles, I rang my dad to see if he fancied doing exactly the same across our home county of Worcestershire. We did it the next week, my step-mum dropping us off in the Wyche Gap, that ancient pass through the Malvern Hills that marks the border with Herefordshire: a sublime experience that I'll cover at a later point.

If there is one path that I would encourage anyone to try, it's this, and every one is bespoke and unique. Beg a lift, take the train or bus, and land two or three days' walk away from home. Turn back, and start walking. Stay in a B&B only ten miles from your front door. See your own back yard in a completely new context. It's the ultimate staycation – and a great way of realising too that for a good walk, you really don't need too much Stuff.

Stairway to heaven: ascending Croagh Patrick, County Mayo, Ireland

7. AND DID THOSE FEET

With the exception of the Coast to Coast, which had been a glimpse into one hall of my own particular hell, every path I'd walked so far had put me in a far more spiritually robust frame of mind. I was keen now to try some paths with an explicitly divine identity, in particular to undertake an organised pilgrimage. With that as the aim, you want to go for the jugular. Although I am normally quite a loner when it comes to walking, when I thought about undertaking a proper pilgrimage route, one of the most important factors to my mind was the presence of others, and preferably in cacophonous multitude. A few years ago, in Saint-Jean-Pied-de-Port, a Basque bulwark of a town on the French side of the Pyrenees, I'd been genuinely moved and amazed at the sight of the legion of pilgrims starting their journey there on the Camino of St James to Santiago de Compostela, nearly 500 miles away on the Atlantic coast of Galicia. They looked so purposeful, excited and united in their mission, and that's what I wanted next. Despite – or perhaps because of – our technological advancement, we seem to need pilgrimage more than ever. 2,491 people completed the Camino in 1985. By 1995, this had jumped to 19,821, and it now easily tops 100,000 a year.

I considered the options nearer home. What about the original great pilgrimage route, as portrayed by Geoffrey Chaucer over seven centuries ago in *The Canterbury Tales*? His motley band of pilgrims, covering all bases from the devout to the debased, caroused their way across Kent from the Tabard Inn in Southwark to St Thomas à Becket's shrine in Canterbury Cathedral. Although the express intention of the trip was meek obeisance to the Christian principles of confession and redemption, it was all conducted with feet firmly scuffed into the earth, the sacred and the profane inseparably commingled. That seems to be an essential ingredient in a good pilgrimage: devotion and wonder, for sure, but with the option of a little light drunkenness and debauchery too.

Aside from the fact that it might bring back unpleasant flashbacks from my A levels, I quickly dismissed the idea of following Chaucer. His pilgrims' most likely route from Southwark to Canterbury was along the Roman Watling Street. This is now the A2 and assorted other trunk roads of varying ferocity, and I wasn't much struck on the idea of plodding through Dartford, Gravesend and the sprawl of Medway towns while ingesting the fumes of countless Polish and Latvian lorries. I pondered a pilgrimage route to England's most famous Catholic shrine, Walsingham in Norfolk. A few folk walk there from Ely Cathedral, a 73-mile tramp under the vast skies of the Fens. The route appealed hugely, not least for its lack of contours, but then I remembered going to Walsingham a few years ago and being quite repulsed by its sickly piety. I looked too at the groups doing the Ely–Walsingham pilgrimage, and that didn't help. Salty

Chaucerian exuberance was what I was after, rather than a polite trundle across the flatlands in the company of people who'd not taken their sandals off since 1986.

The Celtic corners of our islands seemed to offer a better chance of faith *and* fun. One of the great realisations about Wales, after ten years of living there, was how Christianity had cannily absorbed and adopted the older ways. Rugged little stone churches, seemingly sprung from the rock on which they sat, had often been built on sites that had already accrued a spiritual significance over centuries, perhaps millennia, before the missionaries arrived. As it is in the buildings, so it seemed in the doctrine: a far greater sense of organic absorption. My local parish priest, a man of belligerent vision and effervescent charisma, wrote a book on the many manifestations of the Goddess in our culture, and has built a little chapel adjoining his house that bursts with gilted icons and incense, a fusion of Eastern Orthodoxy, Hinduism and Christ in a damp Welsh meadow. I'd found comparable fusions in the Pictish kingdom of north-east Scotland, in the bypassed bits of Cornwall and, once you peeled back and peered under the festering fundamentalism, throughout Ireland.

Ireland! That was it. If there was one place in these islands where I might find the Christ and the *craic*, it was the Emerald Isle, where the church and the pub remain as one. Once that realisation had come, the answer to my quest became obvious. Much as I share the scepticism towards what Jim Perrin calls the 'capitalist construct' of our obsession with 'conquering' the highest, the largest or the longest, when it came to a proper pilgrimage, size really was everything. I needed the biggest, most tumultuous there was, and that could only mean Reek Sunday up Croagh Patrick.

There are lots of ingredients that make up the perfect holy mountain, but the single biggest is its shape. A sacred mount must draw the eye and hold it there, in awe, in aesthetic delight and in slight terror too. It must embody both beauty and a certain haughtiness, which is why so many great holy mountains sit at some distance from any other sizeable peaks, for they are scene-stealers and do not like to share the stage. Symmetry is good, even if seen only from one or two vantage points. These too will acquire subsidiary holy status and become outlying pinpricks of the light that generation after generation of worshipper has accorded the peak itself. Looking from the mountain from other angles, it is often best if it appears in many different shapes and guises, a reminder of the shape-shifting truths at the heart of any faith system. Travel the full circle around a holy mountain and it should, in turn, appear forbidding and welcoming, impenetrable and comely, and all the time iridescently beautiful.

Croagh Patrick, or the Reek as it's known locally, succeeds on all fronts. A 2,510ft (765m) cone of quartz, it rears out of the landscape at the bottom of the island-spattered Clew Bay on the wild coast of County Mayo. The rounded shoulders of the Connemara mountains sit at a discreet distance, leaving Croagh Patrick to wallow in its own glory, commanding land, sea and air – not that you can always tell which is which. The boundaries between them fuzz in the ever-changing light, as sea mists roll in, clouds billow over, sunlight bursts through in day-glo shafts and rainbows shimmer briefly into life. No-one can resist the holy pull of the Reek. To climb it is as much a part of the Irish identity as is doing the Hajj to Mecca for a Muslim. Especially on Reek Sunday, the final weekend of July, a date that harks back to the ancient Celtic harvest festival of Lughnasa, when anything between twenty and thirty thousand people sweat and grind their way up its unyielding slopes. And although the Reek's origins as a place of pilgrimage far pre-date Christianity, the Roman Catholic Church has done everything in its power to appropriate the mountain as one of its own. There might be many a pagan overtone, but the journey would be played out against the backdrop of muscular Papism, in all its shredded splendour.

Returning to County Mayo would be a thrilling prospect too. I'd been there only once, 20 years ago, but stayed for weeks, so bewitched was I by its landscape and life. It was high on my list of places I'd enjoyed so much that I was nervous of returning, lest the experience prove anything other than utterly magical and shatter the precious memories. That 1991 Irish trip was possibly the happiest of my life, as I was 24 years old and had just waltzed out of the world of proper jobs, after barely two years of even trying. Two spiky guidebooks under my belt, published to near universal indifference, I was nonetheless convinced that the world would eagerly lap up my observations about it. Ireland was to be the first of an endless series of award-winning books by the firebrand young writer, and in the months leading up to it and my six weeks travelling around the country, I soaked myself in Irish history and literature and filled two massive notebooks with my earnest musings on it all. And there they stayed, the publishing industry proving strangely immune to their genius.

The venue and time for my pilgrimage presented themselves, and so did the method of transport to reach it. There was only one possible way to get to a Catholic pilgrimage in Mayo, and that was to fly into Knock Airport, the Virgin Mary's own international aviation facility. As befits a name that sounds like the start of a joke, the airport has been the butt of incredulous laughter for decades. Since it opened a quarter of a century ago, it has had four names: Knock Airport, then the Monsignor Horan International, after the local priest who came up with the grand idea of sticking a runway on top of a foggy, boggy mountain in Mayo, then the Connaught Regional Airport, and now the Ireland West Airport Knock. And it's nearest to Charlestown, not Knock.

Who's there?

Absolutely feckin' no-one, went the sardonic reply. The idea that folk would choose to fly into the peat bogs of western Ireland, and all because the local priest thought his village could do with its own airport, was an Irish joke that shot around the world in the 1970s and early 1980s. The people of County Mayo weren't laughing though. They trusted Monsignor James Horan to come up with the goods; his track record certainly suggested he might. The Monsignor was devoutly local and a brilliant populist, capable of coming up with ever-grander schemes to enthuse his parishioners. In one of his earlier parishes at nearby Tooreen, he'd bullied the GPO in Dublin into opening a post office there, and then, convinced that it was partly a lack of social opportunity for young people that was driving them out of the west, built them an outsized dance hall. It became one of Ireland's most famous venues of the 1950s and 1960s, though not entirely for the reasons Father Horan had anticipated. For over half a century, legend has persisted that one night the Devil himself attended a dance at the Tooreen Hall, whisking some local colleen off her feet before disappearing in a sulphurous cloud and a brief glimpse of cloven hooves. A drama of the supposed event was the 2009 Christmas-night blockbuster on TG4, the Irish-language TV station, and included some ageing gobshites insisting that they had witnessed Old Nick's dirty dancing and malodorous departure one far-off night in 1958.

Difficult though it is to pick out hard truth from the mists of time and the even denser fog of Mayo mythmaking, a more prosaic explanation comes from a tract that had just been published at the time by the Catholic Truth Society, called *The Devil at Dances*. This had fulminated angrily against the Church organising sinful dances in country parishes by weaving a clumsy allegory about an actual visitation by the Horned One to a western village hall. Somehow, the story stuck to Tooreen: one theory is that this was thanks to some concerted smearing by a rival dance promoter eager to squash the success of Fr Horan's new hall. This rival was none other than Albert Reynolds, future Taioseach. True or not, it didn't kill Horan's hall: quite the opposite. Now infamous for its diabolic visitation, Tooreen became one of the busiest dancehalls in the land, the acrid tang of rising rural hormones the perfect olfactory complement to the satanic sulphur.

In 1963, Horan became the curate – and shortly afterwards, the parish priest – at nearby Knock, transforming the rundown village into a shrine of global renown. In August 1879, the Virgin Mary, together with St John and St Joseph, had manifested in an apparition to a group of villagers on the gable end of their dowdy parish church. Knock had been a fairly low-level shrine ever since, but Horan was determined to elevate it to the Catholic Premier League, a name synonymous with Lourdes, Fatima and Medjugorje (incidentally, all destinations served by Knock Airport, alongside more secular shrines such as Gran Canaria and Alicante). A vast shed of a new church, dedicated to Our Lady, Queen of Ireland, and able to hold a congregation of 10,000, was built and consecrated in 1976. In a PR masterstroke, Horan succeeded in securing a visit to celebrate the centenary of the 1879 apparition by the charismatic new Polish Pope, John Paul II. The Monsignor expertly capitalised on the publicity, using it to add some considerable traction to the idea of a holy airport for Knock.

Buoyed by the post-Pope euphoria, the government swung in behind the Monsignor. The Minister of Transport, Horan's old sparring partner Albert Reynolds, performed a sod-cutting ceremony on 2 May 1981 – the lump of stringy turf he pulled out, and the spade with which he dug it, are preserved with all of the solemnity normally accorded to a saint's relics in the airport's arrivals hall (arrivals corridor, if we're being picky). An election soon followed, which resulted in a change of government and a change of heart regarding the airport; true to good Catholic teaching, the new government pulled out at the last minute.

The people of Knock were not to be ignored, however. Rallied by the man in a dog collar and hard hat, they poured on to the unpromising peaty peak of Barr na Cùige, levelled the ground and began to lay the runway themselves. On 25 October 1985, two jets took off in the only direction they knew, from Knock to Rome. More flights followed; not many, but enough to quieten the worst of the scoffers. On 30 May of the following year, 20,000 cheering Mayomen attended the airport's official opening by the swaggeringly bent three-times Taioseach Charlie Haughey, who loved to play up his humble Mayo origins. Just two months later, Monsignor Horan died suddenly on a pilgrimage to Lourdes. Not a great advert for the healing powers of Lourdes, but a terrific boost for his immaculately conceived airport, and it has gone from modest strength to strength ever since.

I've always loved the story of Knock Airport, one Monsignor against the world. It worked too: an utterly marginalised economy at the very edge of Europe was given a blood transfusion. In a Westport gift shop, I mentioned to the dotty lady owner that I was flying back home from Knock. 'Ah, praise be for the airport,' she wheezed back, as if breathing the Catechism. There have been numerous books about the story, and even a musical. Its inevitable title – though no less brilliant for that – is *On a Wing and a Prayer*. It can surely only be a matter of time until the Hollywood movie, its paddywhackery dial turned up to 11.

My plane swung in low over the squelchy sump of eastern Mayo and banked down on to the top of the hill. From the air, the terminal building looked like Lego, an impression that doesn't shift much on entering it. Inside the main hall was a perky little blue booth, with a sign on top reading 'KNOCK SHRINE OFFICE'. A few intriguing posters were displayed, telling punters that while it was all well and good getting excited about the Virgin's 1879 appearance in the village, they were not to believe any more recent sightings claimed of her at the shrine.

This was a coy reference to the hullabaloo of autumn 2009, when Dublin healer and *soi-disant* mystic Joe Coleman declared publicly that Mary herself had appeared to him and promised that she would be back at Knock on the afternoon of 11 October. Twenty thousand pilgrims came to see. Expectation and excitement built up as Coleman secreted himself in the basilica. He appeared outside, and processed through the crowd holding a huge crucifix. Folk trampled on each other to touch it. And then the sun came out from behind a cloud. People started clapping, and saying that they could see the Virgin in it. Cameras and eyes were pointed straight at the sun. After a minute or so squinting at it, people started to see strange shapes and had the sensation that the sun was spinning around. They shrieked and hollered. It's a miracle! Or it could have been the warning signs of retinal detachment: cases of solar retinopathy soared in Ireland in the months after. Either way, Coleman announced that Mary had enjoyed herself so much, she'd be back again on 31 October. Only about a quarter of the crowd came back this time, and it wasn't quite as sunny. It had caused enough of a ruckus though for the Church to put up posters at the airport and distance themselves from Coleman and his visions. The Archbishop of Tuam stuck a tart message on his website: 'Unfortunately, recent events at the Shrine obscure [our] essential message. They risk misleading God's people and undermining faith. For this reason such events are to be regretted rather than encouraged.' It would seem that the Blessed Virgin has an Appear By date on her, except of course when she returns as an image in a tree trunk or a pizza.

This was exactly why I wanted to go and do my pilgrimage in Ireland. A country where some nutter could make thousands of people travel across the country to convince themselves that they had seen the face of God in a cloud is somewhere that takes this stuff deadly seriously. A place where people might sink to their knees, burst into tears, shriek in Latin or tongues and wave their stick at the heavens. You just wouldn't get that in the C of E. The week before I left, an old episode of *Father Ted* had been on TV. In it, Mrs Doyle is heading off on her Lenten retreat, which includes a pilgrimage up St Patrick's Hill, a barely disguised Croagh Patrick. Dougal asks Ted what's so special about the hill, and Ted replies: 'Ah, it's a big mountain. You have to take your socks off to go up it, and once you reach the top, they chase you back down again with a big plank. It's great fun.' Mrs

Doyle is not impressed: 'Oh, I don't want it to be any fun at all, Father. I want a good, *miserable* time.' My sentiments entirely, and I was sorely disappointed that it wasn't Ryanair operating the route I needed into Knock.

Croagh Patrick took its name from the 40 biblical days and nights that St Patrick spent on its summit in AD 441. He'd travelled there from Ballintober Abbey, 20 miles further inland, along an ancient track that is believed to have been constructed to ferry druids and pilgrims from the seat of the Kings of Connaught to the holy mountain. The path, called the Tóchar Phádraig, or Patrick's Causeway, has been re-opened over the past 25 years, though it passes across 63 different pockets of private land and is only freely open on a few days of the year. One of those days was Reek Sunday, and the Abbey was organising a pilgrimage for those who wanted to process to the Reek along this venerable route, before joining the rest of the throng ascending the mountain. I signed up immediately, and booked a B&B for the weekend in Ballintober.

It all fitted: Ballintober Abbey had played a major part in my fondly remembered trip of 20 years ago, for I'd had two start-lingly different experiences there just a couple of days apart. The first was with a friend, a very English and very Anglican priest, who had come visiting me in the west from his job as a chap-lain in a Cambridge college. We'd landed in Westport, County Mayo's sweetest honeypot, full of folksy young Europeans twid-dling their tin whistles in pubs that jumped with music. This was pre-Celtic Tiger Ireland, even pre-Eurovision and Riverdance, but there was definitely a sense that the country was swelling with pride and a new confidence, for both traditionalists and lib-erals. The previous summer, in the World Cup that saw England tiptoe into the semi-finals before the inevitable penalty ejection by Germany (actually, West Germany: it really has been that long), Ireland, under the sainted tutelage of Jackie Charlton and a crack squad of genealogists, had made it into the quarters. 'That did it,' a man over breakfast in a Galway B&B had said to me a year afterwards. 'That made us think that, finally, we were as good as anyone else.' The same year had seen the surprise election of liberal lawyer Mary Robinson as President of the Republic. Mayo's own Mrs Robinson was proving a catalyst for a long-awaited social revolution, and Ireland was on the cusp of becoming the coolest place in Europe.

To my friend, the Reverend, it was still all a bit of a shock. On the train to Westport, his eyes had nearly leapt from their sockets at the sight of people fingering their rosary beads as they quietly murmured Hail Marys – 'Good God, it's medieval,' he whispered to me. A ferociously bright, angular man, he had no soft edges or small talk. Going into a Westport pub, he pushed me in front of him, hissing, 'You go first – you seem to know how to talk to the indig pop.' 'To the *what?*' I replied. 'The indig pop – you know, the indigenous population. You talk to them.' I flew through the door on the end of a bony shove. On the occasions that he did chip in to a pub chat, it was mainly to deliver a dry monologue against the patriarchy of Popery or the fetishising of saints. It didn't always create quite the mood I was hoping for.

From Westport, we hired bikes and pedalled over to Ballintober. In the churchyard, biblical tableaux had been recently built with an impressive literalness: there is a suburban rockery garden to represent Gethsemane; the house of Elizabeth, mother of John the Baptist, contained a sewing machine and a dresser piled high with tea crockery; an empty cave – with signs that read 'He Is Not Here' and 'He Is Risen' – demonstrated the Resurrection. The Reverend could barely contain his disdain. 'It's all just tasteless mumbo-jumbo,' he grumbled. When we reached a modern stone cromlech annotated with a sign stating that this represented the Assumption, he exploded. 'Exactly!' he hissed. 'The Assumption! That's all it is – one big bloody assumption!'

Less than a week later, and with the Rev safely back in his more familiar assumptions of Cambridge liberation theology, I returned to Ballintober, on a coach tour organised as part of the George Moore Summer School. Moore (1852–1933) was a precocious and contrary scion of Mayo Anglo-Irish gentry. He'd escaped his native land at the first opportunity and headed to sample the absinthe and hookers of Paris, while churning out the occasional book of withering memoir and some provocative new realist novels. News reached his incredulous ears that things were stirring back in the old country. A literary revival, spearheaded by the likes of Yeats, Synge and Lady Gregory, was pumping intellectual fibre into the fight for Irish independence. Moore swept imperiously back to Ireland, installed himself in Dublin and hurled himself into the thick of the action. This had been the period that I'd been studying particularly keenly, and I was thrilled to see that my time in Mayo coincided with the summer school.

The coach trip, from the car park at Claremorris train station, was the first event of the weekend. I arrived early and was welcomed like a long lost friend, none more so than by an unshaven Dublin academic, who lurched on to the bus, spotted me and plumped noisily down by my side. Despite being hungover from the welcome session the previous night, he spray-gunned me with spittle, trenchant opinions and some libellous asides about our fellow summer-school attendees. After nearly an hour of bouncing around the Mayo lanes, the coach pulled into Ballintober Abbey, a few miles up the road from the burned-out shell of the family's Moore Hall. The Professor took one look at the glutinous Crucifixion scene at the Abbey's entrance. 'Fuck this,' he said. 'Let's have a drink.' It was 11.05 a.m. The bar opposite the Abbey had just opened, and in no time he'd ordered a Guinness for me and a Smithwick's and a Jameson's chaser for himself. I'd not managed half the first Guinness when a second, and before long a third, landed at my side. A bearded head, slightly swimming in and out of focus, peered around the bar door. 'Ah, there you are, you two,' it said, and not with any hint of surprise. 'Coach is off now, come on.' I downed the third pint almost in one, and prayed that I wouldn't be sick.

If the Professor had been voluble on the first leg of the trip, now that he was fortified by three pints and three whiskeys, there was no stopping him. He told me of a thwarted love affair with one of his male postgraduate students in Dublin, fixed me with a watery stare and slid his hand over my knee. For the rest of the weekend, he showered me with drinks and books, wrote poetry to me and told me some of the best gossip and the funniest, filthiest jokes I'd ever heard. On his insistence, I stayed with him on my way back through Dublin a few weeks later. On his insistence, I shared his bed. On my insistence, I all but stuck a bolster down the middle and primly rebuffed his hourly advances. Next day, as I prepared to leave for the boat and home, he presented me with a poem that he'd written in those dark, frustrated hours: 'It is time to prise the lock apart / into the secret garden / which I address / on a sombre and ardent night. / The love-charged baton / crescendoes in eloquent silence'

(I don't think I could have resisted the 'garden/hard on' rhyme myself, so fair play to him). In defence of my cock-teasing, I was 24, as prissy as porcelain and secretly convinced that there would be many other men who would want to write poetry to me. There weren't, as it turned out.

I've long ago lost contact with the Reverend, and the Professor is, I gather from the all-mighty Google, now dead. I thought of them both fondly as I surveyed the stark walls of Ballintober Abbey. The lavish new biblical scenes that had so appalled the Rev had mellowed with age, though not as much as I had. In my 1991 notebook, I'd called Ballintober 'the Alton Towers of the Catholic faith', but it all looked rather sweet to me now. In Elizabeth's House, the crockery-filled cave that had so amused me back then, I read an explanation sheet that detailed the Irish concept of *muintearas*, roughly translated as 'hospitality'. 'In the old Gaelic tradition the door was left open and food and drink were left on the table for the passing stranger . . . for often, often, often went the Christ in the stranger's guise. *Muintearas* signifies welcome, warmth, hospitality and care.'

Two hundred yards up the road in my B&B, I was receiving *muintearas* by the bucket-load. I'd booked months earlier, as soon as I decided to walk the Tóchar Phádraig, but was dimly aware when I got there that there was some degree of surprise at my arrival. They had a family wedding going on, as well as a houseful of Dutch tourists. No matter: I was fixed with a pot of tea, home-made scones and fruit cake, and eventually asked if I'd mind taking their teenage daughter's bedroom for the weekend. The girl in question was sitting in the kitchen in her pyjamas, texting her mates and telling us what a fierce night the previous evening, the wedding day of her cousin, had been. She gave away her bedroom without a mutter of complaint – 'Ah sure, I'll just sleep where I fall this weekend.' Only the next day did her mum, truly the most capable hostess I've ever met, admit that they'd been expecting me the following weekend.

Reek Sunday didn't so much dawn as become gradually less grey. 'Ach, it's sure to clear,' said my landlady, peering out into the drizzle. I was too excited to care, and wolfed down my breakfast before heading up to the Abbey to join my fellow pilgrims. I was hooking up with Patsy, a friend from Galway, who'd done the Tóchar five Reek Sundays earlier, with around 15 others. Now there were four times as many of us shuffling around the massive nave with our sandwiches and drinks. 'Amazing what a recession will do for people's faith,' whispered Patsy.

Father Frank Fahey appeared, to give us the pre-pilgrimage pep talk. The rector of the Abbey, he is a priest surely cast from the same redoubtable Mayo mould as Monsignor Horan. At the Abbey for the past 30 years, it was he who rebuilt it from a shell, who designed the biblical scenes around the churchyard that had so horrified my Anglican friend and who, piece by piece, had reconnected all the paths of the Tóchar Phádraig to Croagh Patrick. Now in his late seventies, he still fizzed with a wild energy and a warm humanity, sending us on our way with prayer, pensiveness and some cracking good jokes. We were not to complain at all, he told us mock-sternly. Whatever the ailment, however sharp the pain, we must turn our moans into the phrase 'Thanks be to God'. His final point was clear: 'And don't forget. This is not a walk; it is a pilgrimage.'

Along the 22 miles of the Tóchar, Fr Fahey has installed 113 stiles, each marked with a black cross, and when we climbed over these, he said, we should offer up a prayer. I was still struggling to differentiate the idea of a pilgrimage from a mere walk: so many of my finest walks I'd thought of as pilgrimages anyway, irrespective of whether the destination had been a church, a stone circle, a view to make you sing, a place to swim or a couple of pints of Parson's Downfall and a bag of chips. Walking with that sense of intent and focus, of revelling in the mud and stones and twigs of now, while also looking forward to the destination, is the only way to do it, and I couldn't think of a particularly new frame of mind to call up for the task of doing my first official pilgrimage.

Luckily, help was on hand at the first stile, taking us out of the Abbey grounds. A plaque to launch the pilgrim on his way has a wonderful quotation taken from the fifteenth-century Book of Lismore:

> 'Going on a pilgrimage without change of heart brings no reward from God. For it is by practising virtue and not mere motion of the feet that we will be brought to heaven.'

The stiles passed quickly and – when I remembered – prayerfully; the day stayed soft, with no long-range visibility. Everyone's mood seemed good, great in fact, plump with hope and the joy of release from real life. Because the group had been so unusually large, we'd been split into four and sent off at intervals. The real keen ones, those with flashy cagoules and proper pilgrimage staffs, pushed forward and disappeared into the folds of green. I left with the last group, mostly locals, save for me and an American student who was writing a thesis on Irish pilgrimages. We ploughed on, sometimes chatty, sometimes silent. At one stage, we were discussing Irish politics, and the level of hatred towards the politicians who had so carelessly broken their economy was bubbling furiously. Talking about a particular minister, one man cursed loudly, 'Oh, he's a complete and utter . . . thanks be to God!'. The phrase became our bleep machine.

You can find the Tóchar Phádraig sporadically marked and annotated in Gothic script on nineteenth-century OS maps. Those tended to be the most obvious parts of the path, rows of ancient flags suddenly appearing beneath our feet in far-flung corners of fields, bogs and woods. At these points I was acutely aware of feeling a deep and resonant echo as we passed, the footfall of centuries. This had been a main route into the far west for everyone: not just priests and pilgrims, but soldiers, bailiffs, farmers, murderers, mourners, pillagers, villagers, the pampered and starving alike. The Tóchar brushes past numerous ghost villages from the famine years of the 1840s: Mayo was the county worst affected of all. In 1841, the county's population was nearly 400,000. It had halved by 1901, and is around 125,000 today.

Although Mayo is a hilly county, the Tóchar remains relatively flat until the mountain itself, stretching its way across a landscape little better described than by the Saw Doctors as a 'soft and craggy bogland'. The line comes from their anthem 'The Green and Red of Mayo', and it had been whirring through my head continuously since the plane had touched down three days earlier at Knock. It's a lot more evocative a description than the next line, about the county's 'tall, majestic hills'. I mentioned that I couldn't shake the song from my brain. 'Ah yes, the hymn to Mayo, sung by the band from Galway,' a fellow pilgrim sniffed.

We pounded lanes, cut through hedges, tiptoed across rickety plank bridges, hopped across flagstones in bogs, tramped down newly laid gravel, ducked down between dry stone walls and swished gorse, bracken and nettles out of the way. Gargantuan cattle, udders heavy, chewed and stared as we passed. Although the path is only formally open for a few days of the year, it has the full complement not just of stiles, but fingerposts and direction pointers as well. It was a rare vista that didn't include one or the other, to the point that we were lulled into a false sense of security and, at one stage, got hopelessly lost when none could be seen. It happened again, not long after the half-way break in the old monastic village of Aghagower, to the point where we, already the last group to go, were seriously lagging.

A 15-year-old Ford Fiesta came bouncing down the lane from the opposite direction. It stopped, and Father Fahey's face appeared out of the driver's window. 'Are you lot the last?' he asked. 'You're a terrible long way behind, y'know. Come on, split yourselves in two and I'll give you a lift the next mile. Some of the others are already arriving at the Boheh Stone for Mass.' This didn't seem right. How could we footsore band of pilgrims possibly climb into a car? Someone else voiced the same concern: 'But Father, isn't that cheating?' 'Ah no, it's not,' he smoothly replied. 'Not if I'm taking you.' I was in the second batch to be transported: three fellas in the back, me in the front seat and the poor American girl scrunched awkwardly on to my lap. 'Getting close is all part of being on a pilgrimage,' Father Fahey grinned at us, as the car scraped up the lane, its chassis periodically glancing off the tarmac. At one stage, he had to conduct a savage hill start, and the smell of burned-out clutch heralded his arrival for the rest of the day.

The Boheh Stone is the highlight of the route. A huge outburst of a rock, it is covered in cup and ring marks. According to

Father Fahey's own book about the Tóchar, it is 'an old druidic stone probably used as a mass rock by St Patrick', and that its many inscribed circles 'show that it was associated with the worship of the sun'. That was written a couple of years before a local man discovered that, when viewing the pyramid cone of Croagh Patrick from the Boheh Stone, on 18 April and 24 August the setting sun rolled precisely from the mountain's summit down its northern slope, a spectacular phenomenon that lasts 20 minutes or so. Together with the winter solstice, these two dates divided the year into near-equal thirds and could well have been crucial in divining the agricultural cycle.

It was a strange thrill then to arrive at this most pagan of stones and see Father Fahey arranging his cloth and chalice across its table top. With his vestment on, he swung into celebrating Mass, after checking who amongst us wanted communion. Not being a Catholic, nor indeed a Christian, I abstained, as did about half a dozen others, but I was happy to chuck in the odd Amen here and there, and mumbled along with the Lord's Prayer, a creed so hammered into my brain that I'll still doubtless be able to dribble it out when absolutely everything else has been wiped clean from my memory. I've only ever been to a handful of Catholic Masses, and they always send a prickle down my spine. In the Church of England of my childhood, people enunciated like Radio 4 continuity announcers, even in prayer, but in Catholic rituals, everyone seems to close their throat down to produce an invocation that's half-voiced, half-hummed. It's strangely effective, and I remembered being both moved and slightly freaked out on hearing thousands doing it together at the Knock shrine two decades earlier, and, a few years before that, when I went with my mate Liam and his family to see the

Pope at Coventry Airport. Not being able to make out the individual words is an advantage as far as I'm concerned: the sound and the feeling are all that matter, washing over me in waves of unfathomable mystery, and I don't start getting annoyed by the overly pious or bigoted bits. It's the same reason that I love going to any religious service in a language I don't understand. Choral Evensong in St David's Cathedral has been ruined now that I've learned Welsh, so I'm always on the hunt for a bit of Latin.

Leaving Boheh, refreshed physically by chocolate and spiritually by Father Fahey's stone-topped Mass, we were within spitting distance of the Reek, but you wouldn't have known it. The great mountain had shown us not so much as a glimpse all day: despite being nearly on it, you'd be pushed to guess where it sat in our horizon. Down every lane that we'd walked, houses called Reek View and the like only rubbed it in. Before long we were steadily climbing up the lane that takes you to the back of the mountain. Most of the thousands of Reek Sunday pilgrims climb from the other side, from the bayside village of Murrisk: there was just us and the emergency services on the landward side. The grey day had solidified now into thick fog and teeming rain, the flashing blue lights of the occasional ambulance looming through the murk only making it even more surreal and jangling our nerves. Chatter had evaporated: everyone was now concentrating on every step.

The age range of our band of pilgrims stretched from the teens to around 70, with an assortment of disabilities and difficulties therein. Mindful of what we'd been told, no-one complained, despite the aching limbs and the bleak provocation of the elements. A couple of times, I caught grimaces of real agony on people's faces, but they'd catch me looking, and those faces would break instead into a smile or a grin, and would ask me how I was doing. In them, I saw some definition of faith, of persistence at all costs and through untold difficulties, and it floored me. I was still on a walk; they were definitely on a pilgrimage. The lane climbed higher, mile after mile, the rain getting steadily worse. When we reached the last point before heading up the sheer slopes on to the still invisible mountain, Patsy's mobile bleeped. It was a text from his wife, telling him that the radio news was ordering people not to try going up the Reek, as it was too dangerous. There were a fair few Mountain Rescue people nearby, for this was their access point too, and they confirmed the order. We could cross over the shoulder of the mountain to meet our bus at Murrisk, but we shouldn't try the difficult last bit of the ascent up the cone to the summit. Like being told to get in Father Fahey's car for a mile, I was quietly relieved and happy to acquiesce.

I'm not sure that I could have made it anyway. To reach the shoulder of the mountain needed a sheer climb of almost a thousand feet, and it killed me. Each footstep felt like my last as we trudged and slid up the stony path, washed over by black, peaty mud. A few of our crowd insisted that they'd still like to attempt the summit, despite the warnings. As if in response, a team of day-glo-jacketed paramedics suddenly manifested through the fog, carrying someone off the mountain in a body bag, on a stretcher. This was the only way they could rescue injured pilgrims, for the conditions had grounded the air ambulance. We watched in silence as they passed in a well-orchestrated two-step down the slope. No-one mentioned wanting to get to the top after that.

Our little path zig-zagged its way up on to the shoulder of Croagh Patrick, where we met the far larger, and incomparably busier, main pilgrim path from Murrisk to the top. Later reports stated that over 20,000 people had climbed the Reek that day, and although it was by now quite late in the afternoon, there were still hundreds huffing and grunting their way up and down. Photos of the Reek, even from quite some distance, make this main path look like a flesh wound gouged out of the mountain's flank, a sensation that holds even when you're on it. The track is vast, gaping and as hard as nails. Loose shale and mud slide down at the slightest provocation. And there's none greater than 20,000 pilgrims in one day, many terribly unfit and struggling, battling their way up the mountain and dislodging yet more loose rockery with their sticks and boots.

Or their bare feet, of course. Within a minute of joining the main throng, I'd seen my first barefoot climber, that celebrated, and rather derided, icon of Croagh Patrick. In recent years, the authorities had been doing their utmost to dissuade the practice, but this was God stuff, way beyond their boundaries, and folk carried on regardless. As we started the long clamber down, we overtook half a dozen or more in the first couple of minutes. I slyly scrutinised all the bare feet as I passed. They were muddy, inevitably, but I was slightly disappointed not to see any sliced to ribbons by the unyielding mountain. The American student and I were both fascinated by the phenomenon, and we ambushed an old fella, well over 60, who was nimbly skinny-dipping his feet over the rocks in front of us.

I wanted him, of course, to be as mad as snakes (or whatever is the Irish equivalent, since St Patrick banished them all from the island in his forty-day stay on the Reek sixteen centuries ago). In truth, he was glowing with an inner joy that was infectious. Not only that: he was more surefooted, curling his toes expertly around the rocks and squishing them firmly into the mud, than I was in my clumpy 150-quid size-ten boots. He fair danced down that mountain, while I skidded and tumbled down like a drunkard.

After the bus ride back to Ballintober, goodbyes were said with genuine depth. We'd come together, a band of strangers, for just one day. But what a day to share. I'd expected piety, perhaps even a little doctrinal dogma. All I'd heard, seen and felt throughout the day was quiet strength, deep affection and great hope, as well as much easy laughter and camaraderie. Over the next 24 hours, though, it dawned that the job wasn't yet done, and that I had to reach the peak of the Reek.

Patsy in Galway felt the same, and a day later he and his wife Helen drove up to Westport, picked me up and we headed to Murrisk. Although not as wet as Reek Sunday, there was that indefinably westerly sensation of claggy greyness, to the point where you could barely tell whether it was actually raining or not. At Murrisk, the full force of the Reek phenomenon is unleashed: cafés, a bar, Catholic tat stalls, stick merchants (buy one for €2, rent it for €1) and mumbling zealots all dotted around a vast car park full of people adjusting each other's gaiters and looking nervously upwards. I'd been slightly sniffy about Croagh Patrick, pointing out to anyone who would listen that it's only 2,510 feet high, and that I can go up and down a bigger mountain than that before breakfast at home (not that I ever have, but the possibility's there). Here, though, you are starting at sea level, right on the shores of Clew Bay and its speckle of glacial drumlins arching from the water like a pod of basking whales. Furthermore, the path is no gentle amble. It lurches heavenwards, hurling contour after contour back to earth with god-like fury. In length, from the car park to the summit, the path is less than two miles, a terrifically short scramble in which to gain two and a half thousand feet in height.

Two days after Reek Sunday, there were hundreds of us climbing the mountain. Anything up to quarter of a million do it every year. Loftily spurned by 'proper' climbers and purist hill walkers, Croagh Patrick is the Princess Di of mountains, the People's Peak, and in many cases, the only mountain that some will ever ascend. To do so is an integral part of being Irish, a damp green Camino conducted for both cultural and spiritual uplift. The mountain was special before Christianity, it has remained so through sixteen centuries of boisterous Church rule, and in these early days of a kind of neo-pagan secularism, its appeal and its pull have not dimmed in the slightest – if anything, quite the reverse. Even those who have long ago abandoned the Church after its miserable succession of scandals still look to the Reek as a penance that must be done. On both days, I was struck by the gangs of teenage mates, the young families and the couples in their twenties who were heading up. Though I'd be lying if I said that I wasn't horrified by the rubbish the buggers leave strewn all over the sacred peak.

It's a really tough climb: relentless and demanding, saving the worst for last. That scramble up the cone, sliding over ball-bearing scree slopes to the summit, is as tough climbing as you'll get almost anywhere, for there is nothing to grip on to and the gradient is sheer. Again, smiles and words of encouragement lifted my knackered legs. Clouds hung obstinately over the summit, so there was no chance of getting the dazzling view of Clew Bay, but that didn't matter. The sense of achievement and fulfilment as the grotty little hilltop chapel hoved into view through the mist sent me soaring; the view on top of that might have been a bit too much. It means also that I'll have to come back and do it again: the next time in the hours up to sunrise. I could see why so many people did this time after time, treading the same path with new hope. It was inspiring, moving and amazing fun. Mrs Doyle would be very disappointed.

While many fine paths play up to our sense of the spiritual, there are a whole load of others whose existence is more explicitly religious, created to oil the wheels of the established Church, in all its pomp and frequent inhumanity. Perhaps the most prominent in this category, and certainly the most notorious and gruesome, are the corpse paths, or death roads.

These were routes for funeral processions, particularly in the early medieval countryside, when larger minsters and churches would insist – mainly for reasons of finance and power – on conducting every burial within a huge area. Radiating out from the mother church was a spider's web of paths used to carry the dead to their final appointment, sometimes the general paths that people used for normal church attendance, but often little used for any other purpose and increasingly imbued with an other-worldly reputation. As the outlying satellite churches grew in size and status, this procedure was gradually abandoned, although it continued into the nineteenth century in some more sparsely populated outposts.

A vast store of legend and superstition hovers around corpse roads. They were where you might see various harbingers of death, such as spectres and wraiths, black dogs, corpse candles and phantom funeral cortèges; numerous accounts survive of such sightings. Less ethereally, one of the most persistent beliefs is that once a coffin has been taken down a path, it automatically becomes a public right of way. Such thinking still surfaces even today in official enquiries held to confirm or extinguish public paths. Public Rights of Way consultant Sue Rumfitt told me of a case she'd attended as a young RoW officer in Bedfordshire in the late 1980s, when a number of elderly witnesses all independently attested to the belief that the path in question was public, because they had heard that 'a coffin went down it'. Interestingly, none of them had witnessed such an event themselves; the information had been handed down as anecdotal local tradition.

The idea has surfaced since, in RoW enquiries in Norfolk, Suffolk and elsewhere, and it remains one of the most persistent myths in our canon of beliefs about our footpath network. It was enough to scare many landowners from allowing funeral processions across their land, although once a path has been established, it was generally treated with the utmost respect, even dread. Corpse paths went unploughed, and were left to become hard and dry, as they would have to be for the task of ferrying a dead body across sometimes punishing terrain. For the coffin bearers, there were numerous customs to which they must cling in the execution of their grisly task. Many believed that the corpse must be carried feet forward. Oftentimes, corpse roads deliberately crossed streams, stiles and crossroads, for these were thought to be liminal places that held the spirits and prevented them wreaking havoc back in this world. It was the terror of allowing the spirit to escape, and then return to haunt old friends and neighbours, that underpinned the most important custom on corpse roads, that the funeral procession must not, under any circumstances, deviate one inch from the prescribed route. Calamity would await those who failed. Is this perhaps one root of the terror that so many people still feel these days about deviating from the official path?

Many of our corpse roads have been ploughed up or built on, but many have not, and their ghosts can be found not just in the misty fringes of our islands, but also in some unexpectedly prosaic corners. Paul Devereux, in his book *Fairy Paths & Spirit Roads*, locates examples at Saintbury in Gloucestershire, Thurmaston on the outskirts of Leicester, across Otmoor in Oxfordshire, near Abertillery in the south Wales valleys and at Brailes on the edge of the Cotswolds in Warwickshire. A fine example can be found at the southern edge of the spreading hinterland of Redditch new town in Worcestershire: starting as Burial Lane in Ham Green and continuing along a bridleway and ancient holloway to the church at Feckenham.

Self-evidently, it is in the less urbanised parts of the land that old corpse paths can most easily be found. The South West is riddled with them, none more famous than the Lich Way across Dartmoor. Lich, or lych, is an old English word for 'corpse', and is more commonly associated with the thousands of lichgates to be found in churchyards everywhere. Such gates originated as the dedicated entrance to the churchyard for funeral processions: their roof would give mourners shelter and a few examples survive of integral wooden or stone slab shelves on which the coffin (or, rather more frequently, the corpse in a shroud) would have rested. The funeral service would begin at the gate, with the priest intoning, 'I am the resurrection and the life,' before leading the party to the freshly dug graveside.

The Dartmoor corpse road sounded fascinating, and I was eager to try it. Its celebrity is due to its considerable length, around 12 miles, the only path crossing this part of the moor from one side to the other. Lydford, on the north-western flank of the moor, was for centuries the largest parish in England, its jurisdiction covering almost the entire moor. This meant that anyone dying in or around the villages on the eastern and southern edges of Dartmoor – such as Bellever, Princetown, Postbridge and Hexworthy – was obliged to be carted to Lydford. The corpse road across the middle of the moor was by far the most direct route, but it was difficult, long and crossed almost featureless terrain.

On a website about the Dartmoor Lich Way, there was some mention about walking it at dusk on a summer's evening. The idea squatted in my imagination, and refused to move. I decided to set off from the west side a couple of hours before sunset on the night of the June full moon, mentally crossing the moor under a fading pink glow and then through silvery beams. In my head, it looked lovely. I checked the calendar and saw that the June full moon fell on a Saturday. Perfect: the Lich Way crosses an extensive military firing range, but the guns are silent on summer weekends. When I mentioned the idea to friends, nearly everyone pulled a vinegary face and said something along the lines of, 'Hmm, rather you than me.' It didn't sound scary to me – well, only a bit. Perhaps it should have done. Mainly, the prospect seemed thrilling, a challenge of wit and spirit, a pilgrimage and a celebration of those who had gone before.

Time and place sorted, and it was immediately obvious too as to the company I wanted. I first met my friend Woody at the annual Queer Pagan Camp (QPC), back in 1999. He's a shaman, a witch, a priest, an artist and a star, and had moved from London to Devon at much the same time that I'd left Birmingham for mid-Wales. As two single urban gay boys launching themselves into the rural outback, it had been good to have each other to lean on over the years, compare notes and shriek with shared laughter at some of our less edifying moments, especially in the early days. After we'd been in our respective idylls for a few years, we almost simultaneously fell in love and settled down with local blokes, people that neither of us would ever have met had we stayed in the urban jungle. I remembered the many nay-sayers when I was preparing to move: a single gay Englishman thinking of upping sticks to Llannowhere! How mad was I? At worst, I'd be lynched, and at best, I was condemning myself to a life of aching loneliness. Even at the time, and without really knowing why, I knew that was rubbish. And one supportive conversation with Woody was worth a thousand hours of clucking from the chorus of doubters.

I outlined my Lich Way plan to him, and he agreed to join me. He was a little freaked out by it, all the same, and warned me to think very carefully about what I wanted and expected from it. One of the most important parts of his spirituality is regular communion with the folk of the land, for to him, they are as real and as present as the milkman or the curtain-twitcher at number 76. At QPC, it would usually be him monitoring – policing even – things like where people pitched their tent, so as not to block the spirit and fairy paths across the land. If you were on gate duty at camp, it was your job to explain this to new arrivals, along with more mundane issues like toilets and meal times. One day, I was on gate duty and a lesbian couple arrived for their first time at the camp. They'd driven from London to our field in west Dorset, and were in a pretty fractious state. One of them could hardly wait to join in, but the other looked like the proverbial bulldog licking piss off a nettle. I brewed up a cup of tea for them on the gate fire and then went through the few rules and regs of the set-up. When I reached the bit about not camping on the fairy paths, the edgy-looking one shot to her feet. 'See, I told you!' she shouted at her girlfriend. 'I told you they'd be fucking nutters! Fucking fairy paths! Hippy wankers!' Within five minutes, she'd roared off back down the lane to London, while her partner stayed the week and had a lovely time. Mind you, a week away from that girlfriend would have been fun if she'd spent it in a cardboard box in an underpass.

The day of the full-moon walk grew hot and sticky. Storms were threatening according to the forecast, and Woody was certain that if they were going to break anywhere, it would be over Dartmoor, and probably at dusk. After all, the moor was famous for its gloomy micro-climate, where fogs can descend suddenly out of a clear sky. His spirituality deals often in the dark of life; mine tends towards a blithe 'Oh, it'll be all right' certainty that, despite the many occasions on which it had been proved wrong, still somehow endured. I gave him Paul Devereux's book, so as to read the quite lengthy description of the route we were to take that night. It didn't help. Ignoring the blood-stirring passages about the Wild Hunt, phantom funerals and the splendours of Coffin Wood, he instead seized on phrases like 'a gruelling journey', 'difficult to navigate owing to marshy conditions', 'continues in an increasingly ill-defined way' and 'poorly defined or, at best, a stranded route in open moorland'. Honestly, some people. Always seeing the negative.

He ramped up our mood of chain-smoking nervousness by telling me a little about his experiences of the folk of Dartmoor. One time, he'd visited Wistman's (or Wiseman's) Wood, a grove of ancient oaks near the beginning of the route and – as its name implies – a place of celebrated magic. There he was greeted by a pack of aggressive folk, warning him away with spears and sticks. After much negotiation, he persuaded them that he came in peace, and they changed instantly into garrulous hosts, escorting him around the wood and showing him all their favourite places. As for the famous pixies (or piskies), he said, they're not the cheery little imps that you'll find leering off the shelves in the local gift shops, but blueish creatures that are 'very spirited', and not always terribly friendly. He'd warned me before that they were particularly fond of cake, so I'd baked a bara brith at home and brought it with me as an offering, worrying only slightly that it was culturally inappropriate to give Welsh delicacies to Devonian piskies. Should I try and rustle up a clotted cream tea for them instead? Woody told me to stop taking the piss.

We drove both cars the hour's journey down to Lydford, leaving mine in a small army car park on the moor's western edge. The drive to Powdermills, our starting point, seemed an awful long way. To the left, the moor looked gaunt and grim, even in the evening sunshine, but nothing compared with the shock of HMP Dartmoor, the most notorious prison in Britain, suddenly looming large and brutal on the horizon. At last, we coasted into Powdermills, parked and set off, giggling a little too shrilly at our crap jokes.

Even though the Lich Way is closed more often than not by army manoeuvres, the path is a fully fledged right of way. And despite countless times when I've learned how untrue it can be in reality, I still found myself looking at the map, tracing the green dashed line and believing in it. Paul Devereux's words of warning about its lack of definition and all-round difficulty were easily drowned out in my mind by the authoritative voice of Ordnance Survey, my much-flawed god. Will I never learn? On the map, the path looked plaintively lonely, edging out over tussocky contours and with only the odd stream and rocky tor to break the monotony, or indeed to navigate by.

At the first tor after Powdermills, Longaford Tor according to the map, we stopped to attune ourselves and make our offerings to the folk. Woody said that he'd already clocked a few interested heads poking up to check us out as we passed by, and when we made the offering, they clustered around. My bara brith was deemed acceptable, apparently, and we gave them a drizzle of tea from our flask to wash it down. They prefer booze, I was told, but sweet tea was a reasonable alternative. The tors, those glorious piles of granite that look as if they have been placed with artistic precision by Andy Goldsworthy or Nils Udo, rippled across the landscape ahead of us, like wave crests atop a swollen green sea. Suddenly I realised that this route was as dangerous, and unpredictable, as the ocean itself.

As the sun slid down in a sultry haze, the temperature barely dropped at all. I was sweltering, the sweat dripping off my nose as we pushed on down into a valley and back up again to the next tor. This was the pattern for miles: you never reach any momentous height, but the constant up and down, through wiry grass and sudden pools of rusty water, was absolutely knackering. The day's over-consumption of fags was also weighing heavy on us both.

My God, but it was impressive. We sat on one tor, having a bit of food and drink, as the sun sank towards the north-west. Ten minutes before it disappeared, I looked around to the opposite horizon, and there was the freshly risen full moon, briefly the sun's identical twin. Both were pink and hazy, squashed at the extremities, one leaving, one arriving, and sharing just the most fleeting moment of perfect synchronicity. We sighed, smiled and felt very blessed, enough even to stop feeling scared for a few minutes.

Paul Devereux wasn't wrong, though. The path was a sod to follow, especially in dwindling light. Even the moon wasn't playing ball. Having risen so spectacularly, it failed to climb high and bright, preferring instead to limp along just above the horizon, the colour of ripe cheese. At times, there was no evidence of a route at all, and all we could do was work out from the map what we were vaguely aiming for and to head as best as possible in that direction. I'm ashamed to say that I hadn't even brought a compass. Though I had remembered my little wind-up torch, and was feeling pretty pleased with myself for that. All the same, we were breaking the cardinal rule of not straying from the corpse road, and I couldn't imagine that it had ever been any different for anyone else.

Occasionally, we would stumble across the Lich Way again, whether as a gravel or grass path, a rough stone cobble, or as a sudden and unexpected little holloway through the featureless sump. It was as clear as day when we were back on the path, you could just feel it. As I found on the Tóchar Phádraig, there was an echoing, bony quality to it, the sound of centuries of human and animal feet booming deep and resonant beneath us. It swam in and out of focus like a distant radio signal, but when it was on, it was very on. And when it was off, we floundered hopelessly. The folk, I was told, were largely leaving us alone. They had long ago surrendered authority on this ribbon of humanity across their moor, for this, Woody felt, had been a human ceremonial way long before the Church muscled in.

He did confess an encounter later on, though, one that I'm very glad he didn't divulge at the time. At one of the bleakest bits in the middle of the moor, when we'd lost the route again and were inching like snails across the squelchy savannah, Woody tells me that the spirit of a dead man, big and hairy, wearing hessian, with mad eyes and a matted beard, suddenly appeared at our side. He wasn't in a good mood either, forever denied the sanctuary of church on account of being a murderer and condemned to spend eternity on the Lich Way. 'You can take me out with you,' he told Woody, who pointed out that he couldn't, as he was protected. 'He's not, though,' said the hirsute murderer, pointing at me, at which point Woody silently threw some protection my way.

Something got through, however, because as we became increasingly lost, and the moon continued to glimmer dimly only just above the horizon, I began to feel really ill. I'd massively overheated earlier, and that nearly always brings on a migraine. And so it was again. It felt as if the jolt of every step were bruising my eyeballs from the inside, and I could barely focus. The map under torchlight swam uselessly in my gaze, all identifying landscape features invisible in the black. I had to stop; the pain was excruciating.

Often, a physical purge helps release the pressure a little, and I was soon retching into the black. My head still pounded, and all I could think of to do was to place it, forehead-first, on the cool grass, and hope that it would absorb some of the heat and pain. Woody later told me that this moment, as I sank to the ground with a moan, was his low-point of the night (amongst some pretty stiff competition), as he wasn't too sure that I'd ever get up again. He put his hands on my head and declared that there was a flint from the folk lodged in my forehead; I'd been attacked. He helped dispel it, and I felt a little better, just about able to continue on our hopeless way.

A long drawn-out hour or two later, the remains of the headache vanished in an instant, at the precise moment when we scrambled over a dry stone wall into a farmer's field. Even if we were miles out of our way (and we were), we had reached the other side of the moor. Relief flooded my body, and the pain just evaporated. I have never had such a strong, and instant, physical recovery from so far down. The dry stone wall, and even the barbed wire that topped it, were the first workings of the hand of man that we'd seen in hours, and they looked just wonderful.

We'd woken the farm dogs up, though. Howling and hollering, they were down in a dip from where a solitary light glowed. It was after one in the morning, and there was nothing we could do but march down there and hope that Woody's protection against the folk of the spiritual realm would work too on the creatures of the distinctly physical one. By the time we reached the farm yard, the noise was tumultuous. A light snapped on in an upstairs window of the farmhouse, and a woman threw open the glass.

'Who's there?' she shrieked. The dogs went even crazier at the tone of her voice. We transmogrified in an instant from pagan subversives into the nicest middle-class boys you'd ever introduce to your mum.

'Oh, hello there,' said Woody, all but doffing his hat. 'Really sorry to disturb you, gosh it's late, but we got, er, well, we got a bit lost on the moor. Sorry.'

Silence. I mumbled a sorry or two in support.

'Er, could you possibly point us in the direction of Peter Tavy?' Not a strapping local who'd come and rescue us, but the name of the nearest village gleaned from the map.

'Down that lane. Keep going.'

The window crashed shut on yet more apologies from us, setting the dogs off again. We ran from the farm yard.

The last bit of the walk, along satisfyingly solid country lanes under a canopy of stars, was beautiful. Even the moon was finally getting its act together by rising high enough into the sky to help us see. There was the small problem that my car was still five or six miles away, and there was no way Woody, whose feet were in agony from knackered boots, could walk that far. We decided that, as soon as one of us had a phone signal, we'd try and find a taxi to take us back to the car.

We shape-shifted for the second time in an hour when the taxi from Tavistock finally caught up with us back on the main A386. Having gone from nomadic rebels to impeccable Cedrics at the farm, we further metamorphosed into swooning Edwardian ladies in the company of the chatty taxi driver. 'You're our knight in shining armour!' we trilled, which he seemed to rather like. He was entirely unfazed to be picking up two idiots who'd 'got a bit lost on the moor' at two in the morning: 'Seen it all in this job,' he said, grinning at us. He told us of folk in T-shirts and flip-flops who ask to be dropped in the middle of the moor ''cos they fancy a walk'. 'Not in that outfit, I won't,' is his standard, schoolmarmish reply. How the Edwardian ladies tittered!

Actually, we were probably near clinical hysteria. It had been the most trying walk I think I've ever done, and that was on a warm summer's evening carrying nothing more than a map, some water and a few Kit Kats. I tried to imagine what dragging

a 15-stone corpse the same way would have been like, on a howling winter's day perhaps. Strung from a bier, the sack of dead
flesh swinging in the wind as your back ached and feet froze
in the gloop. Perhaps some people used a cart, and spent large
parts of the awful journey alternately tugging the wheels out of
the hungry mud and bouncing them over sharp rocks. People
must have died making that journey. Would church rules, condemning people to this torture for no good reason save for their
own sense of divine right, allow that the new body be let in to the
graveyard with the old? Or would the poor, broken bastards be
forced to do it all again next week?

Not much better than the idiots in flip-flops, I had seriously underestimated the moor. It had seemed impossible that
somewhere so savage could sit at the heart of Devon, that lush
landscape of cattle and clotted cream. Snobbery played an inglori-
ous part too: my devotion to Wales, taken to new heights (and
depths) from a decade of living there, had produced a sour little
assumption that there was nowhere truly wild left in England.
England's little piskies had the last laugh on that one.

The northern equivalent of the word 'lich' is 'lyke', and reading
that, a distant recollection detonated. The Lyke Wake Walk was
a name I'd not heard in years, and it instantly brought back memories of *Blue Peter* presenters grunting and grimacing their way
across the invariably sodden North York Moors. In the late 1970s,
it had seemed that every scout pack, charity group, rambling
society, Rotary Club and TV beefcake was stomping through the
heather from Osmotherley to Ravenscar. This, we were always
told, was far more than a mere walk; it was an endurance test,

a challenge like no other, for to qualify for membership of the exclusive club of successful Lyke Wakers, you had to complete the 42-mile trek in under 24 hours, usually necessitating overnight walking. Even better, and even darker, it was overlain with a neo-pagan patina of ancient ritual, for this was said to be an old coffin path to the sea, passing as it does the odd Bronze Age burial mound and stone cross. Some groups even upped the ante by dressing as undertakers and carrying a coffin. In my early teens, it had been the biggest, most famous footpath in the land, yet it had all but disappeared. To paraphrase another great relic of the Age of Beige, whatever happened to the Lyke Wake Walk?

The walk, sometimes claimed to be the first named long-distance path in the country, began in modest circumstances in 1955. Bill Cowley, a farmer from Swainby, between Middlesbrough and Northallerton, had written a piece in that August's edition of *The Dalesman* magazine laying down the challenge of walking across the moors to the sea in one day. The idea had come to him in a flash, he said, earlier that summer when he'd climbed to the top of Glaisdale Rigg, the ridge between Glaisdale and its splendidly named western neighbour, Fryupdale. From the lofty top, he'd suddenly imagined lines of the ancients trekking their way across the moor, from one weathered old cross, standing stone or ancient mound to the next. Cowley was an engaging and passionate Yorkshireman, always able to join the most insubstantial of dots into a seamless swagger of local pride. He'd gone to Cambridge, where he formed the Yorkshire Society, led the 1957 Yorkshire Himalayan Expedition and, since returning to farm his native patch, was active in the Yorkshire Dialect Society.

At noon on the first of October that year, Cowley and 12 others set off from Osmotherley and headed east, threading their way along sheep paths through the heather. The party camped at seven that evening at Hamer, and set off again at 3.30 a.m, reaching the coast at Ravenscar, midway between Scarborough and Whitby, at 11 o'clock the following morning. The Lyke Wake Walk, and its irresistible mystique, was born.

Word spread fast. In the early days, it was almost entirely local: the first logbooks of the walk, which were kept in cafés at either end for people to sign in their times and experiences, are full of entries by groups from bodies such as York Technical College, Middlesbrough GPO Telephones Division, a Stockton-on-Tees scout pack, the Apprentice Training Centre at ICI's Wilton works, Selby Round Table and the Darlington Young Liberals. The unlikely sounding outfit of the East Yorkshire Mountaineering Club features a few times. The few southerners who took it on fared fairly dismally, none more guaranteed to make a Yorkshireman crack a thin smile than a party from the London Region of the Youth Hostel Association, who, in 1961, curtly confessed to the logbook that they 'did not take magnetic variation into account – ended up in Middlesbrough'.

In the logbooks, the glowering presence of Bill Cowley looms over every entry. The first one started with a request to fill in 'details of route, times, conditions and names of walkers on a separate full page for each attempt'. That was crossed out, and 'CANCEL THIS!' scrawled across in Cowley's looping hand. He gave an arch explanation: 'The Puckrin family are taking up too much space!' Indeed, the first eight pages of the logbook are all Puckrins. In a foretaste of the obsessive tendencies that the Lyke Wake Walk stirred so massively later on, Arthur Puckrin in particular seemed hooked on it, and on 9 July 1961 did the route in 6 hours, 39 minutes and 20 seconds. 'NEW RECORD (Beat this!)'

he inscribed proudly. Cowley added a gruff note: 'Can't accept seconds – agreed at 6.40.'

At the end of every year, Cowley would tot up the number of walkers who had completed the route and scribe the result into the logbook. Keeping to the funereal theme, he called himself the Chief Dirger, and granted titles such as 'Anxious Almoner' to his closest acolytes. Any man who completed the challenge in the requisite time could apply to become a fellow dirger, and to receive a black-edged 'condolence card' to prove it at a shilling a pop. In the first three years, 191 did it and then the numbers started to climb quite markedly: 112 in 1959 alone, 255 in 1960 and 790 in 1961. Well over 90 per cent of them were men. Women who'd completed the trek weren't granted dirger status, and were simply called 'witches' instead.

There was a breezy levity to those early days. Bill Cowley himself did the route numerous times, including on skis during the Arctic winter of 1962–3. He sounded at his most spirited recording a trek in November 1961, when he and regular fellow dirger Campbell Bosanquet left Osmotherley just after midnight, arriving in Ravenscar at 2.40 the following afternoon, in time to catch the 3.16 train back for an evening cocktail party. En route, he records, they'd enjoyed ham sandwiches and coffee at 3.30 a.m., sausages and mushrooms at 8.15, 'a pint of iced nectar at Beck Hole' at 10.45 and 'another at the Flask (not quite so iced)' at 1.40. It was all a bit of overgrown schoolboy fun, but that couldn't last.

A month before this crossing, the Lyke Wake Walk had been featured for the first time on television, when a crew from the BBC programme *Tonight* came to film it. Over the next decade or so, other TV crews, journalists and writers followed, and soon the Lyke Wake Walk was a national legend. Numbers swelled exponentially, peaking in the lighter months of May and June. In June 1975 alone, 3,141 people completed the route, including Hungarian-born Louis Kulcsar of Stockton-on-Tees, for whom it was the 110th crossing (three of which were barefoot). He's still doing it, and has now racked up around 200, the official record. It's believed that 1978 was the peak year, when anything between twenty and thirty thousand completed the walk, the vast majority of them going west–east from Osmotherley, and most of them starting in the dead of night. The muttering of discontented locals, furious at being woken up almost nightly by excitable gangs of soldiers, scouts and Rotarians, became an inconsolable roar.

As the popularity of the walk grew, so did the hoodoo surrounding it. Despite there being no evidence whatsoever that this had indeed ever been used as a coffin path (and it seems unlikely that any funeral procession would carry the dead over 40 miles), Bill Cowley's imaginative take on history was given as hard fact, and repeated mantra-like across books, newspapers, radio and television. Merchandise, such as coffin-shaped cufflinks, ties and headscarves for the 'witches', flew off the shelves. Regular gatherings were called 'Wakes', with suitably morbid entertainment laid on. The highest accolade, allowing you to wear purple robes at Wakes, was as a 'Doctor of Dolefulness': to qualify, you had to have done at least seven crossings, one of which needed to be in the winter and one a solo unsupported trek, meaning no teams of thermos-bearing car drivers to meet you at appointed halts. Photos of the Wakes in the 1970s show a curious mix of grizzled Yorkshire farmers, a few bald bank managers taking a walk on the wild side, some wiry fell runners and a generous sprinkling of bearded prog-rock pagans getting quietly wassocked on real ale. These took place against a backdrop of black candles, coffin-shaped menu cards and skull-painted drapes. With its coterie of hardcore fanatics and pedants, its pages of tightly held rules and invented customs, the Lyke Wake Club started to look distinctly cultish.

It was increasingly obvious that Bill Cowley had created a monster, and the backlash came quickly. In the hot summer of 1975, a fire on the heather-and-peat tinderbox of Wheeldale Moor burned for a fortnight. As always, blame was swiftly, and on no firm evidence, lain squarely at the feet of walkers; calls were made for the Lyke Wake Walk to be banned outright. Richard Hamersley, Land Surveyor to the Duchy of Lancaster, slyly pointed out that 'the route of the walk is not a statutory footpath, and serious thought will have to be given as to the legitimacy of this activity.' He was being slightly disingenuous, for around half of the path was on recognised rights of way, the remainder, mostly in the eastern section, on well-worn (and well-mapped) permissive tracks that had been used since anyone could remember. In Hamersley's mind, there was no doubt who was to blame for the fire: 'This week I collected no fewer than 69 cigarette ends in a half-mile random stretch of the route. If this is indicative of the whole length, there must be some 5,600 cigarette ends recently smoked along the walk. No wonder that during the recent dry weather a fire of this magnitude has occurred.' The following summer, 1976, was hotter and drier still, and an agreement was reluctantly brokered to suspend the walk for the duration of the drought.

The first winds of trouble only made the Lyke Wake Club retreat further into its pound-shop Hallowe'en grotto. They put a proposal to the Countryside Commission that the route should be recognised as an official Long Distance Path (LDP), which was immediately rejected. Never mind, for it gave ample chance for the polishing of Yorkshire chips on square shoulders: the Chief Dirger himself denouncing the decision, and stating that it 'reflects the typical Southern, bureaucratic attitude of people who would not recognize a walk if they saw one'. In fact, the Countryside Council had already plotted an alternative walk, the Cleveland Way, over much of the same ground, combining it with a final coastal flourish from Whitby to Filey. After the Pennine Way, this had been Britain's second official LDP, opening in 1969. But that was dull and square, man, authority's preferred route and not for the self-styled swashbuckling dirgers and witches of the Lyke Wake.

As now happens with Wainwright's Coast to Coast walk (which shares some of the route, and much of the spirit, of the Lyke Wake), the lack of official recognition only seemed to make it even more attractive to some. Numbers continued to grow, peaking at the tail end of the 1970s. The walk was barely off the box, and it became by far the number one charity challenge in the country. It was these that killed the Lyke Wake more than anything, for they were often huge groups, walking five or six abreast, prompting a member of the local National Park Committee to say that 'twenty years ago, the Lyke Wake Walk was just a sheeptrack. Now it is wide enough for two tanks to cross side by side.' Worse, every charity-sponsored walk came complete with a sophisticated back-up support system of refreshment and medical teams, to be found bouncing around unfamiliar moorland lanes in minibuses all through the night. Increasingly often, an ambulance would have to join the throng.

Sensing only a thin scatter of population, many walkers – already fired up with the shouty sanctimony of doing it all for charity – were oblivious to their devastating impact on the taciturn local community.

In May 1982, the North York Moors National Park, never the most radical of organisations, set up a Lyke Wake Walk Working Party to investigate what should be done. The remit of the group was clear and stated at the outset, that 'it is stressed that if a substantial reduction in use [of the Walk] is not achieved, the National Park Committee will have to consider complete closure.' Dr Roy Brown of the National Park heaped up the hyperbole: 'Within a few years the whole area will be a desert if something is not done quickly.' This is an interesting one, for while the track was undoubtedly eroding quite markedly in places, is this not exactly how our much-loved ancient holloways and green lanes were initially created? We wouldn't have much to coo over now if our ancestors had been quite so squeamish.

The report concluded that numbers doing the walk must be reduced by half, at the very least. The Lyke Wake Club tried to do its bit by creating alternative routes, the Shepherd's Round and the Hambleton Hobble, but they never really caught on, for people had bought into the myth of the Lyke Wake that the Club had so assiduously nursed and weren't prepared to be fobbed off with sloppy seconds. Ordnance Survey were told to take the route off their maps, which they duly did. TV crews were turned away. Charity teams were discouraged, while those from the police, army and cadet forces – a significant proportion of the total – were firmly told to go elsewhere and find other challenges. Even Bill Cowley acknowledged the necessity for action, saying, 'I feel very sad that it has come to this, but it is the only way.'

And it worked: almost instantly, the number of Lyke Wakers plummeted.

After the drastic cull of 1982, numbers started to rise again, and when, a decade later, the National Park Authority set up another working party to discourage overuse of the route, one of the most vociferous of the Lyke Wake Club's officials fired off a tetchy letter to the *Darlington and Stockton Times*. In it, he told of an American tourist who'd written to the National Park to ask about the Lyke Wake Walk. The officer who'd replied had told him that it wasn't on official rights of way and that 'permission should really be obtained from the landowners.' He then went on to criticise the creeping mentality of council-approved waymarked routes, writing 'for some reason, the vast majority of walkers seem to be unable to place one leg in front of the other unless the route has a fancy name, badge and completion certificate' – a very good point indeed, until you remember that it was the Lyke Wake Club that pioneered such things, and were still enthusiastically marketing them.

Cowley died in 1994, aged 78. While his steady hand was on the tiller, there was still – just about – a sense that the Lyke Wake Walk was little more than boyish high jinks that had got slightly out of control. Some of his lieutenants, though, didn't seem to share his easy-going sense of perspective, and furiously guarded everything about both the walk and the club. This came to a head as the 50th anniversary of the first crossing loomed in 2005, when a tight cabal of 'senior members' decided to call it a day and kill the club. A splinter group vehemently disagreed, and decided to launch themselves as the New Lyke Wake Walk Club. This was inaugurated at a dinner in the Queen Catherine Inn in Osmotherley on the first of October 2005, precisely 50 years since Bill Cowley's first walk. Forty-two miles away on the very same night, at the Raven Hall Hotel in Ravenscar, the old Lyke Wake Club held its final Wake and disappeared from the map. Not entirely, though, for the commercial trading arm, purveyors of all that coffin-shaped tat, the 'fancy name, badge and completion certificate', plus a whole load more, continued and still trades today.

It was not an amicable divorce. The new group was regularly characterised by the old as being full of southern softies who didn't understand the highly autarkic culture of the North York Moors. The ghost of Bill Cowley was regularly invoked in the spat, with both sides contending that they were acting as he would have wished them to. Claims and counter-claims streamed through the local papers and rambling magazines. Although hostilities have largely ceased now, and a few hundred people continue to tramp the route each year, there's still an acrimonious whiff hanging over the Lyke Wake Walk – worse even than the diabolical sulphur of an Irish dance hall or Father Fahey's incinerated clutch. Never has the Lyke Wake Walk's mournful iconography looked more pathetically appropriate.

Up the Brum: the Birmingham Main Line Canal, near Wolverhampton
Photo by Roger Kidd

8. WHERE DIRT MEETS WATER

In common with just about everyone else who spent a large part of the 1990s tugging on a spliff, I'm a huge fan of the late American comedian Bill Hicks. Pirate videos of his gigs were almost inevitably playing in the dark Birmingham rooms, curtains drawn against the sunlight, in which I wasted happy years. Hicks, whose brand of comedy was brutal yet pierced with the sharp light of truth, was a hero to us all, and we would swap lines with the same nerdy enthusiasm we'd swapped football cards 20 years earlier. Even through the fug of those years, I can remember that there was only ever one routine of his with which I disagreed, the basis of which was the opening line: 'The beach! The beach – let's go to the beach! Ah man, what is it about the beach? It's just where dirt meets water.' Apparently, he recanted on this view before he died. I only hope that his change of thinking came after some transcendentally magical days by the sea.

As an island nation, we are pulled towards the coast by a centrifugal force beyond our control. For those of us from the grubby middle of the country, for whom the sea was but a distant dream, this force is nothing short of mythic. Every family holiday to the seaside would include a hard-fought battle in the back seat to win the 'first glimpse of the sea' competition, one which I, hunched defensively over my OS map, would take as a challenge to my navigational skills. Not that the map was much help: a sudden peek of a distant sea in the nape of two hills could come almost anywhere, and would not be spotted amongst the flat contours and colours of the OS.

Years ago, I climbed Carn Llidi, a rocky outcrop at the western extremity of Wales, just beyond the tiny Pembrokeshire city of St David's. There's a stone seat sculpted by nature at the top, which gives you a phenomenal view of the Atlantic shimmering off into the distance, and I was looking forward to settling in it, enjoying a quiet smoke and watching the sun go down. As I neared the top, I saw to my annoyance that a couple had already bagged my spot. Getting nearer, I noticed, as they stared out to sea, their look of hypnotised wonder, like some syrupy image of children at prayer from a Victorian Bible. It was a look I knew well. 'You're not from the Midlands, by any chance, are you?' I called out. ''Ow did yow know?' the bloke hollered back, in a broad Black Country twang. 'Er, just a hunch,' I replied.

Carn Llidi sits above one of Britain's best-loved rights of way, the Pembrokeshire Coast Path, established as one of the first tranche of National Trails in 1970. The idea had dated back to 1951, when local naturalist R. M. Lockley explored the possibility of linking together existing cliff-top and beach paths around the county, and filling in the missing gaps. Lockley was also instrumental in the creation, the following year, of the Pembrokeshire coast as a National Park, still the only one in Britain whose geography and character is almost entirely coastal. This helped cement in the national mind the idea that the coast of Pembrokeshire is uniquely blessed, and somehow the best of all. It isn't: lovely though it often is, there are finer stretches of seaboard elsewhere in Britain, even in Wales. No matter, though, for this early boost to its credentials still plays out today in the enduring popularity of the county, and of its coast path in particular.

You need a certain frame of mind to want to walk any coast path, but especially the 186 miles (300 km) of the one that skips around the frilly edge of Pembrokeshire. Despite my starry-eyed Midlander's love of the sea, it's a frame of mind that escapes me. I honestly cannot think of a more pointless long walk than this one. The county is a peninsula, jutting square-jawed out into the sea from the south-western corner of Wales, but that one peninsula comprises dozens of smaller peninsulas, meaning that often the stark choice is to walk a slippery cliff-top for three or four miles around a windswept headland, or cheat and cut across its neck, sometimes a distance of just a couple of hundred yards. Not only that, the path goes up and down like a whore's drawers, through rickety steps, startling vertigo and muddy slides, rarely having much of a flat stretch on which to stroll, breathe easy and take it all in. If you walk the whole path, from the outskirts of Cardigan to Amroth, on the county border with Carmarthenshire, you will go up and down a total of 35,000 feet. And after weeks of effort, blisters, mud, sunburn, stings, gales, shitting seagulls and aching calf muscles, you'll reach Tenby, just a few miles short of the end, and there a mocking road sign that states:

reminding you that you could be back where you began, all those days and all that pain ago, within three-quarters of an hour.

It takes a special kind of mind – a rather calmer one than mine, I suspect – to appreciate that sort of exquisite torture. Perhaps I'm just too much of a dilettante, or cursed with the attention span of a goldfish, but at the end of a two-week walk (the average time taken to do the entire Pembrokeshire path), I'd like to feel that I'd actually gone somewhere, that I had progressed through different landscapes and taken with me a cumulative sense of wonder at how they all fit together. Mile upon mile of seabird sameyness, up and down, down again and then up a bit more, would snap my sanity, I feel sure. But it is for these very same reasons that many people adore paths such as this. Its sheer repetitiveness and constant proximity to the endless horizon of the Atlantic acts as a fortnight-long Zen meditation. It is, to some, a kind of ultimate challenge, to be locked in the now, to walk only for the journey and not for the destination. And if you've ever been to Amroth, you'll know how doubly true that is.

All the stranger to my mind, therefore, that anyone would want to tackle the South West Coast Path (SWCP), Britain's longest single waymarked trail at 630 miles (1,014 km). The official start is at Minehead in Somerset, then it threads all the way down the northern coast of Devon and Cornwall, then all the way back along their southern coasts and that of Dorset too, finishing at Poole Harbour. The South West is by far Britain's favourite holiday playground, thanks to its comparatively mellow climate and plethora of good beaches – things that are, in other words, best enjoyed at a very leisurely pace. I've walked various sections of both the Pembrokeshire path and the SWCP, and quite wonderful they were too, but the idea of doing either in its entirety fills me with horror.

The section of the SWCP that I've most wanted to see for years was the one perhaps least connected to the sea itself. The seven-and-a-half-mile slither between Seaton, Devon and Lyme Regis, Dorset picks its way through unstable cliffs and landslips, past ruined houses long since demolished by the caprice of Mother Nature. Due to its inherently precarious character, it is beyond cultivation, and a semi-tropical wilderness has grown up there, one so dense and primeval that only the occasional glimpse of the sea, far below, is gained from amongst the deep greenery. This is the Undercliff, and it has held a special place in my heart since studying John Fowles's classic novel *The French Lieutenant's Woman*, for A-level English, a quarter of a century ago.

One of our teachers – a gaunt, rather ascetic New Zealander, now sadly dead – knew all too well that the best way to drag a group of lumpen Worcestershire teenagers towards an enthusiasm for Fowles's book was to hit the button marked SEX. This he did with dry aplomb, making us read out loud all the bits where Charles Smithson, the soon-to-be-unbuttoned Victorian hero would delve deep into the Undercliff for assignations with the wild eponymous heroine, Sarah Woodruff (or Meryl Streep in a red fright wig, as she is rather better known). The fertile, damp, earthy Undercliff was everything that the prim cobbles of nearby Lyme Regis were not. It was abandoned and licentious, a steamy green Hades. It was, I think, the first time that I made the connection between a place and its sensual, even sexual, possibilities.

Finally heading to Lyme, a full 25 years later, I came from Woody's house on the edge of Exmoor, and decided to take a look en route at some of the east Devon resorts that had also long been names to which I wanted to put faces. Not really knowing my Exmouth from my Sidmouth, or my Ottery St Mary from my Budleigh Salterton, I decided to trust in the map to tell me. On the OS Explorer, Budleigh Salterton looked appealing: there was something about its leering cliffs, crooked lanes and genteel detached villas that drew me in. Not marked on the map, but even more of a pleasure to discover, was the town's nudist beach. That'd be a symbol I'd like to see on the Explorers. Far more useful than a picnic table or yet another cruddy visitor centre. They could even differentiate in the pictograms whether it's a nudist beach where you have a chance of keeping your dignity, or very firmly not. Budleigh Salterton's would be in the latter category. It's a steep shingle beach, so that if you go for a swim, you have to get out by catching a wave to crash you on to the pebbles, and then scramble on your hands and knees to safety before the next wave gives you an unexpected enema. By the universal law that most of the people on a nudist beach are the ones you'd least like to see naked, it's not a pretty sight.

The OS version of Seaton, by contrast, showed it as spreading away from the sea in a splurge of what looked like interwar housing estates, a tedious delta of Acacia Avenues and Wordsworth Drives. Even the prom looked moribund on the map, and when I arrived there next morning on the bus from Lyme, in order to walk back through the Undercliff, the notion was proved depressingly right. Lyme looks terrific on the map, and so it is. Tight knots of alleys, cuts, tiny streets and warehouses tumble down assorted hills to the beach and to the outstretched claw of the Cobb, the town's massive medieval harbour wall. It was there that we first meet the French Lieutenant's Woman herself, swathed in a jet black cape as she stared out to sea and the waves crashed all around. And if you're not picturing Meryl Streep at this point, you're probably remembering the Scottish Widows advert that shamelessly plundered the movie.

In *The French Lieutenant's Woman*, the path into the Undercliff is ascribed an undeniably moral, or rather immoral, quality. To the monstrous Victorian archetype, Mrs Poulteney, it is, quite literally, the road to ruin. To Charles, it is a way of such beguiling temptation that he is unable to resist parting its ivy fronds and plunging in. You get the picture, I'm sure, and Fowles ladles it on ('an English Garden of Eden') with lip-licking gusto.

It is not just the uniquely jungle-like atmosphere that gives the Undercliff path its heady scent of musky eroticism. History has only augmented the sensation. On Christmas Eve 1839, the greatest landslip of modern times ripped this coast apart, as eight million tonnes of farmland, in a tranche nearly a mile long, detached itself and slid two hundred feet down towards the sea. When it finally juddered to a halt, it had created new chalk cliffs and stranded grass-topped pillars, their freshly exposed whiteness dazzling all who came to see. A vast chalk canyon half a mile wide separated the mainland from the sheared-off section, which quickly became known as Goat Island, a Satyric invocation to a place beyond the rules. A natural lagoon formed at the bottom of the landslip, and Parliament even debated building a deep-water harbour there, though it soon filled with rocks and earth from the initial slide and its after-shocks.

For the tourism business of Lyme Regis, the 1839 landslip could not possibly have come at a better time. The Regency finery of Jane Austen's era, when Lyme came alive as the post-script to the season in Bath, was a fading memory. The Cobb had been spectacularly ruptured in a storm of 1824, blowing five ships out to sea. Although soon rebuilt, better and deeper harbours were springing up all along the coast. Modern sea-side tourism seemed to be the only answer, and, to that end, the resort invested in four bathing machines and braced itself for the future. The Landslip – it was soon capitalised – catapulted it into the big time.

By 1839, the fashion for the picturesque was everywhere. Scenery should be wild, noble and dramatic, and what could possibly be more dramatic than land that had ripped itself asun-der with a mighty roar and a bone-stirring shudder? Even the mountains of Scotland, Wales and the Lakes couldn't compete with that. Visitors came in their droves, on foot, by pony and trap, and by chartered pleasure steamers from Weymouth, Exmouth and Torquay. Locals hired themselves out as guides, embellish-ing their stories of That Fateful Night a little more with every threepenny bit proffered. But the greatest entrepreneurs were the two farmers on whose land the slip had occurred. The paths that soon grew up to steer the visitors around the Landslip – one for the gentlemen, and a less vertiginous one for the ladies – deliberately passed through both farms, and visitors would be efficiently divested of a shiny sixpence at each. Some tried to escape the charges and find their own way, often straying on to the land of a third farm, Little Bindon. The farmer there also charged the going rate of sixpence. Look-outs were employed to ensure that no-one escaped.

The Tourism Enterprise Award for 1840 must however go to James Chappell, the owner of Bindon Farm, on whose land the majority of the Landslip had occurred. By the summer after the slip, up to a thousand tickets a day were being sold, but he saw the potential for even more, and organised a fair for 25 August, culminating in a celebratory reaping of the corn that had continued to grow on Goat Island, the section that had sheared off his fields and now sat in strange isolation hundreds of yards, and a yawning chasm, away. As an added incentive to spectators, the most buxom young ladies were chosen to wield the first scythes, and, by the end of the day, you could purchase – and plenty did – a framed certificate with a few ears of the special corn affixed to it by sealing wax. Through the day, the many beer tents and food stalls, the jugglers and balloons all did a roaring trade, and the evening resounded to the sound of music, dancing and, as darkness fell, no doubt other kinds of merrymaking in the more secluded corners of Goat Island. According to the *Dorset County Chronicle*, 10,000 people had come that day. The Landslip was a goldmine.

So much the worse, then, when the owner of Pinhay Hall, newly built a mile or two from the Landslip towards Lyme, suddenly closed the Undercliff path that linked the town to its cash cow. Although it had been used for centuries by fishermen, stone quarrymen, farmers, labourers, smugglers and Preventive Men, those employed to hunt them out, Mr John Ames of Pinhay was having none of it. He had ideas about building his own arboretum, and didn't want to see it ruined by a daily invasion of erotically charged 'Erberts and 'Arriets. He threw up a wall across the path, declaring that it was not now, and never had been, a right of way.

Lyme Regis seethed. A townsman, Joseph Hayward, decided to take Ames on in the courts. Three different cases took place in swift succession in Exeter, eventually coming down on the side of Hayward and the town. Ames had built a huge bonfire, to be lit as a final two fingers to the townsfolk on his expected victory, but instead he was landed with a court bill of £10,000. Hayward's costs of £1,500 were soon wiped out by an active fundraising programme from amongst Lyme's grateful population. In fury, Ames instead threw up eight-foot-high flint walls through his estate and funnelled the now legally proven right of way through the dank little gap between them.

The Landslip's fame and allure lasted well into the twentieth century. When the tiny little branch railway from Axminster to Lyme Regis was finally opened in 1903, its only intermediate stop was near the hamlet of Combpyne. The station was proudly christened 'Combpyne for Landslip', a name that lasted until the Second World War. Landslip Cottage, now reduced to a few ivy-clad stumps, continued to dole out afternoon teas to visitors into the 1950s. But by then, it was nigh on impossible to see the very features that had made the Landslip such an attraction in its early days. The blindingly white chalk-cliff faces had dulled, the natural harbour was long silted up, and everything was choked by dense vegetation that had been busily reclaiming the broken land for nature.

Today, the area of the landslip - Goat Island and the Chasm, let alone the lagoon - is abandoned to the elements. They are off limits, both officially to preserve the Undercliff's status of nature reserve, but also practically, for you would be ripped to shreds by gorse and brambles if you tried to get through on the paths that the Victorian trippers gouged so effectively out of the newly exposed slopes. Coming from the Seaton end to the west, the Landslip area is only about a third of the way to Lyme, and as I stood and read the interpretation board, drily regurgitating the facts and figures, I gazed up at the still-impressive cliffs of the Chasm, now cloaked in green. Gulls and buzzards circled overhead, but their shrieking began to sound like happy visitors clambering in awe over the rocks and terraces. Awe, and possibly a subterranean pulse of lust. 'Bindon Cliffs: Where the Earth Moves' – even the interpretation board, decorated with its logos of multiple funding agencies, is slyly titled with a nod to its sensuality.

The Landslip – still marked as such on the OS map – comes right at the outset of the Undercliff part of the walk back to Lyme. It's a good introduction to the exuberant fertility of the path, which courses through dense thickets of ash, maple, beech, ivy and what could well be triffids. Yet again, the weather had seen fit to act in the most appropriate manner for my route. In this year of paths, it had been uncanny just how perfectly apposite the conditions had been for each walk. Not a drop of rain had fallen on me in eight April days on the Ridgeway (and the Icelandic ash cloud had cleared the skies of planes for six of them). My walk across Wales had taken place in luscious warmth, with decent cloud cover to prevent me burning on the most open or knackering stretches and luminous sunshine when in the lanes, the woods or the ancient holloways. The night walk across Dartmoor had been under a cloudless sky and a full moon, albeit a slightly shy one. Even the torrential storm on the dreaded Coast to Coast had done its job of permitting me to give it up as a bad job. And in the Undercliff, rain the previous night had dampened everything down, but now a searing, steamy heat was wafting round me as I moved quietly through the jungle. It felt, smelt and sounded so exotically unEnglish. To the Victorians, this must have seemed like a taste of the Empire itself.

This was all the more unexpected when the previous couple of miles of coast path had been so tediously Little English. Seaton promenade, a concrete wall between a shingle beach and drab apartments, was deserted at 9.30 on a midsummer morning. The path then climbs up to a golf course, where the potholed car park makes all too clear the local way: the spaces nearest the club house were reserved, in pecking order of proximity, for the Secretary, the Captain, the Seniors' Captain and the Ladies' Captain. Behind the doors of Dunroamin or Ocean View down in town, someone was plotting the day when that car-park space will be mine, *all mine*.

Golfers had been on my mind a lot while I'd been walking. Mark Twain's immortal observation that 'golf is a good walk spoiled' pretty much sums it up for me, and I'd hated the bits of path, particularly on the Ridgeway, that had taken me across golf courses. As I lumbered past, dripping in sweat and weighed down by a tatty rucksack, I could feel the waves of impatience pulsing off the neatly coiffed, time-is-money businessmen forced to wait until I'd gone. On one course in the Chilterns, I'd been told off for going the wrong way. 'The path is up by the thirteenth,' a snooty lady hissed at me, shooing me out of the way as if I were a cat crapping in her begonias. Golfers and walkers, I concluded, must be almost mutually exclusive circles on a Venn diagram, for there is something almost inherently antipathetic in each towards the other – aesthetically, if nothing else. I'd rather stand and gaze at a landfill tip or a bus station than a golf course. They make my eyes ache, with their fussy uniformity and fake countryside pretensions.

After climbing over the golf course itself, and annoying a few middle managers, you skirt some cornfields and pass a sign warning you of the harshness of the walk from here to Lyme. It's the coast path, but there is no access to the coast, and no way off inland either. You are locked into a six-mile green corridor. The temperature continued to climb as I pounded the copper groove of the path, up and down rough flights of muddy steps, around gargantuan ash trunks, over their roots and through creepers and clearings. Just occasionally, the milky-blue sea would appear far below, its soft splash a welcome, if frustratingly unattainable, antidote to the intense mugginess. The sweat poured off me, and mindful of the overheated headaches that tend to crucify me in such circumstances, I stopped pretty much every mile in order to cool and dry off. By the time I finally reached Lyme, I'd drunk two litres of water, and my head was still throbbing. It was well worth it, though. Twenty-five years after having my teenage hormones recklessly stirred by John Fowles's take on the Undercliff, their rather creakier fortysomething heirs had twitched in eager accord.

Thank God I'd walked in the direction I did, though. After the furtive, oozing jungle of the Undercliff, popping out of it into the seaside starch of Seaton would have been a horrible shock. Dropping down into Lyme is a definite change of tempo, but it's a destination still odd enough to maintain the illusion that you've left normality far behind. I sauntered to the end of the Cobb, along its hunched serpentine back, before ambling down the bright little prom that links it with the town centre. This, I was chuffed to find, was named Ozone Terrace, a fine memento of chin-up Victoriana. If Seaton fancy rebranding their prom, I'd like to suggest Bromide Boulevard.

For all my lack of enthusiasm at the idea of doing a whole coast-path walk, there is something wonderfully anti-prissy about them. Just look at the cover of any OS Explorer map to see the officially prescribed ways in which we're supposed to interact with our countryside – on a bike, on a designated bike trail, in a helmet; on horseback, through the heather in a hi-vis tabard and a helmet; perhaps climbing a rockface, in shoulder pads, knee pads and a helmet; in a small sailing boat on a Home Counties reservoir, in a lifejacket and . . . you get the picture. In fact, you've got the picture, probably dozens of them, the grinning faces of corporatised leisure all fully concordant with section 14, paragraph 6 of the relevant health and safety legislation.

By contrast, take a coast-path walk, and hear the existential howl of your flimsy mortality every couple of minutes. Some of them are spectacularly terrifying, the unfenced path snaking its way along vertiginous, unstable cliffs and down muddy scree slopes, with just jagged rocks and the restless crash of the ocean to break a fall. In these cotton-wool times, it hardly seems possible that they're still legal, let alone to be yet further encouraged as the plans for a nationwide coast path tiptoe forwards. I recently heard a talk by a warden from the Pembrokeshire Coast National Park about their coast path. It was basically a litany of deaths, injuries and problems landing the helicopter ambulance. Apparently, injuries peak in the autumn, when seal pups are born and walkers go that little bit further to have a good look through their binoculars or to take the perfect pho . . . to . . . *bump.*

Dicing with danger is good for us, and paths, for all their quiet charm, can offer some unexpectedly hair-raising experiences. After the Undercliff, the one section of British coast path I was most keen to try was the Elie chain walk, in Scotland. Part of the splendid Fife Coast Path, the section at Elie is a kind of *via ferrata*, or 'iron way', where you have to haul yourself up and down cliffs using chains bolted into the rockface. It is great fun: enough of a challenge to demand real concentration and give some hairy moments, especially if you're prone to vertigo, yet easy enough for most to attempt. The path is also supremely beautiful, as the chains take you into coves and gulches that you'd never reach otherwise, and have you hanging above pounding blue waves if you time it right. It's no idle leisure path either, for the chains were initially installed sometime in the early twentieth century to allow local fishermen access to remoter corners of the coast.

Purists will sniff at the idea that Elie is a proper *via ferrata*, as you don't have to clip yourself on to the chains and there's little danger of a serious injury. There is a commercial one now in the Lake District, along an old slate miners' path, but for proper terror, you need to go abroad. The most infamous *via ferrata* in Europe is in the Tatra mountains of southern Poland. The Orla Perć (Eagle's Path) was established in 1901, and climbs up sheer rock faces to over seven and half thousand feet. Dozens have died attempting it. Even that doesn't qualify as the continent's most terrifying path, though, a title that surely belongs to El Camino del Rey (King's Path) in Andalucia, southern Spain. A one-metre-wide walkway built in 1905 on to the side of a sheer cliff, it was originally used to ferry workers between two hydro-electric schemes. Parts of it have completely crumbled away, leaving just a metal girder to edge along, with a drop of up to 700 feet below. Even looking at the various videos on YouTube of young desperadoes walking the *camino* was enough to make me swoon.

Welded as they are to totting up their Munros, Nuttalls, Marilyns and all the other sub-divisions they've invented for Britain's modest mountains, Wainwrighty types would contend that Britain's most dangerous path is something like Striding Edge on Helvellyn, or one of its fellow glacial arêtes, such as Crib Goch on Snowdon or Carn Mór Dearg on Ben Nevis. These knife-edge paths have all the right ingredients, and there have been accidents galore, but I think my nomination for the country's deadliest path is coastal. It's still marked on the map as a right of way, but unless you really know what you're doing, your chances of surviving it are slender.

Even on the OS, it looks like no other. Crossing the shifting sands of Morecambe Bay in Lancashire, the path arcs out from Hest Bank, ploughing a course so determined that alarm bells start ringing, for, more than any other path on the map, it looks to be all theory and no practice. The smooth line courses across seven miles of sandbank, mudflat and estuary, disgorging itself on the other side of the bay at Kents Bank, to the south of Grange-over-Sands. Before the turnpikes and railways, this was the only route across to Furness from the main body of Lancashire; a coach service ran six days a week until the railway opened in 1857. One of its last trips saw ten farm workers drown on their way to a hiring fair, when the coach driver, who was reported to be drunk, lost control in the middle of the sands and was subsumed by the tide.

Standing at Hest Bank, on the edge of the bay, I watched

the sea sweep in. At first, it was low tide, when there are 120 square miles of sand in the bay, gleaming gold and silver against the fantastical backdrop of the Lakeland fells. Within half an hour, the whole bay was covered by water, and as I watched it race in faster than any man could escape it, I shuddered at the thought of being caught out there, in the cold, in the mist, in the gloopy half-world between land and sea. Remembering the 23 Chinese cockle-pickers who drowned there one winter's night in 2004, so lost and confused and far from home, I felt physically sick.

The map makes it clear: 'WARNING – Public rights of way across Morecambe Bay are dangerous. Seek local guidance.' Signs on the bank make it equally plain: 'Do not attempt to cross without the Official Guide.' Since 1963, that's meant digging out Cedric Robinson, the Queen's Guide to the Sands, a post that dates back to the sixteenth century. It comes with an honorarium of £15 a year, the tenancy of Guides Farm, overlooking the sands at Kents Bank, and a modicum of danger: at least one of his predecessors has drowned on the job. Using nothing more sophisticated than a lifetime's knowledge, a stick and a whistle, Cedric steers some 10,000 people a year across, mainly on charity walks (it seems to be today's version of the Lyke Wake Walk, which is reason enough to be cautious). The designated route of the path on the map is irrelevant, as the river channels and quicksands are in a state of constant flux; every crossing is different. When the railway first arrived, numbers crossing the sands plummeted. Tramps continued to use it, however, and sometimes the Queen's Guide of the day was known to give a tramp the rail fare to get across, so that he wouldn't have to bother. This became something of a legend in the tramping fraternity, and others soon showed up in some number to claim their free pennies.

Should it still be marked on the OS? I'm not sure that it should, for it must invite people to think that it's more passable than it really is. I tried walking out where it's marked on the map, and couldn't get further than a couple of hundred yards before coming across wobbly sands, apparently firm bits that suddenly gave way and treacherous, fast-flowing channels of water. When the first local authority definitive maps were being drawn up in the early 1950s, the path wasn't included, but the local secretary of the Ramblers' Association lodged an objection, which was upheld. When the route was reclassified in the early 1990s, there were suggestions that it should, for the sake of both safety and wildlife, be extinguished, but again rambling fundamentalists, glued to their dogma of once a path, always a path, managed to stop the idea after a lengthy, and expensive, public enquiry. Perhaps the most avid amongst them could exercise their right with a lovely Boxing Day walk on the path that they've so bravely saved. Sticking to the exact line on the map, of course. And without Cedric.

Not only are we surrounded by water, internally we drip and gush from every pore. Fly over Britain and it's the sunlight suddenly glancing off the surface of so many rivers, canals and lakes that both impresses and moves us the most. On a global scale, our rivers – and indeed all of our natural features – are tiny, but within our own insular microcosm, they are mighty.

Being the capital's grubby sewer, and the waterway in which we are most encouraged to admire our national reflection, the

Thames is the river that bags most of our national adulation. The only consolation for those of us infected with an inverted snobbery against southern England is that, however much it is lauded and loved, the Thames will never be as long as the Severn. It will always be in second place. There are many in Ireland who have the same pride that the Shannon trumps both of Britain's major rivers.

Both the Thames and the Severn have named paths following them, but it is the Thames Path that has been elevated to the status of National Trail. It was first considered as one of the first wave of long-distance paths in the early 1950s, but took until 1996 to be officially completed. Passing as it does some of the most sumptuous real estate in England, there were plenty of ruffled feathers to be smoothed about the idea of having the hoi polloi walking past their boathouses and helipads. Not that such problems were anything new. In the 150 miles between Cricklade and Teddington Lock, the path crosses the river 28 times; a hangover from the days when wealthy landowners refused to allow the towpath through the end of their garden, forcing bargees and their horses across the water on ferries as the path switched sides. If you want the spirit of the Thames Path, look no further than the brass plaque facing walkers at the foot of a particularly lavish garden in Dorney Reach, between Windsor and Maidenhead. 'No Stopping – Right of Way Only' it barks, and who would dare disagree?

The path itself has a slightly different profile to most other long-distance routes. For starters, the people walking it are generally younger than you'll find elsewhere, especially in London, where the largest slice of the demographic is 25–34-year-olds. They also feel unable to put a foot into a boot without tweeting and blogging about it, uploading their photos of every boat, bridge and bar on to Facebook and/or bespoke websites especially created for The Project. It always is The Project. They make it sound as if they're hoping to crack the Enigma code or solve the Middle East problem, rather than take a gentle, flattish stroll through southern England. And not even that, for many of them. Terrified of the lands beyond Zone 6, they're only doing the stretch from Hampton Court to the Thames Barrier, but boy, do we hear about every inch of the way. And see it photographed. Videoed too, if we're lucky. And measured. And mapped; interactively, of course. Looking at all that is more exhausting than doing the bloody walk. Takes longer too.

I take the mick, but I adore walking in London. As a student there in the late eighties, I'd often roll home on foot from a night's excess in the West End, past the pimps and dealers of King's Cross, the goths of Camden, through the kebab alleys of Kentish Town, and the au pair avenues of Hampstead and Highgate. These were the occasions when I most felt part of the city, one tiny cog in a gargantuan, greasy machine that never stopped roaring. The drunkenness helped, I think, blurring the harsh edges of daytime into impressionistic splashes of neon and reflections in puddles. With the collars of my leather jacket turned up against the cold, I shimmied through, feeling like Morrissey, but probably looking more like a walking Soft Cell album cover.

These days, my London walks are a little less dissolute. One of the best lately was from the Tower of London to Hyde Park Corner, via some of the many lovely eighteenth-century churches and old alleyways of the City, and the gluttonous boulevards of the West End. It was hearing my excitement about this walk that made my partner agree to accompany me on the Thames Path from the Barrier for what was planned to be a full day's romantic promenade into central London. We landed on the north side of the river, in order to take a look at the Thames Barrier Park, and then realised that we had to cross the water to reach the path. The nearest option was walking up to catch the Woolwich Ferry, a treat I'd long been keen to sample. I can't say he looked too excited by the prospect, and the flyblown streets of Silvertown, its derelict railway and the belching silos of the Tate & Lyle plant didn't much help, but the rust-bucket ferry across the river was fun, and Woolwich looked interesting. Until we docked, anyway.

I'd promised him breakfast, and pulled out all the stops by getting us a bacon bap from a caravan in a car park. It was enough to send us on our way to North Greenwich and the Millennium Dome. This is another place I'd never been to, and it both fascinated and horrified me. I felt as if we'd been shrunk, like Raquel Welch in *Fantastic Voyage*, though instead of being pumped into a scientist's arteries, we'd been dropped into an architect's model. And one that they'd given up on half-way through, by the looks of things.

The Dome, that cathedral of political hubris, might well have been rescued and reborn as the O2 Arena, but it was still looking mighty tatty, with stains leeching down its sides and acres of redevelopment debris surrounding it. That's all to change, though, at least according to the massive hoardings everywhere advertising this as yet another brand-new waterside quarter of London. The images were all of glossy people surfing on laptops and sipping lattes in funky bars, bluebells in woods, ducks splashing and sunshine dancing on water – well, isn't that exactly what springs to mind when you think of Legoland houses built on a reclaimed toxic sludge pit? 'Greenwich Peninsula: A place where you can' was their slogan. Fill in your own punchline.

This demesne of plasticity and promise was a strange contrast with the gruff solidity of the river itself; the wharves, factories, chimneys and container ships, even the reed beds, swans and geese. Across the water, the towers of Canary Wharf glittered icily, looking way beyond reach or even belief. 'This is great, isn't it?' I enthused to my cariad. 'Hmmmm,' he replied, which I took as a yes. We turned the corner of the peninsula and headed down towards Greenwich, but the Thames Path wasn't playing. Signs announced a diversion, but it soon petered out and left us wandering hopelessly through industrial estates, along a busy dual carriageway, past cranes and concrete mixers, under CCTV cameras and hoops of razor wire. Eventually, after many wrong turns, we landed in the gentrified streets that announced our imminent arrival in Greenwich. 'Er, I think I'll go and see the Chelsea Physic Garden,' he muttered as we sank a pint in the Cutty Sark Tavern on the quay. He was off before I could say, 'But hang on in there, it's Deptford and Rotherhithe next.' Returning that evening, he pointedly compared the two halves of his day: my trip in the morning through noxious mud and rusty dereliction, his trip in the afternoon along perfumed walkways and shimmering walls of fern.

So much for the Thames. The Severn is my river – I grew up by it, went to school right next to it and have its source just a few miles from where I live in the otherwise foreign mountains. When I was considering moving to Wales, the Severn was the thread that kept me linked to all that had come before: it was the liquid guarantee that my old life and my new life could be bridged. I've paddled and swum in it, waded through it, fallen into it, skimmed stones across it, picnicked and gossiped and canoodled on its banks, sailed down it in dinghies, a narrowboat, a raft, a kayak, a party boat and even, between the two Severn Bridges, a 400-tonne sand dredger.

The Severn Way is the path that attempts to follow the river from its source on Pumlumon, a mountain disguised as an upland sponge, squatting like a fat, dripping toad in the very middle of Wales. On any old map, from the fourteenth-century Gough Map to those derived from the Tudor splendours of Saxton and Speed, Pumlumon is shown as Snowdon's equal, despite being only the 49th-highest peak in Wales. It wasn't the physical reality of the mountain being mapped, but its reputation; a place to bewilder and disorientate invaders coursing into Wales from the east. It's likely too that such cartographic prominence was a nod to the mountain's place as the birthplace of two great national rivers, the Severn and the Wye. The Severn Way steers quite a haphazard course, for there are many stretches of the river jealously guarded and out of bounds, so that you can sometimes walk it for hours without actually seeing the Severn itself. With only the slightest hint of disingenuousness, this is presented on the website promoting the trail as 'the Severn Way does not simply follow riverside paths, but is routed to help the walker make the most of the countryside.' There is a point there, I suppose, for sometimes it is good to break the hypnotic allure of the water and see a little more of the context of its sinuous course.

The best bits of the Severn Way, though, are undoubtedly the riverside stretches. Once it gets into its stride, the river is such a languid beast, and to follow it for mile after mile, with no need to check the map or work out where's next, is an easy thrill like no other. My finest walk on it was the most recent, a day in May with my dad strolling from Worcester back up to his home near Stourport. We'd started the previous day on the Malvern Hills, at the border of Worcestershire and Herefordshire. Far below on the plain, the Severn beckoned us. It was a huge relief to meet it after a hot day's walk across the dusty fields, even if we were doing so at one of its least appealing spots, directly beneath the new bypass bridge to the south of Worcester. We had to cross the bypass during evening rush hour, a moment that brought home just how quickly – in less than one day's walking – we'd become completely desensitised to traffic. Dad and I stood timidly on the pavement, waiting for a break in the traffic that never came. Stone-faced drivers glared at us incomprehensibly as they slid by. After about ten minutes of nervy near-starts, a coach driver on the far lane took pity on us and stopped his bus for a couple of minutes, until there was enough of a break in the nearside stream of cars to let us scurry across.

Walking into Worcester, the path was diverted through the old wharfside district of Diglis. This is yet to be tarted up into some futureslum marina: the recession has stopped much of the transformation for now, so that half-built showpiece apartments sit under a carapace of new weeds. But there have always been plenty of people living down here, in streets of redbrick terraces tucked alongside little factories and warehouses. Diversion signs soon vanished, but suddenly the more powerful pointers of ancient memory brought it all back.

'This is the football field where I scored my only ever goal,' I squeaked to my dad. My sporting career must have been a sore point for him. A keen rugby player, he'd been desperate for a baby boy to follow in his studs, and had got me instead. At the age of eleven, I was the tallest in my class: this – and only this – had helped me inadvertently win the 100 metres dash on sports day. The rugby teacher pounced, and I was briefly placed in the First XV to bring a bit of speed to the front row. My strategy to get out of the team was to be as useless as possible, to drop every catch, trip over my own feet, squeal like a girl in the line-out and collapse the scrum if needs be (creating a sweaty, panting pile of lads was just an added bonus). There was no need to pretend. I was pathetic, and sent instead to play football, the school equivalent of the remedial class.

Even that was graded, and I was at the bottom. The better kids were sent over the river to the school playing fields, spectacularly located alongside the Worcestershire County Cricket Ground on New Road. This is always cited as one of the loveliest grounds anywhere, with its eternally Constable view of river meadows crowned by the soaring Gothic of the cathedral. Those of us in the bottom group were packed off instead to the Diglis Rec, a scabby mud-bath of a pitch enclosed by terraced streets and industrial estates. Failing miserably to do anything of interest with the ball were me and the other bookish jessies, together with the lads in bottle-bottom specs, the ones with one leg six inches shorter than the other and one gang in oversized old-man's shorts who always coagulated around one of the goal posts, discussing algebraic formulae. Even amongst that illustrious crowd, I only ever managed one goal, but it is etched indelibly into my recollection, for there will never be another.

There were more memories of my sporting inadequacy as we made our way back to the river's quay. Rowers from the school and city boat clubs swooshed past in the late-afternoon sunshine, lighting up the river with aqualine diamonds from their oars. I'd brought my partner here for the first time a year previously, on another perfect May evening. We'd sat on the lawn of the neighbouring hotel, sipping gin and tonics, watching the sun dapple on the Severn as the sculls glided noiselessly by. At just that moment, the deep bells of the cathedral began their peal towards the strike of six o'clock. I think it was quite an eye-opener for him, the son of a Welsh hill farmer. 'God, this is like England in a bottle,' he gasped. We laughed; it really was. Bronzed, confident people barked into their mobiles from behind designer shades. Ice tinkled in glasses; a heron soared by. Everything – the lawns, the flowers, the river, the faces – looked as if it had been starched and pressed. And the gap felt as wide now as it had then.

I've always loved Worcester's quayside path from Diglis, as much under grey skies and winter floods as on a bright-green May evening. In fact, the regular floods were probably my favourite, because this often meant sport would be cancelled, if the school playing fields on the opposite bank were under water too (although still firmly in the bottom group, I'd graduated by now from Diglis Rec). It was no guarantee, however. Frequently, we were sent wading along the towpath, through fast, filthy water, in order to reach the bridge and the other side. Various sports teachers seemed to compete in just how high they would allow the water to be before grudgingly calling off the afternoon's running around. A quite terrifying thigh-high was deemed acceptable by some of the more Neanderthal members of staff – almost inevitably, the ones who also taught geography. I don't think there ever was a member of the geography department who didn't teach sport as well; it was obviously deemed the softest touch for the intellectually compromised, a fact that always rankled in me. You never found a PE teacher in the physics lab.

Down by the Water Gate, from where the cathedral ferry plied across to the other side (a practice occasionally revived lately), there are numerous plaques and carved stones in the sandstone wall, recording the maximum height of various Severn floods since 1672. Despite the breathless insistence that our water levels are rising and that floods will be both more frequent and more deadly, the wall stoically refuses to confirm or deny it. 1672, two days before Christmas, was the first mark, and it is still the highest, well over six feet above the towpath. Then, in order, come 1947, 2007 and 1886. Global-warning sirens could doubtless find a pattern there to alarm us. Those who believe the exact opposite probably could too.

The difference between the Severn and the Thames can best be seen in the towns and cities that line their banks. The Thames, Father of the nation, comes to its triumphal climax through London, after having watered mellow Cotswold burghs, rich and plump as far back as the medieval wool trade, the dreaming spires of Oxford, luscious market towns like Abingdon, Henley and Windsor, and the capital's most prestigious outer burbs, such as Richmond and Kew. With the sole exception of unlovely Reading, it is a 200-mile thread of luxury, desirability and the most consistently expensive property in the land.

Not so the Severn, its supposedly senior sister. The Thames spends the nation's cash, while the Severn earns it. The great river-side palaces of the Thames – Kelmscott, Cliveden, Windsor Castle, Hampton Court, Ham House, Westminster itself and Greenwich – are the epicentres of power and prestige. Its Severnside equivalents – Elmore, Ashleworth, Chaceley, Ribbesford, Dowles Manor, Dudmaston Hall, Attingham, Powis – are new money incarnate, the homes of industrialists and chancers, those destined never quite to make the grade. And although there are plenty of handsome towns along the route of the Severn, almost all are a little blowsy and chipped around the edges, battered by successive waves of wealth and poverty. The river's three great county towns – Shrewsbury, Worcester and Gloucester – have many handsome corners, but often laid cheek-by-jowl with dereliction and some truly grotty post-war development. One of Britain's most handsome Georgian streets, Bridge Street in Worcester, is a fine case in point: the classically proportioned houses thick with grime and dust from three lanes of traffic hurtling down to the main city bridge.

After a night at a farmhouse B&B to the north of Worcester, Dad and I walked the last section home. In the distance, we could hear the thrum of traffic on the main A449 dual carriageway, a road we'd both ploughed up and down thousands of times. For ten years, I'd commuted to school every day by train on the same route. Yet neither of us had ever walked it, despite this stretch of the Severn from Worcester to Stourport being the riverside walk of your fantasies. It is stunning. Sometimes, the path snuck surreptitiously through dark little woods, over tree roots and stiles, at other times it shimmered into the distance as a green swathe through buttercup-filled meadows. Bluebells, anemones, campion and comfrey danced in our wake. Clouds of pink and white hawthorn blossom leaned down to meet us, and all the while, the flat beer-coloured river sidled quietly by. It was like walking through one of those sentimental Edwardian watercolours you see on the walls of pubs.

There were also copious hints of the world that appeared from the other side of the Great War, in the shape of the chalets and other nuggets of arcadia that littered the banks. These are everywhere along the Severn, much-needed boltholes for metal-bashing Midlanders, for whom the coast was an unimaginable distance away. Some had been craftily rebuilt into more permanent structures, many remained as basic and wooden as the day they were knocked up, only the addition of a satellite dish nodding to the modern world. Dinghies, picnic chairs, gnomes, flags and barbeques were squeezed on to rickety verandahs, while old cars rusted away alongside. The chalet sites, often strung like a cheap necklace along the riverbank, alternated with the more regimented atmosphere of the caravan parks, squadrons of big metal boxes lined up like tanks. Leathery pensioners in shorts and sandals nodded politely as we trotted past.

The workaday spirit of the Severn showed itself again, when the path veered away from the riverbank for a mile or so leading up to Thomas Telford's bridge at Holt, half-way between Worcester and Stourport. I'd managed – and not for the first time – to misread the map, so we ended up having to scale gates and hurry through the middle of a busy quarry, past young workers picking asparagus in a dusty field, before being reunited with the official path and led right through the middle of a strange cluster of light industrial units: a caravan sales office, a catering company, an equine supplies set-up, a charity headquarters and who knows what else, all getting on with it in the quiet of the Worcestershire countryside. As an ex-pat Midlander, I always feel absurdly proud of these odd little industrial estates that you stumble across almost anywhere in the region. Queen Victoria famously demanded that the blinds be drawn as her train passed through the smouldering hubbub of the Black Country, but she didn't know what she was missing. These numerous units, churning out widgets, sprockets, gizmos and thingummies galore, fascinate me, and I'm always glued to the window as the train trundles through any part of the West Midlands, full of ignorant appreciation of these hives of entrepreneurship by the line. People still making stuff! In this day and age! It seems little short of a miracle. That they're probably manufacturing bits of weaponry for dodgy regimes is where I choose to draw my curtains.

One of the many blogs about the Thames Path that I read called it 'a 180-mile pub crawl'. It's a good point. Waterside boozers are some of the best of all, the presence of unhurried swans and weeping willows somehow hypnotising us into kicking back and having another round, and then perhaps – oh, go on – another one after that. No worries about breathalysers when you're walking either. On the Severn Way with my dad, I'd purposely chosen our overnight stop for its proximity to a remote riverside pub that I'd loved in my early drinking days, but hadn't been back to for 20 years. He'd never been at all, and I was nervous that it would have changed beyond recognition. It hadn't, not in the slightest, and we had a wonderful evening in there, eating hearty stew and drinking well-earned pint after pint of Flowers IPA, while the pub's peacocks crowed outside and the setting sun turned the river into pink fire.

The relaxing quality of paths by water is their strongest card, and it's in marked contrast to the nerdy competitiveness on some of the upland trails. They are also the paths that most easily lend themselves to sensual suggestion. 'Footpaths are our routes to a licensed intimacy with the landscape, to a carnal knowledge of nature,' wrote poet Kim Taplin, and it is far easier to appreciate her point in a luscious water-meadow than a force nine gale on the side of a craggy fell. I remembered the steamy fertility of the path through the Undercliff, with the sea plashing gently far below, but walking through the landscape in which I'd grown up reminded me too of my clunky schoolboy attempts at seduction, most of which seemed to occur on out-of-sight waterside paths.

There was the Severn, of course, but rather more frequently, it was on the extensive Midland network of canal towpaths that I, and many of my mates, had our first snogs and gropes. Before they were transformed by ersatz waterside apartments, the canals were semi-derelict threads of illicit possibility – not just sex, but bottles of cider, ciggies, a much-prized joint if someone had managed to nick a tiny blim from their older brother. They formed an alluring no man's land, beyond the grumpy rules of adulthood. Our Narnia, our *Secret Garden*, was reached through a broken archway in a Victorian wall, through muddy puddles and thickets of nettles.

The possibility of sex, even if it came only in finding some jettisoned copy of *Forum* on the towpath, raised also the possibility of danger. Paths anywhere could be tainted with this, but none more so than the towpaths or the alleys, snickets, ginnels and shuts that twisted their way through every urban wilderness. The reputation is still there today. Although you are far more likely to be flashed at or felt up on the Tube or in a motorway service station, it is paths that are instantly demonised on the thankfully rare occasions that something awful happens on their route. Even when it hasn't, siren voices still demand the closure of urban paths, just in case. A favourite place for kids to gather and let off steam is enough to bring on the hysterical opprobrium, for who knows what they might get up to if we don't put a stop to it now?

This is the Nicholas van Hoogstraten mindset, the idea that paths are places only for flashers, perverts and reprobates. It's the golfer-rambler split again too. Walking paths, themselves a penetration of an otherwise unattainable landscape, can indeed be a woozily erotic experience, and who's to deny that bubbling over perhaps into quiet coitus in a shady nook? Chances are it won't, but no harm in letting the possibility carouse through your veins. Perverts, say the men who do the decent, normal thing by shagging their secretaries in Premier Inns just off the M1, and getting the boys from the golf club to cover for them. What kind of weirdo gets his kicks that way when there are five lap-dancing clubs in the vicinity and two pages of escort ads in the evening paper? The kind who's too tight to pay, that's who. Thinks sex is free! Bastard.

In an age much less brutally sexualised, the paths were where you went courting, and waterside strolls were the most romantic of all. To writers like Henry James, Alfred Tennyson, William Wordsworth, E. M. Forster, Flora Thompson and Edward Thomas, paths were used as both settings and metaphors for erotic charge. In many of his works, most famously *Lady Chatterley's Lover*, D. H. Lawrence made much of the connection between illicit trespass on land and forbidden pleasures of the body. And in the Wessex of Thomas Hardy, the public paths were often the venue for idle, hopeful dalliance. Almost all of the various courtships in *Far from the Madding Crowd* – its title even tailor-made to the theme – take place on paths, such as the 'sunken groove between the embowing thicket' where Gabriel Oak lures Bathsheba in order to warn her against Sergeant Troy.

My teenage years hadn't only been about canal-side fumbles, fags and cider; I'd nurtured a pretty serious Thomas Hardy habit for a while as well. Digging out my old books, there was one I'd never read, and it promised much on the subject of paths. *The Woodlanders* is set around the village of Little Hintock, deep within the 'fine old English gloom' of a great Dorset forest. The characters and the paths through the wood are both carefully delineated in a strict order of respectability: on Midsummer Eve, the 'hoydenish maiden of the hamlet' (i.e. village bike), the splendidly named Suke Damson, lures dastardly Fitzpiers into her gusset by leading him as she 'glided on her path, the moon whitening her hot blush away'. When hero Giles Winterbourne is forced by bankruptcy into a distant hovel, the only way his true love Grace Melbury can reach him is along 'the mossy cart track under the trees which led into the depths of the woods'. No good can come of it, of course, and with grinding Hardyesque inevitability Giles dies shortly afterwards, having taken, all too literally, the wrong path.

Even the way of walking, and not just which route they took, becomes indicative of social status in Hardy's highly charged microcosm. Grace's parents fervently hope that she'll achieve a better class of marriage than to stockman Giles. 'Fancy her white hands getting redder every day, and her tongue losing its pretty up-country curl in talking, and her bounding walk becoming the regular Hintock shail-and-wamble,' her father laments. His wife's reply is legendary: 'She may shail; but she'll never wamble.'

Shailing, wambling and a whole host of other more earthy activities can be much enjoyed on what is probably my favourite footpath anywhere. Deep down in the south Wales valley of the

River Hepste at Sgwd yr Eira, the 'fall of snow', there is a path running behind the curtain of water as it tumbles down from an overhang of rock. If you're feeling particularly bold, you can even dive from the path, through the waterfall, and into the plunge pool below: an intoxicating thrill when the afternoon sun is hitting it square on and you have to launch yourself through a glittering wall of water. The path behind the fall is on the map as a fully fledged right of way, and was a useful short cut for drovers on their way from Carmarthenshire to the east. Cattle, and perhaps pigs and sheep too, would generally have been coaxed through the river, but some must have needed herding along the wet limestone ledge, the crash of the water drowning out the bleating, the squealing and the shouting of the drovers.

Sgwd yr Eira is a popular destination for walkers, probably the most loved of all the magical waterfalls in this narrow limestone belt at the base of the Brecon Beacons. One special ingredient is that it's at least two miles from the nearest place to park a car, which immediately rules out the vast majority of day trippers. I once spent a baking June afternoon there, lazily cooling off in the plunge pool and idling away hours on a sun-grilled rock platform. A dozen or two people came and went during that time. Most were couples, and nearly all arrived in thunderously bad moods, at least 50 yards separating them, tense and tetchy after sniping rows and numerous wrong turns. Clouds of flies hung over every sweaty forehead. Migraines had started, relationships almost ended, for the paths to the waterfall run through dense forests, and getting lost is a near inevitability. But the magic began to work almost immediately. Wordlessly, each couple would gradually begin to gel back together. Little glances of contrition turned into broad smiles, cooler brows and – before long – furtive searches of the woods for a quiet place to cement their reinvigorated enthusiasm, perhaps even with some of their own bleating, grunting and squealing. A path and water are a fiendishly potent combination, one to stir the most primal of senses, and thank the gods for that.

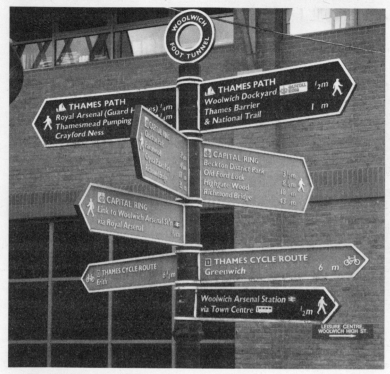

'Which way now at Woolwich?'

9. THE STILE POLICE

You're never alone on a footpath. Really, you're not. There are whole armies of people just out of view, dedicated to defining it, mapping it, marking it, measuring it, arguing over it, trimming it, cutting it, diverting it, refusing to divert it, promoting it, signing it, defending it and – last and, it seems, somewhat least – walking it. These little slivers of common land, wending their way across the jealousy guarded patchwork of the British countryside, might seem to the casual eye to be the physical embodiment of unchanging simplicity itself, but that is often just tricksy illusion. Our footpath network is as fought over and frenetic, as subject to the whims of fashion and fancy, as any other part of our national infrastructure.

At the front line of the battle are the assorted Rights of Way (RoW) officers employed by almost every local authority in the land. In my own county, there are around 20 of them, although it doesn't sound quite so many when you remember that this is Powys, bigger than 31 sovereign independent nations, and with over 6,000 miles of public rights of way, the largest total, along with North Yorkshire, of any British local authority. At the other end of the spectrum are various urban unitary authorities, where responsibility for the few dozen miles of rights of way is sometimes part of the parks division or the museums.

Bringing all of these local authority workers together is the Institute for Public Rights of Way (IPROW), an organisation that, in these days of swingeing public-sector cuts, is feeling beleaguered indeed – as are its members out in the civic centres and county halls of Britain. Cutting expenditure on RoW teams is an irresistibly soft target to most politicians, for it is certain to provoke far fewer grim headlines than axing a child-care centre, a few teachers or the weekly dustbin collection.

I was warned, therefore, to expect dark clouds of doom when I attended the recent IPROW conference in Cambridge. This is the annual get-together of local authority RoW officers plus a sprinkling of consultants, speakers and exhibitors. Civic belt-tightening meant that the conference was about half the size of the previous year's, but there were still around 80 of us there, and with an impressive array of job titles straight out of *The Office*: Rural Network Manager, Rights of Way Improvement Plan Officer, Enforcement Officer, Principal Access Officer, Public Rights of Way Manager, Senior Definitive Map Officer, RoW Team Leader, Access Assistant, Estates Management Officer, Public Rights of Way Warden, GIS Officer, Greenspace Manager, Countryside Access Officer and Strategic Countryside Access Officer, Head of Recreation and Access, National Trail Executive, Projects and Enforcement Team Leader. I would have liked those with 'Enforcement' in their job titles to have looked more the part, but everyone seemed to be drawn from a pool of quite kind, vaguely progressive types wanting to make the world a better place, even if that meant having to wear a fleece branded with your county council logo and whatever meaningless slogan they were using these days.

It hit me suddenly that, had things worked out only slightly differently, I'd have been at that conference as a mildly harassed RoW officer from some obscure unitary authority in the Midlands ('North-East Borsetshire: Right at the Heart – *of Life!*'). There were quite a few folk there who looked like me: balding and greying fortysomethings clinging to the last vestige of their radical youth by still wearing Doc Martens and keeping an earring in. Twenty years ago, when we were tiptoeing uncertainly into our careers, the public sector RoW movement was undergoing considerable expansion, as it has continued to do up to the current era of cuts. People who liked maps, looking stuff up in records offices and a bit of a walk, and whose blood bubbled at the blocked paths they encountered thereon, charged like right-on bull elephants into the growing RoW teams of local councils, certain that they had found both a job and a cause.

One delegate, who'd come to her post after years in a dog-eat-dog corner of the private sector, sighed to me that, lovely though many of her fellow RoW officers were, they were a bit hopeless at the nitty-gritty bits of the job, namely standing up to entrenched opposition, be it from long-standing landowners or other vested interests. She singled out a particular delegate for praise. 'He's an ex-copper, and he does the job exactly as you'd expect an ex-copper to do,' she said. 'He serves a 28-day enforcement order on anyone who's wilfully blocking a path, looking them straight in the eye as he does it, and explains it in crystal-clear detail. They know that he means it, and he'll be back to check exactly twenty-eight days later. He has a very high success rate, while many of the others . . .' She tailed off, but I knew precisely what she meant. Someone who'd come into the job from a marketing background told me that there was a critical need to market rights of way to their potential customers. 'Doesn't that already happen?' I asked. He grunted. 'Just look at them. Nice people, but not sales folk.'

In an attempt to launch the conference with upbeat aspiration instead of depressed scythe-sharpening, the first session split us into six groups, each one given a random piece of household ephemera, boxed and wrapped beautifully in some sheets of a local authority's definitive map. Our instructions were simple. We were to ponder the gift and see in just how many ways we could link it with rights of way and the budget pressures of the moment. Nothing was too oblique or tangential; we must think, even dream, the impossible.

Inside our box was a foot-long plastic cable tie – the sort you use to, well, affix one thing to another. There was a sheet of instructions too, but these were ignored as the group charged headlong into freeform thinking about the many and varied ways our footpath network could be compared to a cable tie. They are both flexible, suggested someone. And simple, ubiquitous and reliable, added someone else. And beautiful, I heard myself offer, not something I'd ever thought about a cable tie before. They can be used for business or pleasure, said someone else. You can join two or more together. We were an orgy of positive thinking, but not for long. 'They're both taken for granted,' someone grumped. 'Remove them and things fall apart.' 'If you cut and cut a cable tie,' someone else chipped in, 'it becomes less and less useful.'

When it came to the report-back session, our group acquitted themselves very well. I'd presumed that we'd come off quite poorly in the gift stakes, having had to waffle around a cable tie for

45 minutes, but it seemed not. The group with the AAA battery didn't have much to say ('we offer an AAA service,' 'we must have energy'), while receiving a plaster with a logo on it made another lot bang on about the idea of commercial sponsorship of particular paths. The Anusol Ridgeway, bring it on. More inspiring were the ideas from the group who had the best present, a small Lara Croft doll, which seemed to act like a shamanic totem to them, inspiring them to ever-greater heights of rebelliousness. 'We need to break rules!' they hollered. 'So much of what we do is inflexible, too rigid and becomes counter-productive! We're too bogged down by legal processes!' I half-expected the session to end in lawless uproar, a flash mob of Rights of Way officers storming out and barricading Cambridge City Council HQ with their fleeces, but we swiftly went on instead to hear back from the groups who'd received a paper clip and a computer lead. It was a heady start.

Twenty-four hours later, I was still in Lara Croft mode, but the mood had passed. I hovered on the edge of conversations, each as impenetrable as any thicket of brambles across a footpath, about Protocol 178s, Schedule 14s, PPOs and THSs. Eyes were ablaze with passion, laced with a very real fear that not only were many of their jobs on the line, but that the painstaking work that had occurred over the past two decades in building up both the paths network and the public's affection for it was in danger of being destroyed. And credit where it is due: it seems unquestionably true that the big battles of yesteryear are largely over now, done and dusted by the growing certainty of landowners, politicians and the public alike that our rights of way network is a Good Thing, and that it needs cherishing. They have done their job well. Goodwill, though, will not open paths and keep them accessible. The glory days of the 2000 CROW Act, and its 2003

Scottish sibling, are far behind us now, and their provisions are slowly being chipped away by legal challenges and dubious precedent from vested interests with no apparent budget limits.

You can always tell a lot about any gathering by its fringe of stalls and interest groups. The Ramblers' Association were there of course, firmly in the thick of the action, but none of the other walking or access organisations. It's not one big, happy, rambly family. In my after-dinner speech to the conference (the price of my admission), I mentioned visiting the Stockport headquarters of the venerable Peak & Northern Footpaths Society. There was an audible hiss from some quarters, like when the baddie comes down the stairs at a pantomime curtain call. I got a small round of applause for observing that the infamous 'Hoogstraten path' in Sussex was not all that interesting; one delegate later told me that he considered the high-profile campaign to be 'mad'.

Other stallholders included salespeople for the ever-growing forest of municipal paraphernalia growing alongside our footpaths. One company specialises in path-specific gates: choose from the Worcester 2-Way (with 'the tried and tested Prosafe Self-Closing mechanism' enclosed in 'an anti-vandal casing') or the Chiltern Bridle Gate 2-Way ('an extra handle is provided so the gate can be converted to a Milton Keynes gate if required'). They also sell stiles, kissing gates, latches, cattle grids, fences, static and retractable bollards, picnic tables and benches made of recycled plastic, and a whole range of barriers, including a strange-looking metal Motorbike Inhibitor (it blocks motorbikes 'whilst allowing access to pedestrians and users of most sizes of mobility vehicles . . . it is recommended that local groups and disabled ramblers are consulted about the siting and the gap that is most suited to them'). I still can't quite picture how a mobility scooter can go through a gap that a motorbike couldn't, and the brochure illustration shows enough space at the sides of the Inhibitor to get a Mini Metro through, but perhaps it's more impressive in reality. At £231 a pop, or £299 if you want it 'Polyester Powder Coated in Moss Green or Black', plus VAT and a 6 per cent increase across the board thanks to the rise in the global steel price, you'd certainly hope so.

Galvanised steel gates have been a boom industry of late, and there are numerous companies churning out variations on the same theme. On paper, they're bland enough, but in situ, especially wedged into beautiful places and alongside the artisanal gates that they've usurped, they become depressingly ugly: a triumph of function over form, the physical manifestation of cut-price thinking. Even their functional victory seems woefully short-lived. Many of the new gates around my village that started this footpath pilgrimage aren't working properly any more, little more than a year after being installed. The commonest problem is that catches have slipped, broken or seized up, so that the gates don't snap shut and tend to bounce back open with the slightest gust of wind, leaving farmers with the furious headache of scattered livestock and even greater tension between them and walkers.

Much as it displays the same kind of one-size-fits-all approach, I was strangely thrilled by the next stall, a company flogging signs. It was just so pretty. A display wall of examples – direction and destination indicators, waymarks, pointer roundels, trail-identity badges – was a blast of bold colours, like the walls of a primary school. Looking closer, the sentiment was all quite primary school too: don't do this, be careful of that, purty pictograms of moo-cows, baa-lambs, bunnies, birds, acorns and flowers. The computer age has made us all far more symbol-savvy, and I was particularly impressed with the various pictograms offered to tackle the age-old problem of shitting dogs. One, which I presume was exhorting people to shovel up the offending heap, makes it look as though they are whacking it with a fly swatter.

Another company offered a product I hadn't even realised existed: electronic pedestrian counters. These – somewhat inevitably, if for no apparent reason, called 'eco counters' – can be placed in special bollards in order to monitor every person walking past, thanks to a 'pyroelectric lens sensitive to the infrared emitted by the human body'. Or pressure-sensitive pads can be buried in slabs or steps, and the information beamed anywhere via satellite, Bluetooth or GPRS modem. All part of the obsession with monitoring and counting that seems to infect every public agency, as if that in itself were the definition of democracy. You'll see it if you ever look at the website of a government department or local council: it's nigh-on inevitable that within seconds of landing on the home page, you'll be asked to fill in a feedback form about it. Someone, somewhere is being paid to collect these mountains of information. Just how useful is it, on a scale of 1 (pointless) to 5 (essential)? Can I give it ½?

The paths on which you're likely to be counted, assessed and monitored are not generally the ones that excite your average rambler. They're often the civic showpiece routes, smooth tarmac or gravel, copious interpretation boards and signs, picnic table stops and designated viewpoints, all opened in a fanfare of photo-opportunity for the mayor, local MP and someone in a polo shirt and trackie bottoms from the health authority. They're paths that look like a road, so as not to scare folk addicted to their cars.

That said, the National Trails love their people counters too, and have been using them for decades. The Countryside

Commission produced a report on use of the Pennine Way in 1971, whose statistics depended much on 'a photoflux counter' and a mechanically switched totaliser placed on a gate, both at Edale. Technology was basic: the report admits that when the figures from the photoflux device were compared with 'visual counts' over a specific timed period, the electronic device had a counting efficiency of only 60 per cent. Nowadays, technology is hugely sophisticated, but the results might not be much more helpful. 'The pressure pads count sheep, dogs, cows and sometimes absolutely nothing, perhaps just a heavy downfall,' one warden told me. 'They're really not very useful, in my opinion, but the bosses love them.'

At the IPROW conference, I heard many people express the idea that, with local authority funding drying up, they needed to tap more from health budgets, and this has been a growing tendency over the last decade. I well recall the first time the trend made itself known to me, walking my dog around Edgbaston Reservoir in Birmingham early in the 2000s. It's a route I'd often done before, but this time new signs had erupted every couple of hundred yards along the path that hugs the water's edge. Each one had a logo of a big, happy heart and told you how far you had walked from the car park, and how far you still had to go if you were going to do the full circuit. Each one also stated something along the lines of : 'You are on a Walk. Walking is Good For You. It helps promote a Healthy Heart. Keep Going! Enjoy walking to a Healthier You!' By the time I'd read this drivel for the tenth time, my blood pressure was soaring.

In fact, paths should be one of the most generously funded arms of local government, so neatly do they fulfil the obsessions and orthodoxies of the moment. Having a walk is good for your health, both physical and mental. It is the ultimate in green and sustainable transport. It gets you out of your little fortress and into a realm where you might bump into a stranger, have quite a pleasant chat and they might not actually try to kill or mug you; it is therefore fabulous for combating loneliness, over-exposure to the *Daily Mail* and for helping foster community cohesion. And by seeing new places (and familiar places from new angles), a walk encourages us to learn about our landscape and our heritage. It's win-win-win-win with a footpath.

The above paragraph is a précis of just about every local authority's Rights of Way Improvement Plan (ROWIP), a statutory requirement of the 2000 CROW Act. All authorities dutifully produced these mammoth documents, intended to show what was the current situation in their area, and their ten-year plan for improvements. My local authority, Powys, managed to spin more or less the contents of that one paragraph into a 254-page, A4-sized book. I've seen quite a few others, and they all follow the same pattern: acres of big photos, lots of meaningless graphs and pie charts, spurious statistics gleaned from tiny, self-selecting surveys, endless repetition and a cavalier approach to good English (and, in the case of Powys, good Welsh too).

On the plus side, they all promise to make the rights of way network more accessible, open and signposted. Of course they do. In Powys, they have come up with the ambitious target of seeing 80 per cent of the network in unblocked, usable condition by 2017. That might not sound much, but it's starting from a hideously low base: they state that only about 35 per cent of the county's footpaths were usable at the time the report was written, around 2005. A couple of years earlier, the Countryside Council for Wales estimated it to be 31 per cent. Bridleways and byways are in better shape, but there are far fewer of them. It's also starting from the point of Powys's gargantuan size: there are over 6,000 miles of paths and byways in a county with a population of just 132,000.

The 80 per cent target is bandied around liberally, but other things in the report suggest that they have no intention whatsoever of reaching it. A statistic that baldly contradicts it slips in almost unannounced, and just the once, on page 117: 'With current base-line capital and revenue management budgets . . . it is predicted to take 38 years to achieve an 80% open and easy to use PROW network.' Ah. And that 'does not take into account any legal costs, Definitive Map work or surface management'. Ooh. Then you remember that the report was written in 2005, before the county council lost 6 per cent of its budget in an Icelandic bank and before the cuts. Hold those boots back a while.

Untangle the deathless language, and another more sneaky puncture in the 80 per cent target appears. In the plan, it is repeated again and again that the majority of people would rather see resources put into the improved maintenance of paths that are already open and used, instead of using the money to open up blocked paths. This spurious contention comes from a stark either/or question posed in their consultative survey: the option of working towards both was not offered. 'The results show that more emphasis needs to be placed on the maintenance of opened routes in the future,' the report states, and not on clearing the vast backlog of obstructed routes. Yet the vote was split only 55–45 per cent, hardly enough of a majority to command such a clear and long-lasting choice. Perhaps the answer comes from the fact that amongst one sector of the survey, landholders (defined as Powys members of the CLA, NFU and Farmers' Union of Wales), the result was 89–11 per cent in favour of quietly ignoring blocked paths. As the 266 consulted landholders accounted for a fifth of the entire survey's constituency, their overwhelming majority was more than enough to swing it their way. Even if a majority in every other interest group surveyed ('general', tourist information centres, town and community councils, tourist accommodation providers) voted for the unblocking paths option, the strength and size of the landholders' vote was sufficient to carry it the other way. That's perhaps what you get in an authority where over half of the councillors are returned unopposed. In my ward, there hasn't been an election since the 1970s. Powys, twinned with Pyongyang.

There's a high 'no shit Sherlock' quotient to these documents too, of course. I can only quote verbatim (the grammar and syntax are all theirs) from the Powys document: 'The ROWIP consultation highlighted the concerns that people have over access to the PROW network by people with disabilities. Respondents were asked to rate the network in terms of access provision. Out of all the different user groups; walkers, horse-riders, cyclists, motor bikers etc, the PROW network was rated as providing the worst service for people with mobility impairments.'

Making everything accessible to everyone is the shibboleth in public services, and you can hear the linguistic squirming in just about every pronouncement on the topic. Most of the ROWIP documents beat themselves up about the lack of disabled people, the lack of young people, or the lack of people from ethnic minorities using their paths, and make vague promises to consult various forums and develop various strategies in recompense.

There's a fine line between being genuinely helpful and plain condescending. Whilst not denying that there is a real barrier between the countryside and many black and brown Britons, it should be remembered that to some cultures, the idea of walking in the country is anathema. Hanif Kureishi said that his middle-class Pakistani family viewed it as utterly demeaning to go 'traipsing about like peasants'. Most of the disabled people I know would not be content merely because the council have built them a nice level boardwalk going 200 yards into a wood, even if it is adorned with Braille interpretation boards and those speakers that you wind up with a crank handle to release recordings of birdsong or sanitised nuggets of local history. They are all too aware that such trails are a poor, and slightly patronising, simulacrum of the real thing.

I have a blind friend who would push me under the wheels of a passing mobility scooter if I ever took her on such a 'walk'. She hates feeling that she is on the receiving end of some sort of Victorian paternalism, and I'm sure that such measures would sit firmly in that category. She is, however, the most wonderful person to go on a real walk with, and not because it makes me feel good to see her little face light up with grateful joy in unaccustomed sunlight, but because she comes out with the most staggering observations as we walk. In many ways, they are more visually rich than anything I ever manage: her ability to marshal all the other senses and conjure up a whole picture of where we are is quite breathtaking, and unfailingly accurate. She feels the path's undulations and its different surfaces, stops to stroke tree trunks and rocks, sniffs and tastes the air for nearby plants, animals or approaching weather, and listens intently to where the echoes fall, the waters rush and the birds crawk. Even on walks that I've done dozens of times previously, I'll see them in a whole new light when I walk with her, a light that seems richer, more vibrant and comprised of many more textures than normal. Walks with her are some of the most totally immersive I've had.

Come back Lara Croft, the people in charge of looking after our rights of way network need you. Every part of every process to do with our footpaths is mired in costly, opaque procedure, institutional buck-passing, multi-agency duplication, vacillating shifts in the political priorities of the day, pointless surveys and head-counting, and rabbit-in-the-headlights terror of lawyers and insurance companies. Against all that, it's a miracle that Rights of Way officers manage to achieve anything at all. Yet they do. But they are going to have to butch up a bit.

The axe is already falling; RoW budgets are being cut by more than half in some cases. The priorities of Powys, so artfully concealed within their Rights of Way Improvement Plan, will probably become the hidden strategy of most local authorities, namely to concentrate on the named and the showpiece paths within their area, at the expense of the rest of the network. There are vague hopes that David Cameron's much-vaunted 'Big Society' will mop up the remainder, and that we'll see groups of volunteers, such as the splendid crew at Kenilworth, popping up all over the country to maintain the paths on their patch. It's a lovely idea. But they were finding it ever more difficult to do the very straightforward work for which they had been established, simply because the forest of regulation had been growing denser and denser by the month. You cannot have it both ways.

As the cuts deepen, there's been no shortage of siren warnings against them. The PR machine of the Ramblers' Association has been cranking out apocalyptic press releases, baldly stating that 'unless something is done we will see a return of the "Forbidden Britain" of the 1960s when access to the countryside was more of a challenge than a pleasure . . . when today's cuts take effect at a local level, walking in the countryside will be taken back fifty years, to a time when you were lucky to be able to reach the end of a path without difficulty.' Absolutely no path is safe, apparently. Adrian Morris, the Ramblers' Association's Head of Walking Environment, even warned that 'we're truly facing terrible times when simple pleasures, such as a walk with the dog, are under threat.' Over in the Open Spaces Society, Kate Ashbrook said that 'the paths will undoubtedly deteriorate and we shall all be the losers.' Amidst all this unspecific sabre-rattling, the best point has been made time and again by IPROW, that cutting Rights of Way professionals is likely to prove a false economy, for without them, local authorities will end up having to spend far more on legal fees and Counsel. Though that, of course, doesn't make for such exciting headlines in the local paper as 'Cuts Threaten Your Dog Walk'.

Of course there is reason to worry, but isn't there always? It certainly seems so for a particular kind of footpath fundamentalist, ever able to turn the issue of the day into a full-scale red alert that they want us all to be terrified by, furious about, or both. I'm a huge fan of the late Fay Godwin, writer, photographer and past President of the Ramblers' Association. Her monochrome imagery of the British landscape is some of the finest ever captured, none more so than in her 1990 book *Our Forbidden Land*. Amongst the elegiac images of trashed landscapes and blocked access, the occasional glibness of her analysis sadly detracts from the bigger picture. At the time, the poll tax was the huge bugbear of the day, and this she returns to on numerous occasions, declaring flatly that it will 'close down many of the village shops which have so far managed to survive', that it will kill crofting and the entire Hebrides as a viable place to live. AIDS was a new panic button to press too, and she asserts, on the basis of one man's bizarre evidence to a Commons committee, that polluted seawater can carry and transmit HIV. And she flaps that philistine Thatcherism is about to see off 'green and thriving' urban jewels, going into loving detail of three over which the axe was hovering: the Kentish Town City Farm and Camley Street Natural Park in London, and the Kirkstall Valley Nature Reserve in Leeds. Twenty years later, all three are still going, stronger and more loved than ever. So when Tom Franklin, Chief Executive of the Ramblers' Association, warns us today that 'in a year or two's time, when the true affects [sic] of these cuts are realised, Britain's landscape will have already started to change. Paths will begin to become overgrown, blocked, closed off and walking will slowly become restricted to a few specially designated tourist destinations,' we should perhaps take it with a cautionary pinch of salt (and a dictionary).

If he's right, though, and only the showpiece routes are going to survive the cuts, then there is a glimmer of good news, for at the rate we're going, there'll barely be a right of way left in the land that isn't part of at least one named Long Distance Path. Their rise has been stratospheric, from the handful of National Trails set up in the 1950s and 1960s to the 1,200 plus now logged by the Long Distance Walkers Association (LDWA). Some routes were dreamed up to fit a historical theme, some a geographic feature, others were named after local luminaries, either famous and long dead or not-so-famous and just dead. They connect churches, battlefields, rivers, mountains, villages, hill forts, castles, rusty lumps of industrial archaeology, standing stones, real-ale pubs, abbeys and railway stations; in other words, anything that gets a walking Brit excited. From the Abberley Amble to the Ystwyth Trail, via the Kinver Clamber, the Myrtle Meander, the Daffodil Dawdle, the Purbeck Plodder, Offa's Hyke, the Trollers Trot and the Seahorse/Skipton/Sidmouth Saunter, the options – and the puns – seem endless. Which of the two Limestone Links, four Jubilee Ways or five Millennium Ways do you fancy? The Dales Way, Dales Walk, Dales Celebration Way, Dales Highway or Dales Traverse? And across the OS map they all spread, a colourful riot of blobs, dashes and diamonds. Though still not Wainwright's Coast to Coast, obviously, the most popular of them all.

The most enthusiastic instigators of new LDPs, though, were the local authorities. When Ted Heath's shiny new counties and districts came into force in 1974, many of the newly minted councils thought that a fine way to cement their name and identity was to create their own paths, often doing nothing more than circling their own boundary. The same has happened with many of the unitary authorities that replaced them from 1996 onwards. While it could be said that such a practice was a fine civic throwback to the notion of beating the bounds, it somehow brings more readily to mind the idea of a dog indiscriminately pissing up the fences that define its territory. All the more so when you consider that the new councils most enthusiastically pursuing the idea were generally the slightly chippier ones in areas with plenty to be chippy about. How many people ever gave up a week of their lives to walk the Solihull Way, the Barnsley Boundary Walk, the Bridgend Circular, the Langbaurgh Loop, A

Coventry Way, the Stevenage Outer Orbital Path (STOOP), the Altrincham Circular, the Rotherham Ring Route, Around Corby, the Doncastrian Way, the Hillingdon Trail, the Taith Torfaen, the Milton Keynes Boundary Walk, the Crewe and Nantwich Circular or the Bolton Boundary Walk (now even more appealing since being taken over by the Rotary Club and renamed the Bolton Rotary Way)?

In local authorities, the paths strategy today remains orbitally minded, though it is literally a case of ever-decreasing circles. These round borough routes, over a hundred miles long in some instances, are now gathering dust on the back shelves, their leaflets long out of print, their monogrammed waymarks vanishing into the undergrowth. For they have been eclipsed by a favourite new toy, the short circular walk. These are routes, anything from a 20-minute leg-stretch to a half-day's hike, that fan out either from car parks or public transport nodes. The paths are even, clean and lit. They are thick with signage, warnings, interpretation boards, kids' treasure hunts, dog poo bins and touchscreens (occasionally, these even work). Many of the more ambitious include things that you can download prior to the walk and play on your iPod or GPS as you shuffle around the circuit. They are to walking what Turkey Twizzlers are to cooking.

These bastard creations would be fine were they not greedily snorting up such a large proportion of the steadily diminishing pot of cash, for all that reassuring gadgetry, spoon-feeding and arse-wiping does not come cheap. But we have to do it, you see, is their response, because our survey said so. And it did. All of those Rights of Way Improvement Plans contain variations on this same theme. People told us that they don't use the footpaths because they're muddy, or scary, or boring. There aren't enough toilets, cafés, signposts, floodlights or car parks. They don't know where the footpath is going. Sort all that out, and of course we'd use them. One day. Maybe.

ROWIP documents have that same tone of voice as some stalwart of *Woman's Hour* trying to talk about urban grime music. They so desperately want to be down with the kids, but just don't have a clue how. Presented with the choice of a way-marked woodland stroll or hanging out with his mates down the Arndale, almost no teenager is going to skip up to the woods, however many MP3 downloads may be on offer. But still the council officers try, wringing their hands with guilty despair at their own fuddy-duddy whiteness, middle-classness and middle-agedness. One of the very newest local authorities, Cheshire East, formed in 2009, thought that this point was worth highlighting in boxed large text in its ROWIP: 'It is very difficult to find info on public rights of way in the area on the internet. If you want to increase the usage of public rights of way in the area by young people then it is absolutely vital that this changes.' Gosh yes, you can see their point. I just googled 'rights of way Cheshire', and it took a full 0.18 seconds to come up with the council's own lists and maps, the Discover Cheshire website, the exhaustive database of the East Cheshire Ramblers and a Wikipedia entry entitled 'Recreational Walks in Cheshire' with scores of links leading from it.

These same faultlines are developing in some of the pressure groups and charities too – even in the hallowed halls of the Ramblers' Association. In 2009, it spent £35,000 rebranding itself in lower-case postmodernism as the ramblers. Losing your capital letters is rarely a good thing. It began with companies that wanted to appear fluffy yet trendy, achingly hip yet responsible eco-capitalists: howies, purveyors of organic surf-dude wear as worn on the waves of W11, were one of the first on trend. As were innocent smoothies, palatable if pricey little bottles of puréed gunk, but almost guaranteed to come up again if you made the mistake of reading the label, with all that 'drink me, i'm really tasty and good for you' simpering. Tellingly, both companies were namechecked as amongst those he most admired by David Cameron, in one of his first big speeches after becoming Conservative leader (he was speaking at the Google Zeitgeist conference, no less; the words 'pig in shit' really spring to mind there). Even more tellingly, howies are now owned by Timberland, innocent by Coca-Cola, and the lower-case band-wagon has had its windmill ripped off and replaced with a turbo engine, courtesy of rebrands such as npower, bp and e-on. And, er, the ramblers.

Leading the charge for the new identity was Tom Franklin, appointed as Chief Executive of the still-capitalised Ramblers in autumn 2007. The whole process has become inextrica-bly identified with him, for the rebranding was his baby and driven through on the back of surveys and focus groups that, as with the councils, were strategically nipped and tucked to tell everyone precisely what he thought they needed to hear. Respondents (it's not said who they were) were asked what they associated with the RA, which produced a predictable roll call of 'retired', 'walking boots and sticks', 'men with beards' and 'an-oraks'. Asked how they should attract members, the unqualified responses included 'modernise', 'make it more trendy', 'do what they can to make me aware of their existence' and 'change their outward appearance'. Shown the old logo, a simple but striking boxed pictogram of a hillside with 'The Ramblers' written above it, the mystery respondents chorused as one: 'it doesn't mean anything to me', 'it looks a bit cheap' and 'it's dated/old-fashioned'. Bullseye!

None of this should have surprised the RA, for Franklin's background is steeped in this kind of stuff. Student Labour politician, Blairite cheerleader and party researcher, he seemed to be heading straight for the Commons and a smooth ministerial career, having become a councillor in Lambeth at the age of 24 and the leader of the council at 30. A newspaper profile at the time quoted an ex-boss of his: 'He cares about poverty and disadvantage, but he will be ruthless to get what he wants, and he is very ambitious. This isn't the end of the story.' It was, however, the end of Labour's rule in Lambeth, for two years later, in 2002, they lost control for the first time in three decades and Franklin became Chief Executive of Living Streets, the urban-walking campaign that had begun life in 1929 as the Pedestrians' Association. From there it was a short hop to the top job in the RA. It's not all been politics and the voluntary sector, though; he spent a few years too in the real world. As a PR executive.

It shows. The new logo, a stylised lower-case letter 'r', will, according to the report, make people say, 'Who's that? The Ramblers? Wow!' as it is 'a radical step . . . desirable to make people completely reassess what the Ramblers is about'. If you think that's exciting, just wait for the strapline that accompanies the logo: 'at the heart of walking' (still no nasty, spiky, unfriendly capital letters). This, apparently, is 'relevant and motivating', 'gives the sense of a charity', has 'emotional warmth' and is 'effective in compensating for, or opening reappraisal, of preconceptions'.

It's possible that the membership would have just about swallowed this guff had the rebrand not precisely coincided with something of a financial and organisational meltdown, as well as a catastrophically malfunctioning new computer membership database. Discontent rumbled like a summer storm, and broke out in a group calling itself the Concerned Ramblers. Brows were furrowed, meetings held, a website set up, the press alerted, and at the RA's General Council in April 2010, two of the ringleaders got themselves elected to the Board of Trustees.

Their launch document, 'The Ramblers in Crisis', spelled out their complaints: the group, they said, 'is composed of truly concerned members of the Ramblers who want to see a restoration of traditional values, coupled with a forward look which will attract new members to the Ramblers'. By traditional values, they may have meant national service and birching, but narrowed it down more specifically to a return to more active campaigning on clearing blocked paths and re-opening lost ones; they claim that 'clear moves to downgrade the importance of these policies have been made in the last few years.' The priorities of Tom Franklin – attracting more younger people, folk from disadvantaged backgrounds and ethnic minorities, running many more urban walks and groups, even joining up with gay walkers' societies – are just not the priorities of folk who live and ramble in the leafy lanes of suburban Britain. It's pretty certain that not many of the Concerned Ramblers were to be found on the recent RA walk around Banksy's graffiti sites in Shoreditch.

Inevitably, the Concerned Ramblers became slightly drunk on their own invective. Stepping up a gear, they let rip in the authentic language of fully capitalised Ramblerhood: 'A namby-pamby tendency led by the CEO to talk about "the walking environment" rather than rights of way, footpaths and freedom to roam has developed.' It 'is clear is that the CEO has no business running an organisation which purports to be democratic' and that 'management . . . is contemptuous of our democracy and unwilling to share problems with the membership.' The minutes of a meeting between the rebel group and the RA's trustees include this even more arch complaint: 'And then there was Tom's presentation at General Council 2009 – the last slide with a supposed Darwin quotation from *On the Origin of Species* – about change in evolution – whereas in fact the quotation did not come from *On the Origin of Species*, was not written by Darwin, did not represent a correct principle of evolutionary theory and anyway the same principles don't apply to organisational change.' I can imagine that would have made Tom Franklin absolutely furious. Not so much the opposition, but the fact that they thought his sleek PowerPoint presentation was a slide show.

The unedifying spectacle rolls on, each side hunkering a little further into its own fortress of intransigence. Savage staff cuts, particularly in the Welsh and Scottish offices of the RA, have resulted in numerous calls for the RA north and west of the border to break away from the London headquarters, but the situation's no happier in England. This battle for the soul of Britain's foremost walking organisation, just as it celebrated its 75th birthday, has been repeated, to some extent or other, in the National Trust and the Youth Hostel Association too, the other cornerstones of an RA member's holy trinity. These battles are always presented as reactionaries versus radicals, but in truth, it's a clash of almost equally conservative orthodoxics: a fussy obsession with hierarchy and tradition in the one corner, and a smug, metropolitan authoritarianism in the other. I can see both sides. But I don't fancy joining either of them.

An ancient holloway in the Olchon valley, Herefordshire

10. LARK RISE TO CAMERON

It was the overpowering whiff of gin that hit first, especially as it was not long after eight in the morning. The source of the smell, a proper Borth *grande dame* wrapped in a shabby kimono, gazed blearily at Mary and me. 'Ah, good morning,' she slurred. 'You have company today, I see. And good morning to you too.' She nodded to the film crew standing behind us, as if this kind of thing happened every day. We all stayed frozen in our positions for a good ten minutes, as Mary and the kimono lady chatted animatedly, even though her pickled logic made no discernible sense. I was fascinated by the movement of her dressing gown, which kept slipping down to reveal acres of leathery embonpoint, before she'd haul it back into place with a rattle of her many bangles and a throaty cough. Out of the corner of my eye, I noticed Emyr flick the switch on the camera; the ramblings of a drunken madam, while potentially worthy of the Christmas outtakes tape, were not going to make the final cut.

As we walked away, I asked Mary why she made such an effort with someone who'd been practically incoherent and had most likely already forgotten that we'd called. 'I'm probably the only person she'll see all day, you know,' she replied. 'It's really important to have just that little bit of human contact.' Mary is the postwoman in Borth, an old mid-Wales fishing village strung out between the sea on one side and a peat bog on the other. Her round, of nearly 500 addresses, is the village's one long street, ruler straight, permanently windswept, and about a mile and half long. I'd wanted to paint a picture of proudly eccentric Borth, and thought that tracking the postie, on what must be one the most difficult rounds anywhere, would be a good way to do it, for none of the houses, their now separated annexes or the little cottages filling tiny courtyards and salty alleys behind, has a number. Everyone's address is Name of House, High Street, Borth.

It was her job as a postwoman that inspired many of the observations of Flora Thompson, author of the *Lark Rise to Candleford* series. The Oxfordshire footpaths were her research ground, for it was there that she saw all life parading by, picking up titbits of gossip as she went. The same paths that echoed to the sound of men crashing and laughing their way to work took on a whole new character in the evening, or at the weekend, when lovers 'would link up, arm in arm, and saunter along field-paths between the ripening corn or stand at stiles, whispering and kissing and making love until the dusk deepened'.

I think of that morning with Mary often, as I walk the dog along some of our old postman's paths. Some days, the real postie passes me on the way, the blur of a wave through the windscreen as he hurtles around the lanes in his Vauxhall Combo. The paths, with their still too-new fingerposts, spider out along the valley, from door to door (or ex-door in the case of the many roofless shells in the forestry). It's this that upsets one farmer in particular. He remembers the postman walking along them, bringing not just the mail but news, views and red-hot scandal. Now he keeps finding startled ramblers edging nervously past his kitchen window, and they can hardly get away fast enough.

Our network of paths is as much an industrial relic as any bit of rusty old winching gear on a canal bank. Paths are spare and lean, not wasting a moment as they find the best way through for the ghostly legion of posties, farmers, miners, traders, priests, tramps, quarrymen, gypsies, milk maidens and factory workers who scuffed them deep into the earth. That we can still trace them and, for the most part walk them, is something of which we should be inordinately proud.

How our needs have changed though. These workaday paths of sweat and grease are now our leisure lifelines. We escape to them, seek solace from them, shut out the gibber and bleeps of the modern world on them. Most of all, we walk them to rid ourselves of the all-pervasive car, something that has changed the landscape, and our relationship with it, far more comprehensively than the enclosures ever managed. Just a few hours walking off-road makes re-encountering traffic such a shock, for it brings home the brutality of the culture on which we've become so hooked. As my year of walking progressed, I became ever more fascinated by how different were the places that you could still only reach by path, and I started to steer my routes to seek some of them out.

Railway stations with no road access have a very singular appeal. There's a holiday jaunt feeling at Berney Arms in the Norfolk Broads, and a Buchanesque sense of foreboding at Corrour station, on Rannoch Moor in the Highlands of Scotland. Just down the road from me is Dyfi Junction, where the mid-Wales line splits north and south. It is just two platforms in the middle of a peat bog, accessed only along a track that soon degenerates into a path, waders and sea-birds suddenly squawking into the air as you pass by. It is also where, for at least 1,500 years, the main ancient kingdoms – and the counties, still – of Wales have met, where the mountains of the north meet the rolling greenery of the south, the scattered hill farms of the east look out over the sea of the west. The beating heart of Wales is a bog-ridden railway station that almost no-one ever uses.

For an even more surreal experience, thanks to its place in the coat-tails of the suburbs, catch a train to Middlewood station, on the line between Manchester and Buxton. Never has a station been so well named, for it is indeed in the middle of a wood – and that's it. No car park, no nearby road, just footpaths and a cycle route radiate out from the platforms, quietly slipping through the trees to who knows where. Just south of the up platform, the Norbury Brook tumbles down a waterfall. Once the train has departed, the sound of the hissing water is all there is to hear. It is the most unearthly, and quite beautiful, experience, and transforms getting a busy suburban train out of Piccadilly and Stockport into a trip on the Hogwarts Express.

Pubs to which people have no choice but to walk are also very special. Folk arrive in a car at a pub, they often stay in their own impenetrable huddle; a reliable rule of thumb is that the amount of fun to be had in a pub is in inverse proportion to the size of its car park. Two of my best pub sessions ever took place in the Isis Tavern, on the Thames Path at Oxford, and the Turf Hotel on the Exe estuary in Devon, both inaccessible by car. It produces a rare, convivial atmosphere, one where everyone is on the same level and is already fairly relaxed when they arrive. I'm yet to manage a pub crawl around the remoter off-road outposts of Scotland, but it's extremely high on the to-do list. The same with churches, and there are many of these, their sanctuary appeal augmented by the fact that you can only walk to them. The fields of Norfolk are particularly stuffed with fine examples, as are the empty hills of the Marches, albeit of a far humbler variety. England's smallest church, at Culbone in Somerset, is an exquisite stop on the South West Coast Path, as is the imposing hilltop St Martha's on the Pilgrim's Way near Guildford.

For the full auto-detox, you can always rely on Venice, of course. The city has charms piled sky-high one on another, but a delight that has sharply increased in recent decades has been its place as a cloister away from the car. As soon as you leave the car parks of the Tronchetto, or the bus depot at Piazzala Roma, you step into a parallel world where the car has evaporated as if it never existed. And not just the physical vehicles themselves, but their plentiful paraphernalia too: the signs, road markings, traffic lights, junctions, noises, smells, the background levels of angst and anger, all joyously absent. You don't even much register it at first, for the city layers on the intoxications with such relish that the absence of cars doesn't compete with the milky turquoise canals, crumbling courtyards and dazzling light of the Serenissima. You notice it when you leave, though. The dream shatters, the bubble bursts as you are spat rudely back into the real world and its slavish addiction to the internal combustion engine.

To a tourist, the lack of cars in Venice is one of its most thrilling ingredients, though we're not, of course, prepared to live without the conveniences cars bring. For the dwindling number of Venetians (the population has now fallen below 60,000, a third of the number who lived there in 1950), it looks far from easy. Get up early, before the daily *acqua alta* of tourists surges through the squares, and you see the gristle and bone of the city flexing itself with a spare efficiency rarely thought of as a particularly Italian trait. Chugging up to the quayside will be flotillas of boats, each stacked with sacks of aubergines and lemons, whole sides of pig and calf, boxes of wine, beer and luminous Aperol, vats of olive oil and vinegar, fridges, cookers and gas bottles, before a small army of men whisk their bounty away on trolleys and carts into the still-drowsy streets. Like a well-choreographed ballet, just seconds after the last one has left, the first tourist parties of the day arrive on gondolas and vaporetti, laughing and pointing their cameras at everything that moves, and everything that doesn't. Another Venetian day is born.

The daily physical struggle to oil the wheels of this capricious machine has some distinct benefits. People-watching over a coffee or a glass of prosecco is one of the finest sports offered by any Italian city, but in Venice you are rewarded by the sight of some of the finest, fittest specimens around. Young Italian stallions, surgically removed from their beloved scooters and cars, display all of the same swaggering bravado that they employ behind the wheel, but here it is forced out in the open, into a far grander arena, and they rise magnificently to the occasion, manhandling carts, barrows and vast boxes with an effortless panache. Young women too: lissom dark-eyed lovelies flick back their hair as they glide carts of laundry five times their size across *piazze* and *campi* – there is no need for gym membership in Venice. Even the older folk keep up, as they must. Over a quarter of the city's population is elderly, a higher proportion than across Italy as a whole, and it's easy to spot the life-long inhabitants. I admired two grey-haired denizens bouncing a boxed 42-inch plasma TV up and over a bridge, even though it overhung their tiny trolley by a foot and a half on each side. The typical Venetian old lady is elegantly coiffed, immaculately turned out and with legs as thin as a sparrow, save for her knotted calves of pure muscle from 70 years of step aerobics.

These tiny little oases in the petrol fumes are a gorgeous anachronism now, turning their very carlessness to an advantage, but for some places it's been their lingering death knell. What happened when the tarmac never came? When the rutted byways, bridleways and age-old footpaths spoking out from every village somehow missed metalling and transformation into brave new roads? This was a more common phenomenon than you'd imagine, and it happened on some pretty substantial routes: the old Oxford–Cambridge main road, for example, was only sporadically tarmaced, and since the 1930s has been gradually reduced to the status of country lanes and footpaths. Villages en route quietly shrivelled and died.

This happened too in the Northamptonshire village of Faxton, a handful of miles to the south-west of Kettering. It was never a major settlement, but Faxton was a parish, with a manor house, two or three good wells, fish ponds, a village green, a few farms, cottages and a row of eighteenth-century almshouses. It really only had one moment in the sun, when King Charles I's soldiers were quartered there the night before the Battle of Naseby.

At the south-western corner of the green, the plain little church of St Denys, with its odd double belfry instead of a tower, had a Norman doorway and font. In this county of often extravagant churches, its lack of ornamentation – Arthur Mee described it as 'plain unto nakedness' in his 1945 County Series book on Northants – was offset only by a florid memorial inside to Sir Augustine Nichols, the Lord of the Manor and Justice of the Peace, who died suddenly on 3 August 1618, the night before he was due to officiate at an Assize Court in Kendal, Westmorland. Rumours that he was poisoned by the lover of one of the men he was due to try – and, given his fierce reputation, probably hang – the following day have persisted since.

Faxton was never an especially blessed place. Exposed on a windy hillside over 400 feet up, the winters were especially punishing. The plague wiped out most of the village inhabitants when the Lord of the Manor fled here from his London abode to escape the disease – unfortunately, bringing with him a servant girl who was already infected. The manor house burned down, after a Faxton farmer's ill-treatment of a gypsy had brought a curse upon the whole village. In 1841, the Census recorded 108 residents. By 1901, this had dropped to 37. The tide was going out, and it wasn't coming back.

The little church hosted its final service just before the outbreak of the Second World War, and was demolished completely in 1959. Whispers circulated throughout local villages that, in its deconsecrated two decades, St Denys's had been used by practitioners of black magic, and this is said to have hastened the decision to raze it to the ground. The perishing winter of 1947 was the final straw for most of the village's beleaguered inhabitants, for it wasn't just the roads passing Faxton by, but mains electricity, gas and water too. Nor was there ever a shop, pub or school. In the early 1960s, Mrs May Bamford, Faxton's last inhabitant, finally succumbed, and left.

On large-scale Victorian Ordnance Surveys, Faxton looks a little too scattered across its blustery slopes, and not at all close-knit or comforting. Footpaths are marked in all directions: west to Lamport, where the mother church to the Faxton chapel-of-ease was found, south to Old, the nearest pub, north to Loddington and east to Broughton. The east–west track was the main one, even appearing as a relatively major road on Thomas Moule's 1836 map of the county. Follow it today and you'll notice something a little odd, in the shape of the smooth tarmac road running alongside, and marked as a private drive. This, the road that finally came when it was too late, heads up to the one solitary house that has been teased back from the brink. Up by the gate of the house, a path – the old cobbled main street of the village – cuts across a field towards a clump of trees and all that's left of the doomed, devil worshippers' church: a truncated octagonal column that records, on each of its sides 'ON THIS / SITE STOOD / THE ALTAR / OF THE / CHURCH OF / SAINT DENYS / DEMOLISHED MCMLIX / ☩.' The cross leered out of the stone, looking like something being brandished at a vampire in some Hammer Horror schlockfest – 'Take that, infidel!' It tickled me, but I still didn't hang around too long.

From the village that died because the roads never came, it's just a short hop across a couple of fields to the village that was born in the back of a speeding car. Mawsley Village, its name harking back to a medieval settlement that died centuries before neighbouring Faxton, is a fast-growing housing estate plonked in the middle of Northamptonshire nowhere. It was started in 2001, and identifies its new-century credentials even on the map, in the pattern of fussy little squiggles and swirls that, on the ground, translate into a set of bucolically named Ways,

Closes and Groves. On a sunny summer Saturday afternoon, I wandered randomly around the village and saw only two other people on foot. The car's the boss in Mawsley.

I first heard of the place as a result of a tangential google. What I was looking for, I can't remember, but somehow I ended up in slack-jawed amazement reading numerous threads and debates on the Mawsley Village Forum. If ever there was proof that the internet is a fabulous way to talk to people far away, but a terrible way to talk to your near neighbours, this was it. Intemperate and inebriate rants, passive-aggressive posturing, unfounded accusations, grudges, whingeing and A-grade curtain-twitching filled screen after screen. The topics that proved most combustible were the predictable roster of dogs (and their shit in particular) and everything to do with cars, especially parking. I hadn't realised that there were quite so many ways in which to get absolutely bloody furious about where and how you leave your car, but the Mawsley Forum soon put me right on that. Even reading it, I could feel my blood pressure soaring, so God knows what it must be like for the poor sods grinding the stuff into their keyboards at their flatpack desk in their flatpack house.

To be honest, I was hoping to make a cameo appearance in the Village Forum myself. There had been a couple of threads headed with things like 'WHITE VAN JJ52 HDG – WHO HE?', posted by upright Mawsleyans who had seen someone they neither knew nor liked the look of in their precious paradise, and wanted to alert everyone else to the fact. Some visitors made it into the threads just because they'd hung around a little bit too long, had said hello to some children or had parked where they shouldn't have (a capital offence if Mawsleyans had their way). And I'm extremely disappointed to report that, despite parking right outside the One Stop shop and leaving my van there *for an entire Saturday afternoon*, despite daring to walk around Mawsley in broad daylight while being guilty of not wearing an England shirt on day one of the World Cup, despite being an unaccompanied bloke in his forties and despite even writing down the odd note in my notebook, no-one felt the urge to cyber-snitch on me. I was gutted. Should have parked in the 'RESIDENTS ONLY' spaces, I now realise.

Mawsley Village, and its growing number of compatriots, are the Tesco Value version of Prince Charles's model town at Poundbury in Dorset, somewhere that he loves to believe is as organic as his biscuits. It isn't. Poundbury is a chemical compound, a sub-urban Prozac, designed to smooth away the edges of reality into a no-peaks, no-troughs azimuth. Poundbury and Mawsley are not bad places, and some of the houses look genuinely lovely, but in order to function, they have had any potential surprise or spontaneity surgically excised from their DNA.

Paths come a long, long way behind roads in Mawsley. There is an old bridleway slicing the very corner of the development, and it was good to see a mum and two kids enjoying it on their bikes, their crash helmets glinting in the sunshine. Less welcome, but more Mawsley, was the couple who nearly mowed me down with a quad bike on the bridleway that brought me back to the village from nearby, long-dead Faxton. And at the northern end there are some meadows into which a path – actually, it's a fully fledged pavement – meanders for a couple of hundred yards. Judging by the comments on the Village Forum, nearly all of Mawsley's thousand-strong population have moved here from towns and cities for their slice of country life, and pavements across fields is as near as they dare get.

The nearest thing to a village green is, naturally, the central car park, around which are grouped Mawsley's fledgling commercial enterprises. There's the One Stop, an antiseptically bright barn housing huge piles of *Daily Mails*, nappies and lager, together with a notice board offering car valeting, yoga and girlie parties where you get your make-up or nails ('Real Gel Extensions!!!') done by Terri or Traci. Should you not be looking quite good enough after that, you could nip across the car park and book an appointment at the hairdressers, Idolz, before heading next door for a skinny latte and naughty bun at The Sanctuary. Meanwhile, your little darlings are bouncing around the Day Nursery, which completes the retail complex. On the internet forum, there's considerable grumbling that the promised pub has never arrived, and that the site designated for it is now being filled with more brick boxes. It's a woman's world, and you get the distinct impression that most of the decisions to move to Mawsley were taken by whippet-thin wives, which their considerably heftier husbands went along with for an easy life.

Nothing can shock us from our complacency quite as thoroughly as a bad photograph. We can suck our gut in a little in front of the mirror and then sally forth into the world convinced that we look that way for the rest of the evening, but then are horrified – and not a little mystified – by the digital image taken only six seconds ago that shows all too plainly how the said gut has now happily freed itself and is having a party all of its own. No wonder people plaster the fridge with these pictures; nothing could put you off that last chunk of pork pie or nicely chilled chocolate bar than the sight of your elephantine alter ego leering from the door.

I've had a few of these photos taken, but none slapped me as hard as one snuck by my boyfriend one recent Sunday morning when we were camping. From inside our camper van, he'd taken a photo of me sitting outside, hunched over a map. There's a look of quiet madness in my posture, a Quasimodo concentration of rounded shoulders, furrowed brow and clenched everything, and all seemingly poured into the OS sheet I'm almost devouring. Worse, he's lined up the angle so as to have me framed by the two stickers on the van's windscreen: one proclaiming our membership of the National Trust, the other my membership (he'd have killed me if I'd enrolled us both) of the Caravan Club of Great Britain. Signing up was an insurance requirement, I feel bound to point out, but it's not much of an excuse, and certainly not enough of one. I'm still debating where I should put this picture as my much-needed warning; where is the equivalent in the house of the fridge door for something that, instead of cautioning me what a fat bastard I've become, shows in gruesome detail what a boring tosser I can be if left to my own devices? I've just asked my partner that very question. 'By your map shelves,' was his immediate response.

One fortuitous by-product of Caravan Club membership is that it brings me something that works as an even more effective preventative than that photo: the monthly members' magazine, its double-spread letters page in particular. Most of the letters start with the words 'My wife and I', and go on to either praise some super new caravanning gadget, something like a tiny kettle that doubles up as a can opener and gets Freeview, or rant fulsomely about the very many horrid ways modern life has gone so hideously wrong. In recent months, there's been a blizzard of letters on one subject: people who dare to walk across their pitch at the camp site. This they – and their silent spouses – insist is a relatively new problem, for in the Good Old Days, no-one, absolutely no-one, would have dreamed of cutting across the corner of your allotted yardage. It's Broken Britain manifesting itself in a neatly clipped field just off the A577, and My Wife and I are absolutely *furious*.

These are the people who would look at a blank wall for a whole day and swear that it's not as good as it used to be this morning. Their whole life is a sagging balloon, fondly imagined as pert and perfect back in the day, but ever since slowly hissing out every last iota of pleasure and possibility. Locked on to this trajectory of diminishing returns, everyone is out to get them, undermine them or rip them off. They'd quite like to put man-traps around the perimeter of their homes, but have had to make do with a few 'No Turning' signs instead.

My haughtiness is, of course, tempered by the very real terror that I will become that letter writer. And liking a walk – loving one, in fact – is no guarantee that I'll avoid the fate. Quite the opposite, it seems, for my year of walking the tracks of Wales, England, Scotland and Ireland had shown all too graphically how easy it is to combine the great outdoors with ever-shrinking horizons. It's quite some feat, in truth, for there is nothing more liberating than progressing through the landscape at your own pace, entirely under your own steam, whilst revelling in both the perfection of nature and the ingenuity of man.

Despite the clouds of doom being whipped up over budget cuts, I'm hugely optimistic about the future of our paths network. Something has fundamentally shifted in the last 20 years: our level of knowledge as to what we have, and an understanding of what it means to us all, have become embedded in a quite new way right across our collective identity. The recent kerfuffle over the sale of English forests has shown quite dramatically just how deep our assumption of access has rooted. It's thanks to a number of factors that coincided almost perfectly. Two decades ago, there was the sudden increase in named long-distance paths, which sparked much interest and a considerable surge in their usage. Around the millennium, there were the debates about the right to roam and the eventual, and long overdue, measures in the resultant CROW Act of 2000, and its even bolder Scottish twin. Hard on the heels of that came foot-and-mouth, whose blanket bans on walking and access served as the most chilling reminder possible of what we stood to lose without our rights of way network. And since then, barely a Sunday night has been free of some lavish landscape porn on the TV, our countryside showcased in its most coquettish glory to a swelling Elgar soundtrack. Garnish all this with growing localism and environmentalism, together with the power of the internet to bring like minds together, and it has resulted in a far deeper connection that is not going to be jettisoned overnight. Neither is it dependent solely on the amount of public money thrown at it. But we're British, so we'll continue to moan and bicker about it, to see loss where there is none and to live in a state of perpetual impending doom, always lurking just around the next corner. It's what we do best.

Along with footpaths, that is. A year of walking, in every landscape and almost every part of these islands, has been an extraordinary experience, one of the purest pleasures I've ever had with my clothes on (though I have of course shed them on one or two remote walks; you've got to keep the likes of Nicholas van Hoogstraten secure in their prejudices). My inner map of our islands has been much coloured in, and the glorious reality of their places and people way exceeds anything even the Ordnance Survey have managed. I'd found too that walking is a surefire way to enhance the landscape, for even places that I was used to looking tired or dull through a moving windscreen took on amazing new hues of subtle interest and beauty as I walked by them. Leslie Stephen, founder of the Sunday Tramps, put it thus: 'Walking gives a charm to the most commonplace British scenery. A love of walking not only makes any English county tolerable, but seems to make the charm inexhaustible.' He's right. I've walked in Hertfordshire, one of my least favourite counties, and it was lovely. So strong is the spell, it might even work for Bedfordshire.

I'm glad too that I waited to do this until well into my forties, for in my younger years, I was in far too much of a hurry to hear the pitch and rhythm of the land, or to wallow in my own insignificance as I crossed it at a steady two miles an hour. Walking is a gloriously middle-aged pastime, and there's no shame in that. It sits alongside gardening, silence, gin, olives and classical music as things most of us take time to ripen into. It cannot be forced. Amongst the acres of PR twaddle in the Ramblers' Association document used to precipitate its glitzy rebrand, there was one tiny glimmer of truth that went entirely disregarded. Asked the question, 'What one thing could the RA do to attract people like you?', one focus group member sagely responded, 'Too young to join. Something to do later in life.' To the officers of the RA, such thinking is treasonable. To anyone else, it's practical good sense, and a pretty sharp summary of the true shape of our three score years and ten. 'The flowers smell sweeter the closer you are to the grave,' warbled the Beautiful South; it was a line that sang in

my soul as I sauntered through the cycle of a British year, drawing limitless inspiration from all that floated by.

None of this is to advocate complacency, though. The threats
to our freedom have always been there, and always will be,
though they mutate with time from one gruesome ogre to the
next. My near-neighbour, the writer George Monbiot, put it to
me that, at almost any given moment in our history, Parliament
is full of that particular age's most venal brand of crook. He's
right, and they've all had a go at regulating our relationship with
the land according to their own worldview and self-interest.
Hoggish landowners begat rapacious industrialists begat bloodless technocrats, all of them seeing both the land and the people
as units to be shifted as and where they saw fit. In more recent
times, the tedious mandarins of the 1970s were elbowed aside by
the city boys and estate agents of the Thatcher age. Once they'd
got what they came for, they shifted to accommodate the marketing and PR gurus of the Blair–Cameron era to package their
greed in ever-glossier assurances and illusions of choice. It's all
PR, and it's nearly all bollocks.

They too will pass, and fade from the scene. But our paths
will not.

Messing with the mind, at Whitchurch psychiatric hospital, Cardiff
Photo by Peter Finch

ACKNOWLEDGEMENTS

The Noam Chomsky quotations are from www.chomsky.info, May 1995 interview for *RBR* magazine entitled 'Anarchism, Marxism and Hope for the Future'.

So many people gave so freely of their time, ideas and special places during the course of writing *The Wild Rover*. In particular, thanks to Audrey Christie and family; Neil Ramsay and all at Scotways; Geri Coop at IPROW and the delegates at their conference; Brian Nicol, Howard Easton, Ian Henderson and their co-diggers at the splendid Kenilworth Footpath Preservation Group; Sian Barnes and colleagues at Powys Council; Anne Taylor at Lancashire County Council; Kate Ashbrook; Roger Jones; Patsy and Helen Cahalan; Gerry Millar; Father Frank Fahey and the pilgrims of Ballintober Abbey; Melissa Coles; Maura and Martin Walshe at Radharc Na Cruaiche; Anne-Marie Carty; Helen Sandler; Jane Hoy; Niall Griffiths; Tom Bullough; Robert Evans; Tony Coleman; Jeremy Grange; Bill Drummond; Rhys Mwyn; Jack Grasse; Meg Thomas; Peter Finch; Jon Gower; John Trevelyan; Sue Rumfitt; Steve Westwood; Sheila Talbot; George Monbiot; Jon Woolcott; Helen Baker; Clarke Rogerson and the Peak & Northern Footpaths Society; Chris Perkins; Paul Salveson; Helen Parker and Julia Griffin; Sue Parker and Andy Knight; Diana Fenton; Susan and Tony at the YHA Ennerdale; Gill at Plas Dwpa and Jane at Carreg-y-Gwynt; Hero Sumner and the team at the John Clare museum in Helpston; Woody Fox; David Archer; Norma McCarten; Julieann Heskin; Caz Ward; William Evans; Peter Finch; Susan Blakiston; Nick Fenwick; Linda Brown; Paul Woodland; Lou Hart; Andrew Gee, Kirsten Hearn; the two Helens at the Ryedale Folk Museum in Yorkshire; Roger Kidd and the regulars at geograph.org.uk. Apologies to those missing from the list, especially the many illuminating people I encountered on numerous paths (and in a fair few pubs).

I am particularly indebted to the staff of the many public libraries who helped with my research, especially in Westport, Machynlleth, Uckfield, Kettering, Ystradgynlais, Crowland, Peterborough, Anstruther, Morecambe, Stockport and Lyme Regis. Dropping in on them unannounced, no question seemed too obtuse, no request too dull for these ever-patient and enthusiastic people. Local libraries are one of our greatest national resources; we let them wither and die at our peril. Thanks too to the staff of the British Library and the National Libraries of Wales and Scotland.

Heartfelt appreciation as well to Helena Nicholls and the crew at Collins, and to my agent Rebecca Winfield for all her sage advice and ability to massage the fragile ego of her clients just when it was needed most. A huge *diolch yn fawr* to friends and neighbours in Esgairgeiliog, a supremely happy home to me for the last ten years, and in particular to Preds for all his unflappable strength and support. Get the jug on, cariad.

BIBLIOGRAPHY

Automobile Association, *Walking in Britain*
Bate, Jonathan, *John Clare: A Biography*
Belsey, Valerie, *Discovering Green Lanes*
Bonser, K. J., *The Drovers*
Cahill, Kevin, *Who Owns Britain*
Chandler, John, *The Day Returns: Excursions in Wiltshire's History*
Clare, John, *Selected Poems*
Countryside Commission, *Pennine Way Survey*
Davies, W. H., *A Poet's Calendar* and *Selected Poems 1928*
Devereux, Paul, *Fairy Paths & Spirit Roads*
Ellis, T. I., *Dilyn Llwybrau*
Fahey, Frank, *Tóchar Phádraig – A Pilgrim's Progress*
Fewer, Michael, *A Walk in Ireland* and *Walking Across Ireland*
Fowles, John, *The French Lieutenant's Woman*
Godwin, Fay, *Our Forbidden Land*
Godwin, Fay and Toulson, Shirley, *The Drovers Roads of Wales*
Grigson, Geoffrey, *The Shell Country Alphabet*
Hannigan, Des, *Ancient Tracks*
Hardy, Thomas, *The Woodlanders*
Hawkes, Jacquetta and Christopher, *Prehistoric Britain*
Hill, Howard, *Freedom to Roam*
Hindle, Brain Paul, *Roads, Tracks and Their Interpretation*
Hippisley Cox, R., *The Green Roads of England*

Horan, James, *Memoirs 1911–1986*

Jennett, Seán, *The Ridgeway Path*

Jones, Roger, *The Walkers' Companion* and *Rambling on . . .*

Kynaston, David, *A World to Build: Austerity Britain 1945–48*

Laws, Bill, *Byways, Boots & Blisters – A History of Walkers and Walking*

Lee, Donald W., *The Flixton Footpath Battle*

Leete, J. A., *A Wiltshire Miscellany*

Looker, S. J. and Porteous, C., *Richard Jefferies, Man of the Fields*

MacEwan, Ann and Malcolm, *Greenprints for the Countryside – the Story of Britain's National Parks*

Major, Norma, *Chequers: The Prime Minister's Country House and its History*

Morris, Chris, *A Portrait of the Severn*

Nicholson, Adam, *The National Trust Book of Long Walks*

Peak & Northern Footpaths Society, *A Century of Footpath Preservation*

Rackham, Oliver, *The Illustrated History of the Countryside*

Ravensdale, Jack, *In the Steps of Chaucer's Pilgrims*

Robinson, Cedric, *Forty Years on Morecambe Bay* and *Sandman*

Robinson, Eric and Powell, David (Eds), *John Clare, By Himself*

Rothman, Benny, *The 1932 Kinder Trespass*

Rowley, Trevor, *The English Landscape in the Twentieth Century*

Salveson, Paul, *Will Yo' Come O' Sunday Mornin'?*

Sampson, Fay, *A Free Man on Sunday*

Shoard, Marion, *This Land Is Our Land*

Smith, Roly (Ed.), *Kinder Scout: Portrait of a Mountain*

Solnit, Rebecca, *Wanderlust – A History of Walking*

Stedman, Henry, *Coast to Coast Path (Trailblazer Guide)*

Stephenson, Tom, *Forbidden Land*

Taplin, Kim, *The English Path*

Thomas, Edward, *The Heart of England* and *Selected Poems*

Wainwright, A., *A Coast to Coast Walk*

Walsh, Pat, *Mayo – A Proud County*

Watkins, Alfred, *The Old Straight Track*

Westacott, Hugh, *The Illustrated Encyclopaedia of Walking & Backpacking* and *The Ridgeway Path*

Williams, Raymond, *Culture and Society*

INDEX

Access to Mountains (Scotland) Bill 57–62, 63, 65–6
Access to Mountains Act (1939) 66–75, 143
Adams, Vyvyan 69–70
Ainsworth, Richard 29–30, 31, 32
Ames, John 253, 254
Ashbrook, Kate 136–7, 138, 139–42, 156–7, 295
Ashcombe Estate 147–51
Attlee, Clement 75, 106
Ayrton Gould, Barbara 79

Bale, Conyers 25
Ballintober Abbey 207–11, 212
Band of Historical Hillwalkers 170–1
Barrow-in-Furness 177
Beamish, Major Tufton 78
Blacks 172–3
Blackstone Edge 122–3
Blair, Tony 82, 91, 107, 148, 177
Bleaklow 21–2, 37, 45
blogs and diaries 87–90
Blue John 53
BNP 19
Boheh Stone 215–17
Borth 305–6
Bottoms path, Flixton 20, 26–7, 28
Brown, Dr Roy 241
Brown, Gordon 80, 82, 107
Bryce, James 57, 58–61, 63, 66
Bryce, John Annan 63
Budleigh Salterton 250
Bush, George H. 82

Cameron, David 82, 109, 176, 294, 300
Camino el Rey, El 259–60
Camino of St James of Compostela 197–8
Camus, Albert 55
Canavan, Denis 81
Canterbury Tales, The (Chaucer) 198
Capurro, Scott 110
Caravan Club 317–18
Carn Llidi 246
car-inaccessible places 307–11
Castle, Barbara 80, 90
Castleton 52–3
celebrities 151
chalk-and-flint 102–4
Chamberlain, Neville 67
Chequers 105–9
Childish, Billy 171
Chiltern Society 111–12
Chilterns 95, 96–8, 102–6, 109–12, 117, 256
Chomsky, Noam 55–6
Churchill, Winston 105, 108
Chuter-Ede, James 72, 74–5
city centres 125–6
Clare, John 157–67
Clarke, Colonel Sir Ralph 77–8
Clee Hills 5–6
Clegg, Nick 176
Cleveland Way 91, 240
Clifton Brown, Brigadier General Douglas 69
Clinton, Bill 82
Coast to Coast walk 87, 90, 174–86, 197, 240
Coleman, Joe 205–6
Concerned Ramblers 302–3

Conservatives (Tories) 19, 57, 59–60, 62, 68–70, 72, 74, 77–8, 79, 81, 109, 176, 177
Cook, Robin 81
Coombe Hill 95, 105
Coronation Street 53
corpse paths 222–34
Countryside Commission 87, 240, 288–9
Countryside and Rights of Way (CROW) Act (2000) 91, 99, 139, 141, 147–8, 150, 191, 285, 319
County Mayo 201–22
Cowley, Bill 235–7, 238, 239, 241, 242, 243
Cranborne Chase 150
Creech-Jones, Arthur 66–7
Croagh Patrick 196, 199–201, 206–7, 212, 218–222
Cumbria, inept tourism 178–80
cyclists 91, 100

Dalton, Hugh 80
Darwen access battle 34–7, 56
de Quincy, Thomas 192
Devereux, Paul 224, 227, 228–9, 230
Dewar, Arthur 72
Didcot power station 114
disabled people 293–4
Donner, Sir Patrick 69
Drovers' paths 126–7
Duckworth, Rev. William Arthur 35
Dyfi Junction 307–8

Eccles, William 26–7, 28
Edale 41, 45, 49, 50, 52, 289
electronic pedestrian counters 288–9
Elie chain walk 259
Ellis, Tom 62–3
Ely–Walsingham pilgrimage 198–9
enclosures 56, 157–8, 160–2
ethnic minorities 292–3
Exeter, Marquis of 158

Fahey, Father Frank 212, 215, 216, 218
farmers 11–12, 146, 195, 256
Farquharson, Robert 61
Father Ted 206–7
Faxton 311–13
Flavell, Brigadier E. W. C. 79
Fletcher, Reginald 67
Fletcher-Vane, William 81
Flixton footpath battle 23, 25–8, 56
foot-and-mouth (2001) 3, 124, 189–91, 319
footpath-upkeep volunteers 17–19, 294

Forestry Commission 12–16
Framfield 9 path 133–4, 136–42, 156–7
Franklin, Tom 296, 300–1, 302, 303
Fraser, Sir Ian 78
Free Man on Sunday, A (Sampson) 42
French Lieutenant's Woman, The (Fowles) 249, 251, 257

gates
around author's patch 2, 10–11, 287
modern plethora 286–7
Gladstone, William 55
Godwin, Fay 295–6
golf courses 250–1
Goring 112–13
grouse shooting 21, 22, 30, 45, 68, 78, 85

Hadrian's Wall National Trail 123–4
Hague, William 81
Haldane, Lord 106
Hamersley, Richard 239
Harding, Mike 33, 42, 43, 90
Hardy, Thomas 275–6
Hattersley, Roy 43
Haughey, Charles 204
Hayfield 43–4, 45–6
Heath, Ted 158, 297
Heilgers, Frank 68–9, 69–70
Hervey-Bathurst, James 155–6
Hicks, Bill 245
Highways Act (1815) 26
Holland 60
Hoogstraten, Nicholas van 133–6, 137–9, 140, 142
Horan, Monsignor James 202–4
Hughes, Emlyn 177
Hunt, Henry 27

Institute for Public Rights of Way (IPROW) 282–6
Cambridge conference 282–6, 289

Jefferies, Richard 120
jogging 82
John Paul II, Pope 204
Joyce, Mary 162–3

Keeling, Edward 77
Kenilworth Footpath Preservation Group (KFPG) 18–19
Kinder Scout protest 21–2, 29, 32, 33, 34, 37–48, 52, 56, 66
Knock Airport 201–6

Labour Party/New Labour 19, 42–3, 57, 65, 66–8, 69, 70, 72, 74, 75–6, 78–9, 80, 81, 91, 106–7, 131, 301
Lake District, shortcomings 186–7
Lake District National Park 49, 175, 181
land ownership and custodianship 152–6
Land Reform (Scotland) Act (2003) 91, 285–6
Lee, Lord 106, 108
Liberal Democrats (Lib Dems) 81–2, 131, 176
Liberal Party 19, 57, 59, 62, 63, 70, 72, 74, 106
Lich Way, Dartmoor 224–34
Limitation Act (1623) 71
Lloyd George, David 106, 108
Llŷn Peninsula 193–4
local authorities 76, 79–80, 83, 158, 281, 290
  paths strategy 297–9
local path inventory, author's 7–17
Lockley, R. M. 246
London walks 264–5
Long Distance paths (LDPs) 76, 80, 83, 84, 94, 101, 130, 240, 296–8, 319
Lyke Wake Walk 234–43
Lyme Regis 250–1, 252–4, 257–8

MacColl, Ewan 34
MacDonald, Ramsay 65, 106
Macrae, Murdo 58
Madison, James 56
Madonna 146–51
Mais, S. P. B. 194–5
Major, Norma 108
Mam Tor 50–1, 54
Manchester 27–8, 32, 34
Manchester Society for the Preservation of Ancient Footpaths 26–7
Mander, Sir Geoffrey 74
Manic Street Preachers 55–6
market paths 124–5
Marshall, Fred 67–8
Mary Barton (Gaskell) 29–30
Maud Heath's Causeway 124–5
Mawsley Village 313–16
Middlewood station 308
Miliband, David 42–3
Millennium Dome 265–6
Millets 172, 173
Montgomery 188
Moore, George 209
Moorlands and Memories (Clarke) 32
Morecambe Bay crossing 260–2

Moritz, Pastor Karl Philipp 192
Morris, Adrian 295
Mountain Rivers and Pathways (Wales) bill 62–3
Murray, Andrew Graham 61–2

National Parks 49–50, 76, 79, 83
National Parks and Access to the Countryside Act (1949) 66, 76–81, 82–85, 91
National Trails 86, 90–1, 93–5, 101, 123, 246, 263, 288–9
National Trust 64, 65, 119, 129, 303, 317
New Mills Millennium Walkway 43
Nicolson, Harold 106
Noel-Baker, Philip 74
Norris, Mr 25, 26
North York Moors National Park 49, 50, 91, 241, 242
nouveau riche 142–5

Offa's Dyke Path 91, 187–8
Open Spaces Society 75, 133, 136, 295
Ordnance Survey (OS) maps 83, 176, 229, 241, 246, 262
  Ellis Martin covers 46
  Explorer 7, 40, 114, 250, 258
  Landranger 7, 129–30
  nineteenth-century 10, 214, 313
Orla Perć 259

Parris, Matthew 81
Peak & Northern Footpaths Society (PNFS) 21, 26, 28, 29, 38, 44
Peak District National Park 49, 50
Peake, Osbert 78
Pembrokeshire Coast Path 91, 246–8, 258
Pennine Way 39, 41, 48–9, 66, 80–1, 84–90, 289
'Pet Lamb Case' 58, 59, 146
Peterloo Massacre 27–8
Poundbury model town 315
Powys Rights of Way Improvement Plan 290–2, 294
Prentice, Archibald 27
Pumlumon 267

Radstock, Lord 161
Raja, Mohammed 135–6, 139
Ramblers' Association 33, 39, 46, 63, 75, 83, 85, 132, 136, 137, 138, 262, 286, 294–5, 299–303, 320
Reynolds, Albert 203, 204

Ridgeway 93–121, 170, 173–4, 182, 250
Rights of Way Improvement Plans
    (ROWIPs) 290–4, 298–9
Rights of Way (RoW) officers 10–11, 223,
    281–5
Rights of Way Act (1932) 84, 157
Ritson, Joshua 74, 143, 146
Robinson, Cedric 261
Robinson, Mary 208
Rogerson, Clarke 21, 29, 38
Roman roads 122–3
Rothman, Benny 33, 39, 42, 44, 45, 46
Rumfitt, Sue 223

Salveson, Paul 32, 33
Sarn Helen 123
Saw Doctors 214
Scottish access legislation 57–62, 63, 65–6,
    91, 285–6
Scott, Sir Walter 60
Seaton 250, 256, 257, 258
Severn Way 266–75
Sgwd yr Eira 277–9
sheep paths 9–10
Shinwell, Mannie 76
Shoard, Marion 157
Shufflebotham, Joseph 31
Siambr Wmffre Goch 15–16
signs and signposts
    on author's patch 1–4, 10–11
    Chilterns 111
    modern plethora 287–8
    Ridgeway 98–9
Silkin, Lewis 76–7, 79
Silverman, Sidney 74
Smith, Chris 81
Smith, John 81, 91
Smith, Sir Herbert 152–3, 154
South Downs Way 91, 115, 117
South West Coast Path (SWCP) 91, 248–9
sporting failures 268–71
Stephen, Sir Leslie 72–3, 320
Stephenson, Tom 38–9, 40, 66, 80, 85, 90,
    94–5
Stewart, Rory 81
Sweeney, John 138–9
Sunday Tramps 72–3, 320
Swetenham, Edmund 63
Swindon 118–20

Thames Path 263–6, 274
Thatcher, Margaret 105–6
Thompson, Flora 306

Tóchar Phádraig 207, 212–22
Tooreen Hall dances 202–3
Trail Fascism 99–101
trespass legislation 70–5
Trevelyan, Charles 63–4, 65
Trevelyan, G. M. 64–5
Trevelyan, George 64
Trevelyan, Katherine 64
Trevelyan Man Hunt 65
Turton, Robin 69, 143–4

Uffington 116
UKIP 12, 109
Undercliff 249, 251–8
urban paths 275–6

Venice 309–11
via ferreta ('iron ways') 259–60
Victoria, Queen 273–4

Wainwright, Alfred 85–6, 87, 90, 144–5,
    175, 184
Welsh Coast to Coast 187–9
'Welsh way' 191–3
walking
    author's childhood 5–6
    benefits 64, 289–90
    Dave's redemption 132
    equipment 169–73
    politicians 81–2
water boards 85
Wayland's Smithy 116
West Midland Safari Park 6
Willey, Fred 80–1
William Clough valley 45–8
Wilson, Harold 106–7
Winans, William Louis 58
Winnats Pass rallies 21–2, 52, 66
Winter Hill protests, Bolton 21–2, 29–34,
    56
Witley Court 152–4
Woody (friend) 225–34
Wordsworth, William 60
working-class
    access campaigns 46
    interest in outdoor life 29–30
    walking organisations and trespass laws
    73
Wright, Ralph 'Vegetable' 23–4, 25–8,
    142–3

Young, Andrew 115
Youth Hostels Association 64, 236, 303